Ten Chimneys

Diana Enright

and

Tanya Ann Hazelton, Ph.D.

PORTLAND • OREGON
INKWATERPRESS.COM

Cover and interior design by Masha Shubin
Interior Photographs © Diana Enright
Cover and chapter illustrations © 2007 Rhonda Riley.

www.inkwaterpress.com

ISBN-13 978-1-59299-283-6
ISBN-10 1-59299-283-8

Publisher: Inkwater Press

Printed in the U.S.A.
All paper is acid free and meets all ANSI standards for archival quality paper.

God gives beauty for ashes.
Is. 61:3

This book is dedicated to Dr. Joseph Garton

Dr. Joseph Garton burst onto the national scene by doing something many of us wouldn't have the courage to consider: placing his personal assets as collateral and securing a seven-figure loan to buy a decaying estate.

For over a half century, hidden within two hundred acres in the whistle-stop of Genesee Depot, Wisconsin, was the haven of Alfred Lunt and Lynn Fontanne: the most revered acting team in American theater history. It was known as Ten Chimneys and the Lunts' frequent guests included Noël Coward, Helen Hayes, Charles Chaplin, Lawrence Olivier, Vivian Leigh, Katherine Hepburn and countless others including a lucky little girl who lived over the hill!

Dr. Garton literally rescued Ten Chimneys from a wrecking ball poised to level the three story, twenty-four room main house including all its contents. Eight other structures on the estate were also threatened by the same demise.

Devoting himself full time, "Saving this historic treasure from this unthinkable fate", Joe became Ten Chimneys interim caretaker. Restoring the entire estate to its 1940s grandeur became his passion. He was a past President of the Madison Repertory Theater and Civic Center Foundation and a former Chairman of the Wisconsin Arts Board.

Known for his tenacious insight into creative possibilities, Joe was also a Madison-area restaurateur, theater historian and passionate arts advocate.

With Joe's gleeful enthusiasm and perfect pitch to excite people and generate the necessary economic support, the Ten Chimneys Foundation was established along with twenty-four prominent civic leaders to form the Board of Trustees. The projected twelve and a half million dollars needed was raised and within seven years Dr. Garton's dream became a reality.

As I reminisced with Joe at the Ten Chimneys' Grand Opening I discovered a kindred spirit who loved Ten Chimneys as much as I do.

"I have to tell you, I think you should consider writing a book Diana," he said during our private conversation. Sadly, Dr. Garton died of cancer in early August, 2003, leaving a priceless monument to theater.

I hope I served you well, Joe.

-Diana Enright

Diana Enright and Dr. Joseph Garton
Ten Chimneys Grand Opening
May 26, 2003

Written for my grandchild, Hailey Erin, who is *my* real life 'Diana'. Like this book, our lives have become a rough place made plain.

-Tanya A. Hazelton

I will not be an old lady who says
I asked life for a penny —
For life would have paid me
Anything I asked of it.

-Anon

April, 1996

Diana, in her early fifties, climbed a spiral staircase, entered a dark bedroom and stopped at the foot of a bed. A breath of cold air crept across the back of her neck, "This is where she died, isn't it?"

Confirming without question, Dr. Joseph Garton nodded his head.

Outside, distant thunder ripped across Southern Wisconsin's kettle moraine, followed by the muted drops of a soft spring rain.

Across the room in an alcove, she saw a floral chintz skirted vanity and walked over to it. She lightly touched an embroidered linen on the tabletop.

Her whole body sagged — a physical force weighed her down — pressed her to sit at the mistress of Ten Chimneys' dressing chair in front of the mirror.

On the table, false eyelashes placed neatly in a small bone china dish were left for nearly two decades. Dust-covered jars of creams and bottles of favorite perfumes were still on trays. Positioned on a linen of alpine flowers as though just used, were a tarnished silver brush and comb.

"Oh my God! After all these years — my edelweiss linen," she sighed. "I had no idea it was this dear to her..." Her voice broke with emotion and her eyes misted.

Respectfully, Dr. Garton cleared his throat and peered at her over his eyeglasses, "My hope is to return Ten Chimneys to the home you love and remember, Diana."

Staring into the vanity's mirror, she looked not at herself, but into the room.

"You never really leave a place you love, do you?" she sighed again. "Part of it you take with you. Part of yourself you leave behind."

CHAPTER 1

The next day in the shadowed quietness of a little chapel, Diana lit a candle. She knelt and, into the soft flame, whispered a prayer. Her best asset was normally a brilliant smile, but she was not smiling as she stood and walked to a stained glass window. Watching a rivulet of rain stream down the colored pane outside, her hand gently stroked the name "Ferdinand Johnson" etched on the bottom panel of glass.

Taking a gardenia tucked behind her ear, she smelled its honeyed fragrance. Placing it on the weathered window-sill near the name, with tears in her eyes, she spoke softly, "From one world's sill to another's door. I'm sorry, Jules. I wasn't able to keep my promise."

The rain stopped as she stepped outside. Standing at the front entry of St. Paul's Catholic Church, she bound a woolen scarf around her neck in the sylvan cold and looked up. The sun peeked out from spent storm clouds rapidly moving across its celestial equator. Above, a giant white oversized cross stretched into the heavens. Built in the early 1870s, the modest white chapel perched on a high knoll.

From her vantage, a typical Wisconsin early spring day was budding with billowed white clouds forming against a deep blue sky. The crisp cold air smelled of wood burning from a nearby hearth; her first of many childhood memories. She brushed the thoughts away for the moment and hurried to a rental car a few yards away where her mother was waiting.

Both she and her mother Eileen were quiet as Diana drove through downtown Genesee Depot. The village, originally a small whistle-stop, hadn't changed since her childhood.

The Depot was located in the middle of thirty miles of Wisconsin Kettle Moraine State Forest. It was an arcadia that time had forgotten. Massive mature oaks lined the main road. Old paint peeled from the town hall and vacant post office. Torhorst's General Store was now a delicatessen, she noted. Perkins' Feed Store sign had disappeared. Union House Hotel, erected in 1861, was still the largest structure. Stag's Tavern was under different ownership.

At the end of town, however, the Milwaukee & Mississippi Railroad Branch Depot bustled with lunchtime activity. Originally built when tracks were laid in 1851, The Depot, now a thriving café, was later moved a short distance to the main road.

Inside the diner, surrounded by a billig of eating strangers, the ladies ordered the special of the day and coffee. From a window table, Diana gazed across the street.

Set back from the road on a huge expanse of lawn was a familiar two-story house. On the large wrap-around screened porch, her sweet elderly childhood friend Lettie Mason appeared for a brief moment. With her shock of white hair always faultlessly combed, she was teaching little Diana her expert crocheting skills, using her atrophied left hand.

There Lettie, stricken with polio as a child, lived and died in her wheelchair. Her widowed sister Iva lived there as well, always near to lift Lettie's twisted body from bed to bath to chair, and offer her a throw to ward off the chill. Diana recalled Lettie's smooth, angelic face holding an ageless beauty without the lines of worry.

Great barren elms cast long diagonal shadows in the late afternoon sun as Diana drove north on Depot Road through Wisconsin's dairy land. A neighboring farmer plowing the familiar green patchwork on his tractor waved at her passing car. The pastures as far as she could see, once populated with huge herds of cattle, were now dotted with only an occasional black and white Holstein.

At a steep rise in the road, the small township of North Prairie appeared in the distance. In the early 1900s Morey Milk Condensery had opened there, employing more than eighty-five percent of the people who lived in the surrounding area. In the late 1920s, Pet Milk Company bought the existing condensery and enlarged its dairy operation.

Diana drove onto a huge empty lot. Unlike Genesee Depot, something had changed in this nearby village.

"I can't believe it, Mom! Pet Milk's building isn't here anymore!"

Devastated, she realized the enormous red brick structure where Pet Milk Company once stood for forty years had been leveled by progress.

Her mother's dim eyes stared without comment. Eileen in her youth had looked much like her daughter; styled blonde hair, well-dressed. Now in her seventies, she wore a neat cotton pant suit with tightly permed grey hair. She had recently suffered several debilitating strokes.

Under sun-filtered green canopies of elm, maple and oak on a narrow winding road, the rental car passed into a dense forest of silver ash.

In a small clearing at the top of a hill, Diana slowly pulled off the road onto a graveled shoulder and stopped the car. She rolled down the car window, closed her eyes and breathed in the cool air. As she wrapped her sweater tighter around herself, like a womb, the insulated forest enveloped her in a familiar comforting silence.

In the distance, she heard a faint train whistle. A twig snapped only a few yards away as a squirrel scuttled up a tree. Diana flashed her brilliant smile and opened her bright, clear eyes.

Across the road she observed the Herrold's cottage. Although Virgel's white aluminum siding still looked new, Louise's favorite color red was missing on the front door. The living room of the cottage appeared enlarged and a garage was added at the end of the drive by the current homeowner. There were only a few bushes left of her grandmother's enormous protective hedge, once surrounding the property. Remaining, however, were the far-reaching shade trees and expansive green lawn her grandfather Virgel had trimmed and mowed every weekend.

Sadly, as with many homes in Wisconsin, Louise's flower and Virgel's vegetable and fruit gardens were gone. She wondered why the front yard looked so empty. Nana's aqua 1940s metal lawn furniture and hammock were no longer positioned under the giant shade trees. This was where the Herrolds spent many happy times with family and friends while meals cooked inside the cottage's small kitchen. What was once a cool place for conversation and rest during the oppressively hot and humid summer days, was now only a memory.

Overcome with emotion, she couldn't knock on the door as she had planned.

Driving slowly along Depot Road, she passed three other solitary houses, as she had done for years on her bicycle. The four familiar cottages on half-acres, set side by side surrounded by meadowlands, remained unchanged.

Shortly, the car stopped and Diana got out to open an unpretentious rough-hewn wooden gate. Continuing down a long winding paved drive, it entered a densely wooded area of rolling hills, with forests rising and falling like swells of the sea. This unique terrain consisting of 'kettles', was Southern Wisconsin's magnificent kettle moraine. Acres of trees, a lake and natural vegetation were alive with colorful songbirds, woodpeckers, white tail deer, pheasant, turkey buzzards, raccoons and squirrels.

The woods grew quiet at the unfamiliar sound of the car's motor. Diana's heart pounded as she seized an occasional glimpse of white appearing and disappearing through the thick trees. A charming wall of rounded field-stone bordered the drive to her left. She smiled recalling Alfred, pleased with his handiwork, describing his layer upon layer of smooth round rock as "his cherub bottoms".

Breaking the wooded stillness, Eileen snapped at her daughter from the passenger seat. "I don't know why we drove so far. You don't know anybody here."

The silence in the car was deafening as the two women, worlds apart but still seated next to each other, advanced slowly down the drive.

In a clearing, Diana caught her breath as a sprawling estate in obvious disrepair finally came into view, partly hidden by generations of buckthorn and forest overgrowth. A twenty-four room, three-story, white clapboard manor with dark green shutters appeared — the great house with its many chimneys — at last revealed itself.

She drove through a rusting, scrolled wrought iron double gate, into the moldering courtyard of Ten Chimneys, home of theater legends Alfred Lunt and Lynn Fontanne.

Instinctively she looked up at a second-floor French door that was Mr. Lunt's promontory. For a brief moment, she saw him standing there watching his guests' arrival. He was a commanding presence in a twill blazer and ascot with an eye patch covering his left eye.

Stunned, she blinked and looked again. Through a broken windowpane, dirty, split lace curtains rustled in the slight breeze.

CHAPTER 2

In a rotting pile of palmate leaves under an immense oak, Diana parked the rental car. An early spring rain returned as she switched off the ignition. Oblivious to the droplets forming on the windshield, Eileen seemed at ease to wait quietly while her daughter concluded her business.

Unhindered by another fresh cloudburst, Diana strolled the grounds of Ten Chimneys carefully watching for her dreaded childhood enemy: poison ivy. Under her footsteps, dead foliage from the fall and winter mulched into decay. The smells of moist dirt were borne again by spring and vivid violets and wildflowers adorned either side of the isolated path in front of her. A blackened tree felled and split in half by a prior lightning storm blocked her progress. As she climbed over the log, undergrowth rustled, shifted and parted. A squirrel peeked out, paused, then darted away.

From a commanding stand of white birch, came the haunting call of a bird. The bird's song emoted loud, sharp, piercing echoes above the trees. Looking up through the branches, Diana spied a proud, red-breasted robin.

The tall, stately trees were unnatural to the region, a gift to the Lunts from Alexander Woollcott, their controversial friend, radio personality and prominent theater critic. Diana had often overheard Miss Fontanne call her gay flamboyant, easily combustible Mr. Woollcott, "the big wind".

Passing the ruins of an 18th century Swedish log cabin, she read aloud a wooden plaque in uneven Old English typeset to the right of what was the Lunt's Studio door.

"Lynn and Alfred live here."

Unlike the natural kettle moraine, the area beyond The Studio showed traces of once well-planned gardens, orchards and landscapes — now barren and untended.

Advancing toward a red and white eight-room, two-story Scandinavian farm cottage, she gazed up at the balcony.

"Hello, Hattie." She smiled through the rain.

Behind grimy windows, Alfred's mother's once-white dotted-swiss curtains hung in gray tatters. Diana recalled bright filtered light flooding into an all-white bedroom. As a child she sat on a beautiful white vanity with yards and yards of gathered tulle over taffeta which she knew must now be covered with layers of canescent neglect.

She remembered Alfred boasting of buying ivory sheep-skins from a stockyard in Chicago for a hundred dollars. She sighed. Dear Alfred was tight like that. His designer, Syrie Maugham, had suggested a thousand-dollar sheepskin rug to complete the stunning 1930s Hollywood white ménage. It was staging Mr. Lunt was after — the effect — not the reality. If something could be made faux, why pay for originals.

In spite of the downpour, Diana continued past a barn and stables, stopping at a greenhouse window. With a circular hand motion, she wiped away dirtied wet film, and peered through darkened, aged glass. The inside once abundant with seedlings and lush greenery was reduced, she noted sadly, to a small scattering of pottery chards. She spied Mr. Lunt's Dutch weeding hoe and wooden gardening stool, up-ended and carelessly tossed in a corner, along with a soiled yellowing paper-wedged hat. On the brim barely-legible black lettering read 'Pet Milk'.

She strode across the wet grass and stood at the edge of an L-shaped pool emptied for years, where Broadway's theater giants once swam and played. Few people other than Diana probably even noticed Alfred had chosen the shape for his last name. The pool was currently filled with moist, rotting debris.

A copper mermaid, unperturbed by the ruins around her, sat atop the cupola of a faded red and white bathhouse. She was a whimsical creature, designed and crafted by Cecil Beaton, British photographer to kings and queens. He was also the Lunt's set designer.

Separating a tall group of muddied weeds — looking for something — Diana grew anxious. Finally, she exposed a soiled four-foot statuette of a young English maiden. Relieved, she wiped dirt from its face and smiled, remembering a summer afternoon long ago.

It was eerily quiet and almost dusk — Alfred's gloaming hour — as she walked down the knoll toward the back of the main house. A single shutter squeaked and swung precariously in the rimy breeze, interrupting the kettle moraine's stillness.

She breathed in a familiar lilac scent at the back terrace where she had often had tea with Miss Fontanne. Lynn's beloved lilac bush with large clusters of little flowers was grossly overgrown. Touching the roofline of the main house, it now enveloped Jules' upstairs apartment windows above the garage.

Walking around to the front of the manor house, she noticed the roof was sagging in the middle, and tares had grown as high as the second floor. Only hulled trunks remained of mature ivy vines that once climbed the trellis and sheltered Ten Chimneys' splendid veranda.

Surprised, Diana saw a laborer hoeing some smilax-looking greenery near the wrought-iron gate. He looked much like Ben Perkins, Ten Chimneys' original caretaker.

"Sir! Are you a Perkins?" She called to him.

Tired and muddy, the man looked at this stranger as if she was daft. Soaked and disheveled from the rain, she brushed wet hair from her eyes. "Please be careful! That's where Miss Fontanne's lily of the valley is planted. Shall I have Dr. Garton confirm this?"

The man shook his head as if to say 'no' and returned to his hoeing in a different spot.

Diana knew when the rain stopped and the sun warmed the earth, Lynn's tiny white baby bells would continue to emerge year after year, long after the childless couple's death.

CHAPTER 3

Under a green umbrella near Ten Chimneys' front entrance, Dr. Joseph Garton patiently waited. He was an articulate soft-spoken professor with a warm inviting smile.

"Delighted to see you again, Diana," he extended a hand in greeting. "Hope you had a restful evening after your long flight from California."

"Yes, I did." She smiled back. "Thank you, Dr. Garton, for meeting me on such short notice. My visit was much too brief yesterday."

He dropped his chin and peered at her over his glasses at half mast on his nose. His eyes twinkled. "Please, call me Joe."

Together Joe and Diana entered the main house. On murky foyer walls a painted Victorian-garbed maid and butler peered at them. The capricious servants presented a cordial and a pineapple. Intended to welcome Ten Chimneys' guests, they were the creation of a close friend, Claggett Wilson, another Lunt-Fontanne costume and set designer.

They side-stepped some ceiling drips and a huge mud hole in the middle of the grand entry floor. Above them, next to a stunning Czechoslovakian crystal chandelier, a bulging leak threatened to pellet the two visitors with dirty water again.

"After all those years, Mr. Lunt was never able to repair that roof leak," she acknowledged.

"It will be fixed at last, Diana," Dr. Garton assured her. "I already have a professional contracted."

Remembering Mr. Lunt's frustration, she nodded, "Alfred will be very pleased."

Ascending a spiral staircase, they passed through a great hall and entered the Lunt's drawing room. To their left was the gay grand Steinway, also painted by Clagg Wilson, where Noël Coward loved to play and sing 'his ditties' before dinner.

In the middle of the room was an elegant matching set of antique chairs. The armrests were worn through to the stuffing and ashen-dust covered the original bright citric fabric. Alfred's mother Harriet Sederholm had gifted them to him when she came to live in the 'hen house', his affectionate term for the red and white farm cottage. Alfred had a rich imagination — but this time his humor was literal — it was originally a chicken coop.

Clagg painted classic scenes from the Bible on the walls in this room. To complement his set designs, Alfred purchased blackamoors supporting tables, statues holding lamps and faces painted on fine china. Even when the Lunts were alone at Ten Chimneys, a cast of hundreds appeared to surround them.

Leaving the drawing room, Diana heard the familiar intricate refrain of a Viennese Waltz. Briefly Miss Fontanne appeared, dressed in a pale gown, seated at a table near a gilded mirror. She was playing solitaire, awaiting Alfred's call to dinner.

"Did you hear that?" Diana asked Joe Garton, now standing in the great hall.

"Hear what?" The professor replied, unaware.

She looked back into the drawing room. The elaborately carved wooden table with playing cards was there, but Lynn had vanished.

"My imagination, I guess," she shook her head.

Joe opened the double doors to Mr. Lunt's Swedish Baroque dining room. "Since you grew up in this area, I'm sure you're familiar with our midwestern farming communities. Much of their activity revolved around supper and conversation. Life at Ten Chimneys was no different."

"Oh yes, Mr. Lunt was the ultimate gentleman's farmer and loved bringing his fresh garden fare to the table." Touching the head of an Italian Majolica Courtesan bust on a side table, Diana laughed. "One evening at dinner when I was a young girl, I placed a napkin over that bare breast in embarrassment. To tease me in my adult years, Alfred was mindful to cover it."

Here, too, Clagg's murals covered walls and ceiling. Above the dining table he painted images of Antoinette, Lynn's sister. Diana noticed each figure progressively revealing Antoinette's face growing more and more gay with drink. In childhood she had not discerned this erotic gradation.

"Do you know Hattie saved every letter Alfred wrote her?" With purpose Joe entered the kitchen and opened a drawer. "We found them all, even one dated when he was five years old. There are copious notes and recipes in here written to someone named Jules. Did you know a Jules?"

Struggling with emotion, not knowing where to begin, Diana nodded her head and opened a tall, thin cabinet door. A handwritten log in Mr. Lunt's own pen was tacked to the inside of the door, his instructions to the staff for the numerous light fixtures on the estate. With Alfred's penchant for detail and a stage manager's precision, every light — no matter how small — was given a wattage designation.

"With proper lighting, a great actor's slightest nuance becomes profound." Diana repeated an Alfred witticism.

In the kitchen stairwell leading down to the garage, she peered into a silent butler and spied familiar discolored spots on its wooden base.

"I don't believe it! The blueberry stains are still here," she sighed. "Mr. Lunt was so angry at me for climbing in with my berry basket."

"You were actually able to fit into this small contraption?" Joe chuckled.

"Well, I was a very skinny eight year old at the time," Diana smiled. "Mr. Lunt was very proud of his 'contraption'. Jules told me it was inspired by a picture in a Sears and Roebuck catalog and it took Alfred many days to design and build. He watched him hammer and nail it together with ropes and pulleys, cursing, 'I'll be damned if I'll pay forty dollars when I can build it with scraps!'"

They both laughed at Alfred's notorious frugality.

"So you did know Jules." Joe was fascinated.

"Jules was one of the finest men I've ever known," Diana admitted. "He was godfather to both me and my son, David. A dear friend to five generations of my family."

Captivated, Joe dropped his chin and again peered at her over his eyeglasses. "We must have a long talk about your Jules, Diana."

Continuing their tour of the manor, they re-entered the great hall Alfred dubbed the Flirtation Room. Fashioned after the romantic intrigue of a French farce, the hall had six entrances leading into a labyrinth of rooms. The Lunt's preferred the open-air windows of Europe, and their French doors with lace curtains opened out to view the courtyard and drive leading up to the grand manse.

"Miss Fontanne and I used to have tea here." Sitting down at a loveseat, she touched the marble top of a hand-carved wooden table in front of her.

A few yards away, her eyes drifted to a small, elegant chest. She strode across the room to it and opened a tiny cubby revealing an assortment of old black well-worn eye patches.

"He hated the thought of wearing eye patches in public in his senior years. But with Miss Fontanne's insistence, he eventually wore them, thinking they might actually look distinguished."

Through an open door, she stepped into the Belasco Room. Quickly returning, she commented, "The casting couch is still there."

Joe's eyes sparkled, "Alfred fell in love with and purchased the entire office originally owned by David..." realizing Diana was deep in thought, he finished quietly, "... Belasco."

She stared out from Alfred's French doors, touching the lace curtain. "This time of day he would be in his garden gathering vegetables for Jules to prepare. She would be in the kitchen arranging gladiolas for tonight's dinner."

Eerily, Diana parted the soiled curtains. Her memories of Mr.

Lunt opened and closed here. From Alfred's bird's-eye view, she envisioned a stage play.

Act One, Scene One

1.1 Enter [Center Stage]: A skinny blonde-haired girl (6) on a new red bicycle. She approaches Ten Chimneys' laundry room door having no earthly reason to trespass on his property.

Act Three, Final Scene

3.3 Exit [Stage Left]: Same girl, now a young woman (25) in a beat-up blue Volkswagen, weighted down with all her worldly belongings including a husband and child.

Intuitively, she has reappeared at precisely the right time to help an old dear friend.

CHAPTER 4

In the late 1930s, to the delight of newlyweds Virgel and Louise Herrold, Diana's grandparents, four half-acre lots went up for sale near Genesee Depot. The parcels were situated at the top of a hill on Depot Road with neighboring farmland beyond and, to the side, lush dense forest. The property was also only a few minutes by car from Virgel's work in North Prairie, so the Herrolds eagerly bought one parcel.

Their best friends, Marion and Rhea Lemon, purchased what they thought was the adjoining lot. Both couples dated together and married the same year. The four best friends presumed to live next door to each other for the rest of their lives, until they were told two other families had bought parcels between them.

Louise tried to talk her new neighbors, the Dables, into trading lots with Rhea and Marion. But she wasn't persuasive enough — or maybe too insistent. Whatever it was, they wouldn't accommodate. Louise incited a couple big flaps early on, then planted an impenetrable hedge around her property and refused to talk to them for over thirty years. In spite of the adult rift, Diana and Martin Dable became best childhood friends.

The Herrolds and Lemons built their houses themselves, brick by brick, beam by beam. Like most survivors of The Depression, they refused to borrow from the bank. In the summer, they laid the stone drive, dug the cellar and poured the foundation cement. When the cold set in that winter, they lived below the ground with only a temporary cover, until enough money was saved to build the rest of the house. The next spring framing began with assistance from Opa Zabel, Louise's German-born widower father. Bob Pietrowski, her only child by an earlier marriage, appeared briefly to help. Secretly, though, Virgel discovered Bob had come home to pinch money from his mother.

On a hot, humid afternoon when the Herrold's house was nearing completion, a stranger strolled out of the dense forest and approached their acreage from the top of a hill. Louise had seen him before. On occasion, usually in the late afternoon, he would appear and disappear into the kettle moraine near the neighboring estate of Ten Chimneys.

Dressed in a sun hat, khaki pants, and white dress shirt with sleeves rolled up to the elbow, the man approached from the opposite side of Depot Road. As the figure drew closer, it was apparent he was a black man. He walked with a light step, a dignity that belied his social status, dabbing his forehead and wiping his hands with a freshly-ironed white linen handkerchief.

In a celebrative mood having just finished insulating their house frame and attic, the Herrolds were resting on their front lawn chairs in the shade. Virgel waved and shouted, "Would you like to come join me and my wife for some refreshment?"

Hesitantly the man considered, then crossed the road and shook Virgel's extended hand in greeting. Both men had a strong, solid grasp. It was apparent they instantly liked each other.

Still sweating from the heat, Virgel removed his small-brimmed straw hat and combed his hand through his thick, wavy hair. "My name is Virgel Herrold and this is my wife, Louise."

"Ach, call me Lu," Louise chirped, handing the man a Manhattan.

Professionally, Virgel was Head Bacteriologist at Pet Milk Company. Socially, he was a man of few words and happily content to stand in the background and allow his wife to take center stage.

Louise Herrold was a large, cuddly, warmhearted woman with

henna-red hair, fashioned like her movie star idol Lucille Ball. Above her deep blue eyes were penciled-thin, over-plucked, arched brows that refused to grow back. Louise was young of spirit and always the life of every party.

"I'm Ferdinand Johnson, but everyone calls me Jules." He was soft-spoken, with a slight West Indies' accent and a kind smile. A medium-built man with short, dark, nappy hair, his skin was a polished light mahogany and his eyes were deep brown pools of quiet wisdom. "Delighted to meet you."

"I already know all about you," Louise chirred. Because there was little she didn't know about her neighbors, she had asked Aggy Pronold about this reserved gentleman. Aggy ran the Genesee Depot post office and was the only person who knew more than Louise about the comings and goings of everyone in The Depot.

Virgel proudly opened his red front door, freshly painted to match the porch and stairs. "My little bride loves red," he boasted. "I hope to be finished before the fall. Would you like to see my workshop in the basement?"

"Would love to." Jules followed Virgel into the house and through the small kitchen. "My father was an accomplished carpenter."

"Lu tells me you work for the Lunts?" Virgel inquired.

"Yes, that's true. I had the good fortune of meeting them in New York, fresh out of the Army. Jules stopped at the stove. "Something sure smells good in here! May I take a peek?" He lifted a lid on a big simmering pot. "What is it?"

"Sauerbraten!" Louise handed him a large serving spoon. "Go on — take a big slurp. No one makes it as good as me, I'll tell ya — huh, Virg?"

"Do you use a special seasoned vinegar for the marinade?" Jules asked.

"Well, I don't know about that," Louise was confused. "I just throw this and that together until it tastes good." She nudged him and giggled, "Good cooks don't need recipes, right?"

Jules chuckled, immediately enjoying this woman's company. Louise Herrold related to everyone with sincerity and affection.

The following weekend Jules helped Virgel hammer up durable white aluminum siding on the house exterior while Virgel began the finishing work on the inside. Louise's brother Hank and father Zabel, who lived and worked together on Hank's large mink ranch in Marinette, drove in from Northern Wisconsin to join in the construction.

That summer Jules and the Herrolds began a close friendship that would last a lifetime.

Chapter 5

Noël Coward phoned Ten Chimneys from London one evening. "Well my darlings, it may be a long time before Rabbit's Bottom sees Grandpa and Grandma again. Think of me. Think of old England. I am thinking of you."

The next day, Lynn Fontanne fretfully snipped another rose and placed it into her gardening basket. "I'm picking roses and our dear Noëllie could soon be lying dead somewhere in Mother England!"

On his hands and knees Alfred Lunt was weeding nearby, a compulsion displayed at inappropriate times that annoyed Lynn almost as much as his gleeful hand-rubbing.

Purposefully, he stood up, dusted the soil from his six-foot-three frame and took his wife by the hand. Without a word the couple walked to The Studio.

Once inside, he placed a record on the turntable and, while husband and wife of over twenty years danced cheek-to-cheek, Glen Miller's band played 'The White Cliffs of Dover'.

There'll be love and laughter
And peace ever after
Tomorrow, when the world is free...

Alfred kissed her tenderly. "Lynnie, we will not open The Studio until Noël is with us again," he promised as the refrain continued to play.

There'll be bluebirds over the white cliffs of Dover
Tomorrow, just you wait and see...

Sometime later as Alfred began to close and lock the Studio door, "Just one moment!" Lynn stopped him. Choosing one flawless rose from her basket, she placed it on an inside window sill.

Daily, as she walked through her flower gardens or rode her horse Franklin on Ten Chimneys' acreage, Lynn thought about her British family and friends. And her frustration over the war continued to grow throughout the winter.

After hearing a Christmas Day broadcast over the radio from the fighting lines of Finland where Russia was bombing Helsinki, the famed scribe Robert Sherwood immediately fashioned a rough draft of a play entitled 'Revelation' and dispatched it to the Lunts. During the train ride home after a benefit performance of 'Shrew' for the Finnish Relief Fund, the Lunts read his initial draft. Sherwood's words so emblazoned the couple that they instantly decided to unlock their Studio and invite Bob Sherwood to Ten Chimneys.

Alfred at once identified with Sherwood's character, Dr. Karlo Valkomen, a Nobel-winning neurologist, who abhorred war. With Lynn as his American wife, Miranda, the acting couple transcended the ordinary speech of concerned parents whose son and fiancée go to the warfront. Upon word of the son's death, the daughter-in-law returned home unharmed and pregnant, turning Bob Sherwood's simple drama into a message of hope. Although killing was morally reprehensible to Valkomen, reluctantly, he fought for this just cause. Courageous, too, his wife remained behind at home in Finland, refusing to return to America.

From Alfred's youth in Finland, the scribe mined the actor's love and in-depth knowledge of language and land. Within three and a half months, Sherwood and Lunt rewrote the play and, with the Theatre Guild's assistance, assembled a Lunt-Fontanne production at Ten Chimneys. During the rewrites, at Lynn's insistence in Scene III, her "coffee growing cold" dialogue was brilliantly transformed beyond the mundane, revealing the tragedy of one's home in an unprepared free country where global assassins penetrate.

With the Lunt's help, the newly titled 'There Shall Be No Night' opened in Providence, Rhode Island, March 29, 1940, and went on to tour and impassion a nation. It was to become a play to end America's isolationism of the war. After seeing the play, Eleanor Roosevelt was quoted: "Alfred Lunt and Lynn Fontanne gave a performance so perfect that I felt I was living in this portrayal on the stage."

Charles Chaplin, after viewing their performance, admitted he, too, was emotionally moved. So much so, he could not go backstage to congratulate his dear friends afterwards.

CHAPTER 6

On a balmy evening in April, still hot from the oven, a raspberry pie compliments of Louise Herrold cooled in the Ten Chimneys' kitchen, filling the room with a sweet, pungent aroma. It was to be served after Alfred's rack of lamb entrée.

"Which wine in our cellar is best with lamb?" Alfred catechized to himself. "Shall it be white or rose?" He was still in his chef's apron, fussing with a pureed raspberry icing to coat the French vanilla ice cream, a perfect accompaniment to Louise's pie.

In the dining room, Jules placed a vase of Lynn's handpicked irises and greenery on a side table.

Nearby in the adjoining room, Helen Hayes and her husband, Charles MacArthur were sipping martinis. Seasoned stage professionals, the couple radiated confidence and always reminded Lynn of a pair of peacocks. Helen's girl-next-door looks and modesty belied her great acting talent and MacArthur, a writer, was known for his boastful, dramatic flair. Although Charles rarely accompanied his wife, Miss Hayes was a frequent guest at Ten Chimneys, visiting several times a year.

"If Alfred starts talking theater insignificance again, I'm going to rant on in detail about my typewriter ribbon jamming in the middle of a sentence..." MacArthur groused.

Jules hurried into the kitchen, "I hear Miss Hayes laughing in the Flirtation Room. I'll finish the glaze, Mr. Lunt. You best run upstairs and dress for dinner."

Alfred untied the apron and was only half-way out of it when Jules grabbed it and quickly disappeared.

Shortly, to the strains of Chopin, Jules entered the Flirtation Room with a silver platter of herring and liver pate. "Mr. Lunt and Miss Fontanne will be with you momentarily," Jules' face was flushed, but his voice composed.

Limping into the room moments later, the brilliant dramatist Eugene O'Neill was met by a respectable silence filled only by the soft, convoluted music. Gaunt and somber, he was drinking prolifically, obviously suffering from a crippling illness.

"Scotch is a curious spirit," he observed. "One more drink and old Napoleon would be a piker!" Amidst scattered laughter, the Nobel laureate raised his glass. "To Helen! It is seldom that a playwright has the privilege of hearing his character realized exactly as he imagined it. You have given me that in your radio performance of 'The Straw'."

"Thank you, Eugene," Helen bantered. "Tis the same part you denied me years ago because of my lack of experience!"

"Rightly so. At that time years ago, you did lack experience!" Eugene's taunt was received with nervous laughter.

Miss Fontanne floated down the spiral stairs, a striking figure, elegantly dressed in a white velvet gown and matching rhinestone heeled pumps. With each step, her shoulder and hip dipped and rolled while her head remained level, her eyes focused. Her gleaming raven hair was twisted back in a psyche knot, bejeweled in a sparkling hair ornament. Perfectly-applied make-up enhanced her translucent English porcelain skin. Her deep-set, red-brown eyes with long sweeping false lashes were hers and Garbo's alone. She placed a cigarette in her black onyx holder.

"You're particularly lovely this evening, Lynn." Awkwardly, Eugene produced a lighter from his jacket pocket.

"Thank you, *dah-h-h-ling*. I wore this little dress in 'The Guardsman'." With elaborate drama, Lynn leaned toward the flame, inhaling and exhaling deeply. "Reminds me of our brief mundane film career. Endless take after take!" she drolled. "I told Universal's Carl Laemmle, we can be bought, *dah-ling*, but not bored!"

Everyone applauded and chuckled. What Lynn did not say, but all acknowledged, was that the Lunts did not compromise their work. They were an acting team, refusing to be paired with anyone else on stage. And their leisurely summers together at Ten Chimneys were not to be interrupted.

Resplendent in black tie, Alfred grandly opened the double doors of Ten Chimneys' lavish dining room. "Same as the day Paul Pioret fitted her. Isn't she beautiful!" Alfred seated Lynn at her place of honor at the table and kissed her hand. "One of the advantages of not having children — right darling?" She jerked her hand away from his lips and smiled broadly for their guests.

Seating himself at the other end of the table nearest the kitchen, Alfred watched each guest take a seat at Lynn's scripted place cards. As Jules poured into bottomless flutes a rare champagne, the legendary thespians managed to conceal their broken hearts over the war in Europe.

O'Neill tossed down another glass of Scotch, attempting to drown the pain of his milk leg, lamenting he had not seen his daughter Oona in anything other than maternity since her Sweet Sixteen. Grumbling something about his son-in-law, Charlie Chaplin, being old enough to be her father, Eugene finally in drunken agitation spat out,

"She's become a God-damn baby machine!"

"Get that man another drink!" Alfred quipped as Jules entered with a soup tureen and expertly ladled crème vichyssoise into each guest's bowl. "Who are you complaining about now, Eugene?" He didn't expect an answer. Everyone knew and no one cared except O'Neill that Chaplin was almost thrice Oona's age.

"We need another bottle of that magnificent..." Alfred squinted to read the vineyard label, "...damned small print ..." he mussed, "... Chateau d'Yquem to celebrate England's imminent triumph over the Third Reich!"

"Here! Here!" Lynn lifted her wine glass.

Placing a small silver crumb brush under his nose, Alfred cleverly remarked, "Remember, Adolf loves The Arts! He even trimmed his mustache to Little Tramp size!" He rose from the table and exited, Chaplin style, with splayed feet and twirled napkin. To all but Eugene's laughter, he clicked his heels and disappeared into the kitchen.

While Alfred routed in the cellar, Jules tastefully placed parsley and mint around the rack of lamb on a large silver tray. From the kitchen he overheard a heated debate erupt about guild membership between O'Neill and MacArthur in the dining room.

"...All of theater knows my spigot hails from an aged Broadway cask..." O'Neill raved.

"...Well, I'll take a union man who fights for his country," MacArthur interrupted, "over faggot writers and actors any day!"

The usually witty, urbane company plunged into an embarrassed silence when Alfred returned to the table wrestling with another bottle of wine and popped the cork. Following him, Jules balanced a laden tray with the rack of lamb garnished in white paper frills and asparagus spears.

Surprised, Ten Chimneys' host arched his eyebrows. "What happened?" Helen cleared her throat, "Well, unions are fortunately — or unfortunately here to stay. I say we oblige. Look at me ... I only intended to cooperate. Then I met my Charlie and, I have to say, sleeping with it isn't so bad," she humored, dabbing her mouth delicately with her napkin. All at the table laughed. Helen's quick wit placed everyone at ease.

Appeased, MacArthur puffed his chest and lifted his glass. It was obvious to all Helen had raised the smoothing of her husband's ruffled feathers to an art form.

Lynn threw her head back and laughed so hard, her unfettered breasts shook. "Helen, *dah-h-ling*, t'would be even better were it published! What's all the fuss, for God's sake! Alfred and I joined The Guild twenty years ago. They had greater literary theatre then — and still do in my opinion!" She smiled beguilingly at O'Neill, making a mental note not to invite MacArthur to her dining table again. She knew Helen was very shrewd and was probably thinking the same.

Deadly serious, Eugene responded. "Listen to what she says,

Helen. Her droll comment at dinner about possessive mothers won me a Pulitzer."

Raising an index finger, Alfred reminded her, "Ah, but you forget Lynnie! The guild's lack of vision almost cost us 'Idiot's Delight' — Sherwood's first!" Affecting O'Neill's style of stage play, Alfred hummed and began to pound the table mysteriously like a tom-tom. Then, with increased volume, "And the chorus chants..." He began with melodramatic ceremony, using his large demonstrative hands to frame his eyes in a brooding expression, "*This* is 'A Strange Interlude'... ."

"...Ah, yes, my social misfits and their illusions..." O'Neill chuckled. "Which reminds me, how is our perilously wild Mr. Coward and his affinities?"

Alfred's drums playfully crescendoed and ended in a rhumba beat. Everyone laughed as he capered about, snapping fingers and kicking heels.

Abruptly, Alfred stopped. "Noël's most recent letter from Goldenhurst says he is enmeshed in a musical about a blithe spirit, I believe he called it." His tall frame stood erect and his dark eyes darted into the corners of the room. When the suspense was finally unbearable, he licked his thumb and index fingers, and snuffed out the dinner candle in front of him.

Standing behind him, waiting a beat, Jules hit the light switch. As the room plunged into darkness there was a collective gasp from the dinner guests. Lynn, holding one flickering candle, slowly, gracefully, walked the length of table to Alfred.

Whispering coyly over Alfred's shoulder, she rekindled his smoking wick. "'Twas Roosevelt's speech writer who brought us 'There Shall Be No Night'."

With the timing of a seasoned stage hand, Jules flipped the switch and the crystal chandelier flooded the room once again with light.

With his duties done for the moment, Jules returned to the now-quiet kitchen. Alone, he sat down at the table and bowed his head. With an explosion of applause from the next room, he quickly finished his prayer with the sign of the cross and began to eat his meal.

Back in the dining room, everyone at table stood up and clapped, including O'Neill, as Lynn and Alfred took their bows.

"I'm highly complimented, Eugene." Lynn bowed again, deeper this time, and threw him a kiss.

The Lunt's renowned Nobelist and Pulitzer-winning guest smiled, pleased with their artful sport.

Under the tutelage and close friendship of giants like First Lady Eleanor Roosevelt and Dame Ellen Terry, Lynn was liberated in mind and body long before America's feminist movement. And, whether she consciously knew it or not, the precision with which she approached her work on stage, and her personal life at Ten Chimneys, was firmly shaping and maturing American theater.

Shaking her head, Lynn laughed to herself. All this worldly wisdom from a poor typesetter's daughter born Lillie Louise in a hovel in Woodford, Essex, England. But, she vowed, Lynn Fontanne, the world-renowned actress of stage, would be her own alpha and omega from her haven at Ten Chimneys. Determined to be the first and last to laugh at the fates of her own unhappy childhood — so much for misfits and illusions, she thought.

Eugene's booming, slurred voice interrupted her reflections. "And a final good riddance to 'The Beast' — Adolf fucking Hitler — with Alfred's excellent vintage!"

All at table joined O'Neill in raised glasses and one final sip to seal The Great Dictator's fate.

Setting his glass down, Alfred rubbed his hands together gleefully, "Anyone for raspberry pie? Picked fresh from our Genesee neighbor's garden."

"Alfred, must you!" Lynn demanded, referring to his hand-rubbing, which irritated her immensely.

Lynn Fontanne could not fault Alfred Lunt's timing, however. It was always impeccable, whether he was emoting dialog on stage, or acting as host and chef of Ten Chimneys.

"Jules," he called, "help me serve, please."

CHAPTER 7

While the war raged in Europe, Russia joined the Allied Forces and Germany occupied Greece. Sherwood diligently adapted the new events for British audiences and, with the Roosevelt's encouragement, the Lunts decided to take "There Shall Be No Night" overseas. Without question, they planned to donate a large portion of their profits to the British cause.

Before they sailed to England, Alfred wrote to Hattie. "Mother, I had to do it. I have always thought of myself as all arse and no character. Ever since the war broke out, I felt I wasn't doing enough. I couldn't get into the Army or Navy. If we can help the Anglo-American relations, that's dandy with us. At least they have living proof an English girl and an American can get on damned well."

Once in London, the Lunts visited often with their close friends, the Oliviers, in their English countryside.

Again, Alfred wrote to Hattie, "We had a heavenly weekend with Larry Olivier and Vivien Leigh. The nicest I believe we ever had. Delicious food and such a warm sweet cottage. Fires in every room, and beautiful countryside to look out on. They have but one maid, but Vivien is a perfect housekeeper. We had the old pre-war breakfast in bed as though the house has six servants. I had a high old time as their garden was full of weeds and I did go to it."

Throughout their war effort, the Lunts visited with John Gielgud, Cecil Beaton, Britain's Greek Ambassador, the Duchess of Kent, Lady

Juliet Duff, the Duchess of Westminster and Winifred Ashton. There were also many luncheons at the Ritz with other English Royals.

One evening the King and Queen publicly appeared in their Royal Box at a performance. But the Lunts also secretly performed 'Love In Idleness' for them at the Royal Palace of Westminster.

They gave public performances daily and their engagements began at precisely five p.m., so theater goers could hurry home before London's mandatory blackout.

When General Patton came backstage one evening, Lynn told friends Alfred was so overwhelmed with emotion, he almost went down on his knees.

His biggest thrill, however, was when Winston Churchill walked down the aisle to his front row seat, flashing his 'V' for victory sign. When Alfred produced a cigar on stage, acting as Cabinet Minister, Churchill stood up and the crowd exploded with applause. The next morning, with Churchill en route to the Alta Conference, a large Corona cigar with the Prime Minister's hand-signed band was delivered to Mr. Lunt at The Savoy Hotel.

Even amidst all of this coronation, Alfred in his humble manner anonymously emptied bedpans as an air raid warden volunteer at St. George's Hospital. He also made hundreds of waffles at the military canteen and, afterwards, washed dishes for the troops.

One night during a performance, a buzz bomb hit the London theater. As a fire curtain fell toward the stage, Alfred grabbed it and righted it — shouting in his high pitched nasal, "Take it up! Take it!" Then, at that precise moment, he recited his scripted line to Lynn, "Are you all right darling?" The audience stood up and burst into cheers holding up the play much longer than the explosion.

From his Goldenhurst estate, they continued to receive regular letters from Noël during those war years. Coward wrote four plays, all the while entertaining British troops. His friend David Lean adapted three of his plays to film in the mid-1940s, the most successful, 'Brief Encounter', was considered one of the best film dramas of World War II. Even after the British troops trashed Goldenhurst, Noël continued to write from a cottage near Dover's white cliffs.

In the early dawn of April 30, 1945, as was their custom, Alfred and Lynn were lying side by side in bed in their suite at The Savoy reading a script. It was another rewrite of 'Love In Idleness' and Sherwood had given it a new title, 'O Mistress Mine'. They were a handsome couple, barefoot and dressed in luxurious white satin loungewear. But their down-at-heel slippers, carefully laid out by Jules the night before, were at the ready on the floor at bedside.

In the hallway, there was a soft knock at their door. "Jules," Alfred whined, "I hope you have our weekly care package!"

Smiling broadly, Jules entered with a breakfast tray and a large brown parcel from Ten Chimneys neatly wrapped and addressed in Ben's handsome cursive.

In great anticipation, Alfred rubbed his large hands gleefully.

"Please don't *do* that!" Lynn laughed. "You *know* how I hate it!"

From the opened box Alfred lifted a coveted array of fruit, meat, vegetables, butter and eggs, and finally found Ben's customary letter.

To himself he read, "Mr. Lunt, I want to get this off my mind at the top. George Bugbee is at it again, disrupting the entire household staff. Jules is much too polite to mention this to you, but here at home I can hardly tolerate it. Promise you'll have a talk with your brother-in-law before the situation becomes unbearable..."

"Alfred, *dah-h-ling*," Lynn interrupted his silence. "I'm every bit as interested in Ten Chimneys as you are... Read out loud, won't you?"

Clearing his throat, Alfred began reading only selected passages, preferring not to fuel Lynn's on-going agitation toward his relations 'the Finns'. "Well, let me see. Ah! Here we go. 'The bulbs are in full bloom and have peaked.' Yes, yes, but what about the hens, Benny? 'In the mornings Lynn's lilac bush is the most fragrant... I place a fresh basket of eggs and an empty can at the front gate... Enclosed is $7.80 in egg money...decided Miss Fontanne could better use this for the war effort...I'm sure at this point, Mr. Lunt, you are exasperated, but I will not disappoint. As you instructed, I fed the hens some minnows, skim milk and a meal of turnip tops and cabbage. They are now exuberantly laying eggs! Also, I have now made sure, as you insisted, even on the coldest days the cow has a sun bath for one to two hours. Yes, Mr. Lunt, giving her access to salt was very helpful...'" Alfred finally beamed, "Now, that's my Benny!"

Listening, Jules poured coffee as Alfred resumed reading, "'...our roses are not yet in bloom, but I am confident they will return from the cold winter much like the glory of Lynn's beloved England from this war...'"

Thinking of home and Ten Chimneys, Alfred's voice grew hushed and his eyes filled with tears. "'We all dearly miss you,'" he read.

Lynn, too, was stricken with homesickness. "Alfred, dear, did I tell you Stanley Phenus came backstage a few nights ago? He was terribly disappointed you could not be found. He looked so handsome in his uniform." She sighed. "He was desperately worried about things back home in The Depot."

"Godspeed we all return home safely," Jules spoke for all.

Outside in the street, a noisy commotion erupted.

"What-the-devil?" Irritated, Alfred put the letter down, jumped from the bed and flung the hotel windows wide open.

In the street below, enveloped in London's early morning fog, a crowd of people began to gather around a young newsboy. "Hitler is dead! Read all about it!" The lad shouted, excitedly, as a mass of people grabbed at his papers.

Incredulous, Alfred bellowed into the street. "Did you say The Beast is dead?"

"No, sir!" The boy screamed back. "I said Hitler is dead!"

"I'll get a paper!" Jules hurriedly ran out the door.

Only moments later still standing at the hotel window, Alfred read the newspaper. Holding Churchill's cigar between index and thumb, he envisioned the last scene of a play befitting The Globe or The Abbey.

WWII World Stage
Battlefield, German Countryside

3.7 Enter [Center Stage]: Allied soldiers with bayonets poised, march to battle onto the World Stage and into the German countryside.

With muzzles blasting and blades clashing, the Allieds overrun the Nazis, killing and maiming as they go!

A Nazi Prison Camp

Enter [Stage right]: Chorus dressed as Holocaust Prisoners. Behind them, chimneys spew a white-gray subcutaneous ash.

(They hiss and chant.)

The Beast! The Beast! Lucifer!
Judas! Iago! Mussolini!
Hitler, do you hear? The shots that
Rang in Mezzegra?
Victory! Victory! Victory is ours!

A Dark Underground Bunker
Berlin

Enter [Stage left]: Shakespeare's 20th century Iago, Adolf Hitler, his companion Eva Braun and a Nazi Officer amidst the muted noise of troops still fighting above them.

Nazi Officer: (A Hitler Jugend, tall, beautiful, blue-eyed.)
I now pronounce you man and wife.
Have you a ring, Herr Fuehrer?

Chorus [Stage right]: (The Prisoners hiss.)
Die Lugeshamluse! Die Lugeshamluse!
The Beast! The Beast!
Ancient Celtic words for all time,
Yeat's Slouching Beast!
War! War! Evil, vile war!

Bunker [Stage left]: Hitler presents from his uniform pocket, not a wedding ring, but a small vial.

Chorus [Stage right]: (The Prisoners shout and hiss.)
With smell of bitter almonds
And taste of golden flux
Victory! Victory! Victory is ours!

Bunker [Stage left]: Hitler lifts the vial and empties it into his mouth, biting down on the crystalline cyanide. Embracing his bride, he kisses her, deeply, passing the poison to her tongue. Their bodies collapsing in spasms, they die.

Chorus [Stage right]: (The Prisoners shout, triumphant.)
Yeat's Slouching Beast is Dead!
The Beast! The Beast is Dead!

Battlefield [Center Stage]: (A funeral durge.) Weary soldiers help their wounded from the battlefield. A dead soldier is placed in a body bag and carried away.

Exit Chorus [Stage right]: Stooped and broken, the Holocaust Prisoners solemnly march across the blackened field.

An emaciated old man falls and a young woman lifts him up. A young woman breaks down in tears while an older man comforts her.

A father, crying softly, hugs a dead child to his breast.

All Exeunt

❧ ✻ ❧

"Shall I get you a light, Mr. Lunt?" Jules asked.

"No thank you, Jules," Alfred stared at the cigar band with Churchill's bold signature. "I think I shall keep the casing precisely the way it is for the rest of my life."

Lynn joined Alfred at the window, as the rimy morning fog lifted and the sun shone through the thick haze. Together they stared beyond the River Thames looking for London's skyline, but none was visible. Engulfed in clouds of smoke were the Houses of Parliament and Westminster Abbey. Rising above the pocked and rubbled destruction of war-torn streets, only St. Paul's Cathedral and the face of Big Ben could be seen.

"I was afraid of the bombs. Yet it wasn't fear of death, but fear of separation..." Alfred took Lynn's hand and kissed it tenderly, "...the terror of being apart from you when something happened."

Chapter 8

After several years' absence, Louise's son Bob unexpectedly returned home with a new fiancée and her little girl. Young Eileen Johnson was a pretty farmer's daughter and Maxine, an adorable four-year-old dressed in a sailor's suit with a head full of curly hair. Ecstatic, Louise thought maybe her Bobby might finally settle down. Although Bob walked with a limp resulting from a childhood disease, he was a physically vital man who unfortunately had quite a reputation as a womanizer.

Bob had a God-given artistic talent but was uncommonly lazy. That summer in an uncharacteristic burst of hope and energy, he helped Louise apply a pretty apple blossom paper to the Herrold's living room walls, and designed, built and installed a large mirror with glass shelves. Pleased, Louise placed her treasured knickknacks on the glass. He also painted a pastoral scene over the Herrold's bathtub of which his mother was particularly proud.

In the late summer, Bob and Eileen married in Louise's newly-decorated front room. With bouquets of flowers and lit candles placed on the shelves in front of the mirror, Louise lovingly transformed her living room into a wedding altar. Little Maxine was thrilled to be her mother's flower girl. The ceremony was attended by less than a dozen people and the only guest outside of immediate family was Jules Johnson.

Only months later, Eileen announced she was pregnant and, by the next spring, she was due to deliver her second child. On April 25th, the young mother's water burst early and when she reached the hospital in Milwaukee, she was already in hard labor.

Bob and Eileen's baby was not willing to wait for her mother to be prepped for delivery. Instead, Diana Lynn Pietrowski burst into the world on the lobby floor of St. Mary's Hospital. Along with her proud grandparents, Jules was also present during the bedlam.

Shortly after his daughter's birth, Bob disappeared again and Eileen with her two girls was forced to move to a small apartment above a photography studio in downtown Milwaukee on the very busy Wisconsin Avenue.

As a toddler, Diana recalls awakening in her bed one night, watching her older sister dial the telephone. The scared seven year old wailed, "Grama Lu? Can you come get us? Mommy's been gone an awful long time. I don't know where she is."

Less than an hour later, spitting fire, Louise swept Diana up in her arms and wrapped her in a blanket while Virgel searched for Maxine's favorite stuffed animal. The Herrolds took the girls home to Genesee Depot that night, and a quick decision was made: Maxine was to return to her grandparent's farm near Neenah in Central Wisconsin while Diana was to stay with her grandparents in Genesee Depot.

While being held tightly in her Nana's arms a few days later, the toddler wondered why she was waving goodbye to her older sister.

CHAPTER 9

Diana stood naked in a bathtub. Six years old and unusually thin with arms and legs the size of tiny tree limbs, she braced herself, shivering. Another wall of tepid water hit her in the face.

"Don't push away, Di," Louise trilled as she scrubbed another layer of skin. "Ten Chimneys! Do you know how lucky you are?" She gushed, "Now remember, Jules said the gates will open at eleven. You can't be a minute late."

"What if I'm late, Nana?" the child asked boldly.

"Well, I don't know..." Nana teased, "They'll close the gates on you, I s'pose."

Her grandmother poured one more pitcher of water over her flaxen head. Diana giggled as her Nana bent over the tub, exposing her garter belt and bloomers from under her cotton housedress.

"Now, don't talk unless you're spoken to," her grandmother lectured. "Be sure to flash your beautiful smile, and remember to say please and thank you."

"I hate my smile!" Diana pouted. "I can fit a Popsicle stick between my front teeth!"

"Don't you dare do that! They'll never grow back together that way!" Nana admonished. Then, "Are you nervous, Di?"

"I'm not scared at all!" Diana wiggled with excitement and splashed the bath water.

"No, No! You dassent do that!" Nana scolded. "You're going to get water on your dad's painting."

Because of Bob's estrangement over the years, Louise obsessively protected her prodigal's painted mural on the wall behind the tub. For thirty-seven years the shower head in the Herrold home, wrapped in a hand towel encased with plastic and secured tightly with rubber bands, was never used.

"Do you think I'll ever be an artist like my father?" Diana pondered.

"Ach, you'll be even better! Now hurry up, Di, I'm going to miss my stories," her Nana said, anxiously.

Everyday her grandmother faithfully turned on her television and watched 'The Guiding Light'. When 'her stories' ended, Louise was full of nervous energy, cooking, canning, freezing, sewing and cleaning the house. She was a classic German 'action juggernaut', a real 'putzfrau'.

Even though Virgel worked in management, his pay was low and their harvest from garden and orchard supplemented his income.

This season Louise's raspberry bushes were bearing abundantly and she had been baking pies all morning. At North Prairie's Fourth of July Auction the year before, she had won a blue ribbon for her raspberry delectable. Jules had raved about her pies long before her blue ribbon and suggested Diana deliver another one to Ten Chimneys for the Lunts enjoyment.

Still bending over the bathtub, Louise wrapped a towel around Diana. "Oh, my aching back!" She straightened up. "Jules was right, no one can bake a pie better than me. If the Lunt's don't love my pie, they're nuts! U-u-u-mpf!"

When Louise Herrold was stressed, she had a nervous tick much like Tourette's Syndrome, forcing her to make a guttural sound and jerk her head from right to left. It had become unnoticeable to those who knew and loved her, but to her it was an infernal source of embarrassment.

Dressed in her Sunday best with an oversized pink bow in her hair, Diana stood on the Herrold front porch holding her carefully-wrapped bundle.

Nana kissed her. "Remember, Di, you have a dress on." As her granddaughter disappeared down the driveway on her bike, Louise shouted and waved, "Be sure to keep your legs together!"

The sun was high in the sky as Diana pedaled her gleaming red Schwinn bicycle down Genesee Road. It was a birthday present, fully-equipped with basket, horn and handlebar tassels. Virgel had bought and restored the bicycle from Pet Milk's plant manager.

Atop the hill with her foot poised on the bike pedal, she took a deep breath. She had discovered, with much practice and only one pedal stroke, how to glide from her grandparent's driveway all the way down Depot Road to the train station.

In seconds, with her arms outstretched, balancing her bike, she was flying into the wind. Up and down the kettles of the moraine, soaring in and out of the woods, she always strained to catch a peek of the mystical white manor and estate with its ten chimneys, rising into the trees like steeples.

From Depot Road, Diana had spent many happy summer days daydreaming, peering through the kettle moraine, trying to see more of the grand estate. Sometimes in the late afternoon a man or woman's laugh echoed through the trees or a strain of music lilted through the air. In later years, she came to recognize many popular Noël Coward and Cole Porter tunes and others like 'Stardust', one of her favorites.

In her child's imagination, Ten Chimneys was the most beautiful place on earth, so perfect only a king and queen must live there. The Genesee locals were proud of the Lunt legend too, and fiercely protected them from inquisitive tourists. You might say the whole community had adopted Ten Chimneys as their own enchanted fairytale.

Every day she passed the hidden estate as she flew down the road on her bicycle into The Depot, but to open the wooden gate and step onto the drive — or even find an opening in the forest — was unthinkable. It was to her hallowed ground.

Today, for the first time, she excitedly pedaled through the opened Ten Chimneys' wooden gate. To savor the moment, she walked her bicycle slowly down a shaded, long winding drive and entered a large courtyard. Carefully, with the toe of her Mary Janes, she flipped the kickstand and parked her bike under a huge oak.

Jules' familiar voice floated to her through an opened window. "Hi, Di! Don't you look pretty! I'll be right there."

Holding her Nana's pie in a favored tea towel, she stood at the main house's laundry room door. Shading her eyes from the noon sun, she looked up. Above her, lace curtains in an open upstairs French door rustled closed.

"Hey! Miss!" Behind her the Lunt's groundskeeper, Ben Perkins approached, walking down the path from the stables. "What are you doing there?" Scared, Diana put the pie on the porch step, scrambled back onto her bicycle and pedaled away.

Jules shouted from the open kitchen window, "Ben, it's Diana from over the hill, delivering a pie from Mrs. Herrold!"

"I'm sorry," Ben called back, laughing."I didn't recognize her all dressed up."

Jules' caution echoed through the woods, "Remember to close the gate, Di!"

From his promontory inside the main house, Alfred Lunt's large, elegant hands opened the lace curtains again. He was impeccably groomed in an ascot and English-tailored houndstooth jacket with his brown hair stylishly slicked back. His enormous, expressive brown eyes watched the young girl depart.

Typical of most actors trained for the stage, Alfred stood ramrod straight, but his exaggerated movements were lucid and precise.

From a side table, brooding, he picked up a silver cigarette case, a cherished gift inscribed by his dear friend and literary giant, Noël Coward. Lifting out an English Oval, he tamped the cigarette and lit it. Inhaling quickly, he dramatically elevated his chin and exhaled a stream of smoke toward the ceiling.

"Jules!" The usual depth and breadth of his eloquent voice became pinched and nasal when he was annoyed.

His major domo appeared in the door well of the Flirtation Room. Jules was dressed in his usual white shirt with rolled sleeves and muslin chef's apron. A towel at his side, folded over at the apron's waistband, was a habit he and Alfred shared from their training at Le Cordon Bleu in Paris, where they both graduated top of their class.

Ferdinand 'Jules' Johnson was not only Ten Chimneys' overseer and premier chef, he was also Mr. Lunt's butler and valet. While touring, he was the theater great's make-up artist and the keeper of his wigs and costumes.

Mr. Lunt continued, "You know all the locals. Who's the young girl?"

"That would be Diana, sir," Jules spoke guardedly.

After a long pause, Alfred goaded him. "Well, do I have to get a drink at Stag's to find out more?"

"Diana is..." Jules hesitated, "...my little god child, Mr. Lunt. Her father abandoned her years ago, and she lives up the hill with her grandparents."

"Child without proper upbringing? And all that?" Alfred sniffed and drew deeply on his cigarette. "Your god daughter, you say. Pretty little thing."

CHAPTER 10

North Prairie's annual Fourth of July parade and carnival was ablaze with newfound American patriotism.

As always, the festivities began with a parade down main street, then moved into an open field near the Pet Milk plant where a stage was erected. Throughout the day for everyone's listening and dancing enjoyment, big band selections, polka tunes and even a couple hymns were performed; and in the late afternoon, a talent show was planned. Diana's accordion teacher, Mrs. Honeyager from Waukesha, had arranged a stage recital for her pupils during the talent show. Rows of tables were set up for food judging and a noon-day bake walk. There were pony rides for the children as well as the carnival amusements. And, in the evening, there was to be a much-anticipated fireworks display.

This year the honor to carry the Pet Milk Company banner in the parade went to the plant manager's daughter, Jean Kirkpatrick, and Diana.

At nine o'clock in the morning, as the drum major whistled sharply once, twice, three times to begin the parade, adults and children alike stood at curbside, waving small hand-held flags along the main street. Amidst cheers, the band exploded into Sousa's Marine Corps Band refrain of 'Stars and Stripes Forever'.

A color guard of veterans began to march forward holding the American flag, flags of the four military services and the American

Legion banner. Fresh from the war, Stanley Phenus, known by the town folk as Stags for his tavern on the main street, stood at attention in his uniform, decorated with a row of gleaming medals. Jules stood next to him, still slim and handsome in his old, immaculate Army uniform. Both men, along with a small contingent of servicemen, proudly saluted the flags and marched in cadence.

Jean and Diana scurried to their places in parade formation at opposite ends of the ten-foot long Pet Milk banner. Diana patted her wild curls into shape. When each girl lifted her heavy pole, neither child was mindful of the disparity, Jean wore a sensible Sunday school dress in sharp contrast to Diana's pink netted formal, lovingly sewn by her grandmother.

Diana was proud of her gown, inspired by Glinda the good fairy in the Wizard of Oz and boasting a hooped petticoat. Nana had also given her a Toni Home Perm, her first hair permanent, for the celebration. But, as Diana walked close to the banner, the hoop kept bouncing up behind her. She struggled in vain to lower it, only to have it instantly pop up again; a predicament for which her Nana hadn't anticipated.

"Look, everybody! You can see Gap-face's underwears!" Butch pointed from curbside. Only a few yards away, Diana's best friends and neighbors, Martin Dable and the Perkins brothers, Dick and Jerry, scowled at him. Frederick 'Butch' Miller was a bully. He was two heads taller than Martin, and even though he was three years older, they were in the same grade at school.

Martin, shot back at him. "How come you don't bully the boys, Butch? Why is it only girls?"

Looking straight ahead, Diana walked down the main street resolutely ignoring Butch's taunts. As the band energetically strutted and blared the rousing Sousa tune, she waved back to her proud grandparents.

Each year many local farmers joined in the merriment by decorating their work tractors and driving them in the parade. Not to be outdone, Alfred disguised himself in an Uncle Sam costume, designed and sewn by Lynn. He stood on a platform behind Ben's seat who, in bib overalls, proudly steered their new John Deere decorated with a 'Yankee Doodle Dandy' theme down the parade route.

Alfred waved to the crowd and threw red, white and blue confetti into the air. "John Phillip Sousa," he leaned close to Ben's ear, "died a happy old bugger moments after conducting 'Stars and Stripes Forever'. I earnestly hope my timing is that perfect, Benny."

Children followed on decorated bicycles with their own parade of pets. Cows, geese, pigs, ponies, birds, cats and dogs, were all lovingly dressed by their owners in Fourth of July finery as the band broke into another march, 'On Wisconsin'.

A few blocks away, the locals quickly forgot the sticky humid air as they approached a long table of home-baked goods. Carefully placing her jiggling lemon meringue pie on a colorful tablecloth, Louise smoothed her hair and her apron, preparing for the noon-day bake walk.

Several judges leisurely strolled up and down the table, tasting each of the entries. One particularly robust judge bit into Louise's pie. "Just tart enough. Excellent! All the way down to the perfectly formed golden beads. Mmmm. Mrs. Herrold, you never disappoint!"

"Oh, I bet you say that to all the ladies!" Louise, smiling and pleased with herself, handed him a tall glass of iced tea meant for Virgel.

After the parade, Virgel strolled across the field, passing the various carnival rides and stopping at the booth games. He sighed as he tossed another ping pong ball into a sea of small fish bowls. He had already sunk ten dollars into this effort, but if he could get three balls in the bowls, he would win a Snow White chalk doll for Diana.

A half hour later, finally mollified, Virgel hurried away to the food booths with a little bowl and one very lucky gold fish. Passing an open field, he admired rows and rows of brightly decorated tractors including Alfred's John Deere — all deserted for cold beers, wursts, sauerkraut and potato salad.

Sometime later, Louise strolled up to her husband perspiring over a blistering hot flame, turning dozens of wursts. He slathered some meaty ribs with barbeque sauce as she handed him a glass of iced tea.

"There sure are a lot of people..." He wiped his brow with a shirt-sleeve and gulped down the refreshing brew.

"Wait til you see the supper crowd. You'll have to cool off in the Dunkin Tank when you're through," Louise teased him, kissing him on the cheek.

The Frog Jumps and Greased Pig Races always created the largest and most excited crowds. But the most popular attraction was the Charity Dunkin Tank. Local politicians, clergy, police and firemen gladly volunteered to sit over a large tank of cool water, waiting for a hardball to hit a button rigged to dump the man of prominence into the water.

After the first few hours, the good-natured volunteers grew tired of getting dunked or, worse, sitting for an hour in the sweltering sun hoping for someone with good aim. Gibby Pronold was in charge of the charity event and its cash box. It was his job to recruit the locals for the hourly dumps. As the self-proclaimed mayor of The Depot sipped his cool beer in the heat, swapping stories with a group of old-timers, Butch, unnoticed, quickly grabbed a wad of dollars from the cash box and scribbled something on Gibby's sign-up sheet.

At four o'clock Martin was surprised to hear over the loud speaker it was his turn to sit in the Dunkin Tank. Being a good sport, he allowed himself to be jostled and herded up onto the high seat. His outlook immediately changed when he saw who was standing with a handful of baseballs in front of him. Butch was not athletic, but he did have a gift for accurately pitching balls, a talent he acquired throwing stones at his dad's empty beer bottles in their yard at home. Laughing, Butch nailed the bull's eye again and again, dunking Martin into the water with his missiles. When his hour was finally up, exasperated, Martin consoled himself with the thought at least he had raised money for charity.

"Just so's you don't think I wasted my own money on you," Butch razed Martin, "I lifted the money for those balls from Gibby's cash box!"

Across the field swinging at a staggering height on the ferris wheel above the trees of the kettle moraine, it was almost sunset as

Diana watched a little cluster of lights come on in The Depot. She recognized St. Paul's church steeple and the scattered familiar patchwork of family farms. No matter how much she strained, though, she could not see the Herrold's cottage or Ten Chimneys. What she could see, however, was a huge supper crowd of hungry farmers forming around her grandfather's barbeque pit.

The gondola abruptly stopped and swung back and forth as another load of passengers disembarked below her. Anxious about her accordion recital to begin in fifteen minutes, she swallowed a last bite of Popsicle and wedged the stick between her front teeth — a nervous habit. Remembering her Nana's reprimand, she pulled at it. The stick was firmly lodged in place. She stared, cross-eyed at the huge beam protruding beyond her nose.

Now grounded and still struggling to pry the stick loose from her mouth, she ran onto the side entrance of the darkened recital stage. Nana was waiting there, fretfully, to help her into her accordion harness.

"Where have you been?" Nana shouted impatiently. "It's almost time to start. The whole class is waiting for you! Have you seen Virgel? He's not here yet, either!" Her dreaded tick returned. "U-u-u-mpf! What's that in your mouth?"

"Nuffing!" Diana ran to take her place with the class.

As Mrs. Honeyager guided her cherubs onto the stage, she placed Diana, one of the smallest children, in center front with her bright red accordion. Mortified, Diana tried in vain one more time to remove the stick from between her teeth.

In the audience, front row, Louise and Jules were saving a seat for Virgel, when Fred Miller, Butch's dad, muscled through the crowd toward them with a beer in his hand.

"I'm sorry, this is saved for my husband," Louise stated, miffed Virgel was missing.

"Tough shit!" Fred replied, as he squeezed his abundance into the empty chair.

She glared at him.

Jules stood up. "Sir, that's no way to talk to a lady!"

Fred stared back at Louise and belched in her face. "I don't see any ladies here!"

"Thank you, Jules, but I'll take care of this." Louise grabbed Fred's bottle of beer, emptied the cold brew in his lap, then pushed him. His arms and legs shot out in all directions as the chair flipped backwards, overturning his huge mass like an upended turtle.

"I only act like a lady around gentlemen!" she retorted.

On stage, Mrs. Honeyager and the children wondered why the audience was applauding before they had even started the recital.

When the spot lights brightened, the kids blared a disorderly version of 'You're A Grand Old Flag' in time to Mrs. Honeyager's baton. A young boy standing behind Diana kept trying to see over her frizzed hairdo. He jumped up and down several times, then successfully blew a part down the middle. The whole audience erupted in jubilant laughter, including Louise. Oblivious, Diana continued her performance, concentrating on her accordion keys.

From the sidelines Butch mocked. "Ha! Ha! Gap-face needs a flag for that pole in her mouth!"

Upset, Louise shouted, "That's okay, Di! You keep playing, honey! Show 'em what you're made of!"

As the recital came to a close, the children, stepping high, exited the stage with a last resounding tune of 'When The Saints Go Marching In'. Louise and Jules jumped to their feet in tears, desperately applauding. The entire audience followed with cat calls, whistles and thunderous clapping.

Moments after the children marched off stage, Virgel appeared. Smelling of sweat and barbeque, with stains on his shirt, he handed the tiny fish bowl to Diana.

"Next year," he apologized, "I'll get your Snow White, sweetheart."

"No, Birgel!" Diana beamed. "I lub my fish!"

At twilight families began to gather on blankets on a grassy knoll for the highly awaited fireworks display. In the darkened sky, first one red, then one blue plume crackled and dissolved on the horizon. Together, two volunteer firemen lit firecrackers by hand with long fire stick torches, continuing their colorful spectacle for more than a half-hour.

When the fireworks ended, as parents collected their blankets and sleepy children, the Herrolds leisurely strolled to their car across the emptying field. All the while carnival booths and rides were being dismantled and packed away in the smoky, sulfur night air.

"Wha happen cho you? Does it hur?" Diana mumbled as Martin, with a black eye and a big smile, swaggered up to her.

"Kinda — but Butch hurts worse." At her shocked look, he laughed, not surprised by the protruding Popsicle stick. "I got Giby's money back, too!"

The children waved goodnight as Virgel steered the old Chevy through the pasture toward the paved road. With each bump, Lu's head nodded up and down as she fell to sleep, clutching her bake walk blue ribbon to her chest.

"A'll caw him Un'cle Cha'lie...Eben ip he's not a boy..." With the fish bowl in her lap, Diana dozed off in the backseat. Moments later the stubborn stick silently dropped out of her mouth and into the bowl.

The next day, Louise and Diana drove into Waukesha and purchased the largest fish bowl they could find at the five-and-dime. They added real plants, colorful stones, and a little porcelain Snow White wishing well. At home when Lu transferred the fish to the larger bowl, she thought for a moment, then placed the Popsicle stick in the bottom, a reminder sometimes things get better on their own.

Uncle Charlie grew into a huge, bulbous, golden nugget and lived blissfully to a ripe old age under Nana's loving care. He even visited the local vet once because Louise thought he wasn't eating well.

Several years later Virgel finally won the carnival chalk doll. Snow White held a place of honor on Diana's glass-enclosed shelves in her bedroom for many years.

CHAPTER 11

The Lunts, in their white satin loungewear, relaxed in bed at Ten Chimneys. Opened on Alfred's night stand was a new Robert Sherwood manuscript, 'The Twilight'. Lynn was still under the bed-covers reading her copy. They had just refused some lucrative radio and movie deals, including a revival of 'The Guardsman', and were in want of a fresh brilliant stage production for their next theater season.

"No thank you, Robert. No story, no situations, no drama, no tears, and not enough laughter to cover," Lynn stated bluntly.

"How on God's earth do we tell him?" Alfred lamented. "My stomach is in agony! I love Bob Sherwood! If his Madeline were still alive, she could ease his pain by calling us every name in the book, plus some he hasn't heard yet!"

"You must write him a conciliatory letter, Alfred." Lynn was always sensible.

Jules entered their third-story bedroom with a breakfast tray. The Lunt's dachshund puppy, newly gifted to Lynn from the cast of 'O Mistress Mine' was eagerly barking and bounding at his heels.

Lynn's eyes lit up and she tossed the script onto the bed. "Lisa, *dah-h-ling...*" The young doxie jumped into her welcoming arms, licking her face. "...a most *delightful* interruption!"

Recently back from Europe, the Lunts reveled in the morning sunlight streaming through their lace curtains. The summer sun cast bright light and tree-filtered shadow onto the English rose wallpaper in the bedroom and beyond into Lynn's large adjoining sunroom. On the sunroom floor, pinned for cutting, were Lynn's carefully-placed pattern pieces for her most current dress design. The war-wise Miss Fontanne had become an expert dress maker, also designing and sewing extravagant window treatments and canopies for Ten Chimneys.

"Alfred? What do you think of this hat?" Lynn stepped out of her closet. Still in white satin pajamas, she had donned an enormous wide-brimmed red felt hat.

Alfred, now up and shaving, could be heard from the bathroom humming. He peeked around the corner, "Yes, yes, darling. But make sure the red pumps are at least three inches."

Lisa dove off the bed, and scampered into the sunroom, leaping from pattern piece to pattern piece. She quickly squatted to urinate, then playfully hopped back onto the bed and into Lynn's arms.

Unaware, Lynn stroked Lisa's head and ears. "When you're a tad older, Mama and Papa will take you with us on tour. Would you like that?" Excitedly, Lisa wagged her tail and licked Lynn's face in thank you.

"I'm afraid Lisa had another accident, Miss Fontanne," Jules whispered. "This time in the drawing room."

Groaning, Lynn doffed her hat, dusting the soft red felt with her fingers. "We must not mention this to Mr. Lunt, Jules."

"Of course, not a word." He picked up the breakfast tray with Alfred's morning coffee, newspaper and the prized Churchill cigar, and entered the steaming bathroom.

Patting aftershave on his face and neck, Alfred squinted into the mirror, examining his face closely. "It still looks like an old douche bag!"

Jules tried to hide his shock. "You are still the most elegant man in theater, Mr. Lunt."

"I am, aren't I?" Alfred took a big gulp of the very strong Swedish coffee and studied his profile, sucking in his stomach. "The coffee's perfect, by the way."

"What have you decided in regard to the Churchill cigar, sir?" Jules asked.

"Encased," Alfred answered decisively. "On my desk in the library."

Jules leaned in close to whisper, "Mr. Lunt, Ben just alerted me squirrels are feasting again in our vegetable garden."

Coffee cup poised, Alfred froze at mid-gulp. He struggled to swallow. "Gather my rifle, Jules, and a good supply of shells."

"What about the cigar Mr. Lunt?" Jules repeated.

Alfred grabbed his treasure and carefully placed it in his top breast pocket. "I'll meet you in the garage in a few minutes." He leaned down and hissed, "Oh yes, not a word to Miss Fontanne! She feeds them biscuits at tea, for Christ's sake! Treats them like they're her pets!"

On Depot Road, Diana opened the Ten Chimney's gate and, with a lemon meringue pie in her bicycle basket, she pedaled up the driveway. Since the war, Louise Herrold had been steadily adding customers to her weekly pie deliveries for extra money. Now older and three inches taller, Diana was no longer concerned about entering Ten Chimneys in her Sunday best. She wore shorts and a tee shirt with her long blonde hair fastened in a pony tail.

"Jules!" She called from the courtyard up to the open kitchen windows. When he didn't answer, she entered through the laundry room and climbed the stairs to find the kitchen empty. This being the last of her deliveries, she was anxious to join her waiting friends in The Depot. She placed the pie on the counter and ran back downstairs to her bike.

As she passed the courtyard gate and reached the drive, several shots rang out and echoed through the forest! In full hunting attire as though he were tracking game, Alfred stealthily stepped from behind a tree to once again take aim. As more potshots rang out, Diana dove out of sight. A bevy of terrified squirrels scattered, most up trees, some under rocks and leaves — and one between Alfred's legs.

Losing balance, he plummeted face-first to the ground. Righting himself, worried, he lifted the prized Winston cigar from his breast pocket and examined it carefully. Seeing it was not damaged, with renewed anger he leaped up, pivoted on booted heel, and bellowed,

"You God-damn *rodent*!" Squinting into the crosshairs of his rifle, he lined the petrified pest up for extinction.

"Don't!" Diana yelped involuntarily, popping up from a pile of leaves, her hair covered in thistle.

Alarmed, Alfred lowered his rifle suspiciously. Focusing on the young girl, he grew disconcerted. "How-the-devil did you get in here?" His concern turned into angry frustration. "Do you realize you could have been hurt?" He commanded in his pinched nasal, shooing her away from his property. "Run along, now!"

She plucked a green tri-leaf off her face as she climbed back onto her bike. Already feeling the sticky sumac all over her body, she whispered to herself, "Uh-oh, I'm in trouble."

Minutes later Alfred entered the Ten Chimneys' kitchen, ballyhooing, "Those damned squirrels must have nine lives! Thanks to your little god..."

Ashen faced, Jules slowly hung up the kitchen phone. "Miss Mary MacArthur was stricken with a high fever and has perished suddenly. She was touring with her mother. Miss Hayes was told it was polio. She was only nineteen. God rest her little soul."

Chapter 12

Side by side, with hushed woods surrounding them under darkening skies that typically precede a Wisconsin storm, Diana and Martin slowly pedaled up the hill toward the Herrold house. That morning Nana had covered her — head to toe — with a white zinc ointment to relieve the poison ivy's intolerable itching.

"Boo!" Martin teased, "You look like a ghost!"

Deep in thought, Diana absentmindedly scratched at a red patch behind her ear and asked her friend quietly. "Have you ever seen a dead person?"

Scared, Martin answered, "No, have you?" His bicycle tire snapped a twig and both children jumped.

"I'll show you." She said mysteriously, parking her bike on the front grass. As they both entered the house, she yelled. "I'm home!" She was just checking — she knew this afternoon was Nana's hair appointment.

Her grandmother's bedroom was dark as she entered. Nana always lowered her window shades in the morning to keep out the summer heat during the day.

Martin remained in the hallway. "Is someone dead in there?"

She ignored him and went to Nana's top dresser drawer, pulling out a faded red Valentine chocolate box. Motioning Martin to sit beside her at the foot of the bed, she opened the lid and lifted out something in tissue, carefully unwrapping it. It was an old card-mounted photograph.

He was disappointed, "Who is that?"

"My great-grandmother," she said matter-of-factly.

"She doesn't look like *my* great-grandmother!" Martin exclaimed. "She's supposed to look old and creepy!"

"She was only twenty-five." Diana touched the picture tenderly. "Isn't she beautiful?"

"Yes," he pulled the fragile image up close to his nose and squinted at it curiously. "Why did they put shoes on her? She's dead!"

"See all the flowers?" Diana paid no attention. "Everything's so beautiful."

"Everything's so dark!" he observed. "But she looks peaceful."

"If it's so peaceful, then why am I so afraid of the dark and ghosts?" She confessed, not telling him the whole story behind her fears.

"Everybody's afraid of the dark and ghosts!" He helped her rewrap the picture. "Who's that?" Martin pointed to Bob and Eileen's wedding picture.

"That's just my parents." Without looking at the picture on her grandmother's dresser, Diana carefully placed the Whitman's chocolate box back into the drawer. She whispered, "Goodnight, great-grandmother," and in the same breath to Martin, "Race you to The Depot!"

Both kids rushed out of Nana's bedroom, through the Herrold living room and back outside onto their bikes as a crack of thunder pierced the skies above the kettle moraine.

"Last one there's a ...!" Diana shouted, undaunted by a fresh cloudburst.

"... rotten dead body!" Martin screamed as they raced their bikes down the hill past Ten Chimneys through the downpour.

Chapter 13

"Jules! Look what I found!" Rain drenched, she rushed into the laundry room at Ten Chimneys and shouted up the stairwell. She darted back outside to her bicycle in the courtyard and gathered an arm load of dripping wet rhubarb stalks and a basket of blueberries.

"I'll see you then, Wilhelmina..." Jules was on the telephone in the upstairs kitchen. The dachshunds were bouncing and clawing at his feet as he held their empty food dish. "Me, too." His face was flushed with a happiness rarely seen.

As he hung up the phone, he called down the stairs. "Di, I can't help you right now! Set it in the silent butler."

"What's that?" She questioned.

Jules yelled above the dogs' hungry yelping. "The small platform in front of you. Just set it in there, Di. And come on upstairs."

Diana climbed into the small cubicle. Alfred never tired of boasting to his kitchen guests how he had built the rope and pulley invention at a fraction of the Sears and Roebuck catalog cost. Rather than wearily trudging household goods up the stairs, it proved very handy in delivering them to the second-story kitchen.

After the dogs were quickly fed, Jules pulled the ropes from the upstairs kitchen stairwell. "My God, child, did you roll a stone into this thing?"

Crouched in the tiny space, Diana giggled when the upward motion overturned her basket, spilling her blueberries.

"Jules!" Alfred's voice exploded from the vicinity of the staircase near the kitchen. "That god-damn roof leak is ruining Clag's mural in the god-damn foyer! Where-in-the-devil did we put the cleaning solvent?"

With a jolt, the platform stopped just as Alfred entered the kitchen. Aghast, Mr. Lunt stared at the small child in his unsafe contraption! It was a very small platform without safety railings and, had she lost her balance, she could have fallen fifteen feet to a cement garage floor below.

"How could you allow this, Jules?" Alfred was horrified. "You do know how dangerous this is!"

"Please, don't blame Jules, Mr. Lunt!" Diana jumped out of the silent butler, fighting back sobs. "I wanted to surprise him! He didn't know I was coming up with Mr. Butler. Look what I picked!" She glanced back at the smashed berries on the platform and was reduced to tears. With small hands trembling, she presented the rhubarb.

Alfred studied the stalks. They were a soft green-red, tender and perfect for stewing. "Where did you find these?" He took the stalks from her, admiring them.

She mustered all her courage. "They were growing along your fence near the road. I just had to pick them for Jules."

"Good decision! We'll serve them tonight." Alfred passed the stalks to Jules, who quickly handed him the missing solvent before he left the kitchen.

Reappearing a second later, Alfred complained, "Don't you think you should go home? I'm certain your grandparents must be worried." Obviously peeved, he disappeared again.

"Don't pay him any mind, child." Jules kneeled down to Diana's height and whispered as he towel dried her damp hair. "He's really a dear man, you'll see." He hugged her tightly. "Di, promise me, don't ever do that again! You scared old Jules half to death! Now, I must prepare Miss Fontanne's tea. Here, have a fresh-baked brownie."

Afraid Mr. Lunt might reappear, the child sat quietly at the kitchen table. When Jules returned, he lifted an iced pitcher of lemonade from the refrigerator and poured them both a tall glass.

"I got a doll from my father today." Diana wanted to share with him. "He promised to take us all out for a fancy Easter dinner."

"Oh, Di, I'm so happy for you. You finally get to meet your father!" Jules exclaimed. "What does your doll look like?"

"She's a ballerina. I have to put her away, though. She's too beautiful to play with." Diana was strangely melancholy.

He disappeared into his apartment adjoining the kitchen to place a 33 RPM album, from a cherished Billie Holiday collection, on his phonograph.

Moments later, they were snapping green beans in a colander as he sang along, "God Bless the Child..."

"Who's that, Jules?" Diana was mesmerized by the woman's mellow, deep, rich tenor and the soulful ballad.

"That's Lady Day."

Outside, as quickly as the storm arrived, it passed through the kettle moraine. Jules opened the upstairs kitchen window and breathed in the clean, fresh air. On the inside sill was a small bouquet of gardenias, often placed there by Miss Fontanne for his pleasure. He returned to the table with one perfect bloom.

"Lady Day always wore a gardenia in her hair when she sang." He inhaled the flower's fragrance and placed it behind Diana's ear.

Naturally curious, Diana stared at Jules' closely cropped head. "Can I?"

Smiling, Jules bent forward. Marveling, she pressed her hand lightly against his wiry curls.

Chapter 14

Lynn Fontanne was humming along with Billie Holiday when she entered the kitchen.

"I'd like to take tea on the terrace today, Jules. I adore the way the bright sun shines through my lilac bush after a fresh rain — reminds me of England."

She noticed Diana, "Well, good afternoon, child! What a lovely bloom." She too picked a gardenia from the window sill and placed a flower behind her ear, winking at Diana.

"May I introduce you to Miss Fontanne." Jules never addressed Alfred or Lynn or any of their adult guests by their first names. He didn't think it proper. "This is Diana, my godchild."

Diana stared at the most beautiful woman she had ever seen. In the open window's sunlight, Miss Fontanne's skin shone like porcelain and her lips were tinted red. She was dressed in a dirndl with her raven hair cascading around her shoulders.

Delighted with the prospect of filling her spring day with this young girl, Lynn asked, "Will you be taking tea with me today, Diana?"

"I would love to!" The child was overjoyed.

Ten Chimneys' hostess lead the way to the back garden terrace and Jules followed, toting a large sterling silver tea service. Miss Fontanne and her young guest sat in the shade of her sweeping lilac bush at a linen-draped table.

"Do you take milk or sugar with your tea?" she asked.

"Yes, please!" Diana answered.

As was her custom, Miss Fontanne poured from both silver servers at the same time. "Mr. Lunt tells me you live up the hill with your grandparents. Do you mind my asking, are your parents living?"

"My mother's away — finding a good job," Diana confided. "I've never seen my father. But he keeps promising to visit soon. I'm told my parents fought a lot and got a divorce. Not at all like my grandparents. My Nana — she's German you know — yells at Virgel sometimes, but can't stay mad at him very long. I love them both very much."

Intrigued, Miss Fontanne stared at her young talkative guest, realizing the similarities of their youth.

"I loved my Irish grandmother, too, very much indeed. Her name was Sarah Ann Barnett. My sisters and I were blessed she lived close by when my parents had their great rows." Lynn stated wistfully, "Mind you, they only had one or two a year of that magnitude, but just the same, she was my comfort. Oh, I was such a little gamin! I would often sneak out of my bedroom window in the middle of the night and creep into the theatre," she laughed. "I remember standing up during the Merchant of Venice and loudly reciting along with Dame Terry her "Quality of Mercy" speech. But we mustn't give you ideas. Another cup of tea, dear?"

Lynn pleasantly surprised herself, recalling an Old English melody her grandmother had often sung to her as a child. "...Lily of the valley, the bright and morning star. He's the fairest of ten thousand ..." She roused herself back to the present with a sigh. "She sang to me before I nodded off to sleep — and she told me the most wonderful stories."

"My Nana tells *me* stories too!" Diana asked, "Would you like to hear one?"

Amused, Lynn smiled and nodded her head.

"Nana said the road behind us used to be called Lover's Lane before our house was built." She giggled and quickly covered an impish grin with her hand. "They would park and neck in Virgel's car.

The old Model-A is still in our backyard. Virgel wants to get rid of it, but Nana says, "No way. It holds too many memories ..." Laughing innocently, she continued, "...The only one who uses it now is my Opa. He loves to sit in it with the door open and smoke his cigars. I think he has memories in the car too. When I ask him, he just smiles."

She paused to take a bite of her cucumber tea sandwich, and bent her head close to Miss Fontanne. "My Nana is older than Virgel, but please don't tell her I told you. She'll get so mad at me." She crossed her index and middle fingers and held them up solemnly to swear. "No one's supposed to know."

Offering Diana another tea sandwich, Lynn whispered. "I'm going to tell you something — I'm older than Mr. Lunt!" Imitating the childish vow, she crossed her fingers, too. "Our secret."

"I just love these little sandwiches!" Diana spouted happily. "Jules showed me how to make them. Would you like to know how..."

Lynn laughed and nodded her head again.

"...You must use fresh baked white bread and cut the crusts off on all sides," Diana continued. "Then cut them diagonally into four pieces, so they look like little triangles. Put a thin layer of unsalted butter and very, very thin slices of cucumber, and sprinkle with salt and fresh ground pepper."

Amused, Lynn watched Diana pop one bite-sized sandwich after another into her mouth, trying to talk in between. "You do almost the same thing to make little asparagus sandwiches. Would you like...?"

Diana took a deep breath to launch into another Jules' recipe when Lynn interjected, "*Tea* to the English is a time of *reflection*, dear. So much more than food and drink on lovely bone china, Diana. It's the assortment of family heirlooms and little chips that make it dearer."

After once more refilling Diana's tea cup, she put some bread-crumbs in her palm, bent down and placed the morsels at her feet. Waiting for just such an opportunity, a squirrel scampered back and forth from a nearby tree and nibbled his fare at a safe distance. A friendlier one ate directly from her hand. Others waited for her to scatter the food on the terrace.

Excitedly Diana watched as the little creatures ran to and fro from table to trees, gathering their cache.

"I'd like very much to show you something that's dear to me." Lynn took the child's hand and they walked up a large hill on fieldstone steps. At the top of a grassy knoll, was a new greenhouse, Lynn's cutting garden and rose gardens. There were also barns, stables, an old log cabin and, to the left, a red and white poolhouse and sparkling blue pool.

"There's another village up here!" Diana gasped. "With a pool!" she clapped her hands joyously. "This is better than my dreams!"

"How do you fill your days, child?" Lynn asked as they strolled to the pool. "Do you know how to swim?"

"No — but I love to ice skate," Diana beamed, "especially with Virgel." She bent down and splashed the water with her hand. "And Nana and I take accordion lessons together. Do you know I'm going to classes all the way in Waukesha to learn tap, toe and ballet?"

"Not too close to the pool's edge. Oh my dear, you *are* multi-talented." Lynn was thrilled. "Perhaps you will dance for me some day in my Studio." Lynn took her hand once more and stepped to the poolhouse.

There, on a plot of grass and flowers, surrounded with ivy and rose bushes, was a statue of a young girl. The child gazed at the white stone maiden dressed in traditional Old English garb, holding a basket. In the surrounding woods beyond, a light gust of wind shook the trees and the leaves clapped their hands.

"Diana, dear. This is *my* dream."

CHAPTER 15

"I'm going to ask Gerty to be my wife, if she'll have me!" Ben's handsome face was radiant. "What do you think, Jules?"

They were in the kitchen at Ten Chimneys, seated at the table, having morning coffee and fresh apple muffins. Comfortable with each other, both were quiet men, used to keeping confidences.

"Do you see her smiling or frowning when you have to drive Mr. Lunt to New York or Chicago at a moment's notice?" Jules was always practical.

"Smiling," Ben laughed. "We're going to keep it small."

"That will be impossible — you and Gert are so loved." Then Jules declared, "Not one guest less than two hundred!"

"There's no way around it, we are forced to invite Bugbee," Ben lamented. "The minute the Lunts go on tour, his personality changes completely. He bosses us around as if he owns the place!"

"Benny, you must start your guest list right now." Finding a writing pad in a nearby kitchen drawer, Jules placed it in front of his friend and asked, "Are you going to invite all the Finns?" Chuckling, he poured them both another cup of coffee.

"How can I not?" Ben answered. "I have no choice. They depend on Mr. Lunt for virtually everything. They are in constant disagreement with one another and have never been on their own. And then there's Carl — who gambles too much."

In a rare moment, knowing he could trust Ben, Jules exposed a

Lunt confidence. "Do you know when one Finn sister was insulted down in The Depot by Mr. Torhorst, she retaliated by telling Mr. Lunt to stop buying meat for the dogs there — because he might poison it."

"I'm not surprised." Ben wrote some names on his note pad then sobered momentarily, "So — when are you and Miss Cooper going to marry, Jules?"

"Someday...perhaps..." Jules hesitated for only a moment, "We both have responsibilities." To change the subject, he happily slapped Ben on the back. "We must plan your bachelor party at Stags!"

"Who's going to tell Mr. Lunt?" Ben smiled expectantly at Jules.

"Tell me what?" Alfred strolled into the kitchen and poured himself a cup of coffee.

"That Gerty and I are getting married!" Ben burst out the news.

"What took you so long?" Alfred erupted, "Here's to our Benny and his bride!" He lifted his coffee cup in a toast. "Miss Fontanne and I have already decided to build you two an awfully grand home! May you be happy in your new love nest! And may our Genesee neighbors, Iona Kock — and the Dingledines — come to visit often!"

The men exploded in raucous laughter.

Ben and Gertrude Perkins were married in the fall when the leaves of the kettle moraine were turning magenta and gold. With a close gathering of family, they said their vows in the small chapel of St. Paul's Catholic Church.

Together, Gert and Ben were a handsome couple. She was a vivacious woman, a local beautician who was often called to Ten Chimneys to do Lynn's hair.

Keeping their promise, the Lunts built the Perkins a two-story stone house. It was a beautiful modern structure on a large hillside lot. The house was built on the southern edge of the Lunt's property, connected by a paved back road. Alfred planned this as a private and convenient way for Ben to go back and forth to work without traveling through town. More importantly, it was a means for his caretaker to keep a watchful eye over the rear hundred acres of Ten Chimneys.

CHAPTER 16

Thoroughly enjoying himself in the coolness of the early evening, Jules relaxed in a lawn chair near Louise's rose garden, her bushes now cut back for the approaching winter. While wisps of leaves fell gently to the ground around him, he sipped a highball with Virgel. A large bushel basket of apples at his feet, he was always the proper guest and had brought a gift from Ten Chimneys for his hostess.

In her small, cheerful kitchen, Louise hummed while preparing a traditional German meal. She stepped to the front screen door and unlatched it to let Nippy, her black and white Boston bull terrier, into the house.

"Pa, come take your medicine!" she yelled. "And Diana — get your coat on!" Louise bent over and smothered Nippy with kisses and hugs. The dog followed her back inside the house. Wherever Louise went, Nippy was underfoot, especially when food was cooking.

About five years before, the adorable stray with little pink tongue and button eyes had shown up one evening at the Herrold's back door while Louise was preparing supper. After he ravenously consumed an entire bratwurst, she opened the door for the small terrier who immediately ran through her kitchen and into the living room, jumping onto the couch where her husband was napping. While Virgel snored, the grateful pup licked happily at his new master's face and 'nipped' at his trouser leg.

Under a shade tree at a folding card table, Opa Zabel and Diana continued their playful, petty argument over her blatant cheating at Canasta. Knowing her Opa was not a gracious loser, she loved to fondly rile him.

"You need to turn up your hearing aid, Pa!" Louise shouted again from the kitchen, annoyed.

Grinning, Zabel whispered to Jules pointing his gnarled index finger into the air. "I hear *every*ting!" Then to Diana, "Sveetheart, it's getting too cold for you."

They went into the house, she for her coat and he to retrieve his bottle of schnapps.

"Mr. Lunt has built a greenhouse." Jules declared as he continued to sip his highball on the Herrold's front lawn.

"What will you grow?" Virgel asked.

"Well, for one thing," Jules admitted, "Mr. Lunt and I will love having cooking herbs year 'round."

"Just imagine this coming winter before the snow even melts being able to harvest early vegetables and flowers for Miss Fontanne..." Virgel began to lose his concentration. A pungent, sweet-sour smell wafted from Louise's kitchen as Zabel returned outside with Nippy at his heels.

Zabel poured a shooter for their guest and offered him the schnapps with a large glass bowl of creamed herring. At Jules' puzzled look, the old German picked up a dripping ice-cold fish chunk with his fingers. "This is how ve do it. Gut appetite!"

Nippy climbed patiently onto Jules lap and watched him eat the whole bowlful, saving one last piece for the lovable dog who downed the morsel in one gulp.

A bit tipsy and already full, Jules licked his fingers. "That was a delicious picnic!"

Louise opened the front screen door and yelled, "Supper's ready!"

Unlike the French fare at Ten Chimneys, the Herrold table overflowed with food. On Louise's brightly colored tablecloth, sat a large platter of sliced Rouladen, huge bowls of hot German potato salad, pickled red cabbage with apples and creamed cucumbers.

When Jules sat down, Louise scooped a gigantic serving of potato salad onto his plate. "We need to fatten you up, Jules!" She pinched his skinny upper arm.

"Like my Virgel, here!" Diana patted Virgel's tummy.

"Ahhh, Rotkraut! Mein favorite! Liebe geht durch den magen." Zabel saluted and threw a big bite to Nippy who caught it mid-air.

"Opa says 'Love goes through the schtomach!'" Diana beamed at Jules, tossing Nippy another bite.

"I'm not an authority on love, but I know how to satisfy a stomach." Jules politely masked a belch with his handkerchief. "Nippy receives more love than most people I know."

"Speak up, Jules, Pa can't hear too good." Louise was happiest when family and friends appreciated her meals. Simple pleasures brought her the most joy. She picked Nippy up and, to her delight, the excited dog licked her all over the face. "Pa always says, 'Never trust anyone who doesn't love children or animals', don't you, Pa? — Pa, turn up your hearing aid!"

"Zehr gut!" Opa gulped his beer from the bottle and winked at Jules. "*Every*ting!"

"Virgel, Hank needs Pa back at the ranch next week." Louise asked, "Can you get the time off?"

"Far as I know," Virgel replied.

After supper, once again outside, Opa lit up a cigar and resumed his Canasta game with his great-granddaughter, Virgel and Jules found their comfortable chairs while Louise served apple strudel. When dessert was finished, Louise brought her record player out to the porch. As the music played in the brisk evening air, she took Jules' drink from his hand and pulled him out of his chair. With Louise leading, they danced a fast cheek-to-cheek. Nippy joined in, barking, twirling and chasing his tail.

Running inside the house, Virgel returned in minutes with their Kodak Brownie movie camera.

"The Lunts take moving pictures, too," Jules grinned.

"Bet Miss Fontanne doesn't do *this* in front of the camera!" Facing the lens, Louise kicked up her leg, exposing her bloomers and garter.

They all exploded in laughter. Virgel laughed so hard, he almost dropped the camera.

"Ach, you get me every time!" At the Canasta table only yards away, Zabel slapped his knee and threw his hand of cards up in the air as Diana laughed uproariously.

"How on earth, Louise, does one begin a mink ranch?" Jules asked as he and Louise continued to dance.

"With two mink, of course. A male and female. Right, Virg?" Louise stopped to balance herself for a moment. She was getting tight. "Oh, my feet are killing me!" She kicked off her well-worn shoes and rubbed her feet. "Hank jets back and forth to New York with his furry friends. And Bea has everything mink you can think of. Coats, jackets, stoles, wraps. Me? His only sister? I'd settle for a collar on my old winter coat, I'll tell ya! All I have is Rudy, my pet mink back on his ranch. I'm dying to touch your hair, Jules. May I?"

As Jules leaned forward to oblige, he noticed her stockinged feet and asked, "Do you have any worn hose, Lu?"

"Oooo!" Louise giggled as she touched his downy locks. "My hose, whatever for? Does it matter if they have runs?"

When the music ended, Jules stumbled a little as he sat back down in the lawn chair and nursed his Manhattan. "Better if they have runs."

"Di, go into my drawers and pull out my old hose," she shouted and laughed. "And bring me my accordion while you're at it." The child returned laden with her grandmother's red music box and a sack full of oversized women's hose.

"This one's for you, Pa." Louise pumped the bellows and began to play an old familiar German tune, 'Lorelei'.

When Zabel sang along, they both started to tear.

"Opa, are you sad?" Diana asked.

"No, my little sveetheart. Never sad. My heart is full of liebe. Your Opa cries sometimes vit schnapps and singing. I miss Deutschland and my Anna. Crying is gut for the soul." Zabel composed himself. "Jules, I vant to take you to Schtags. Sing songs. Trink gut bier. Get you a mug." He winked and quietly whispered, "Maybe find you a voman."

Before Jules could answer, a fast-paced jitterbug tune interrupted him. Diana had placed another record on the phonograph and quickly tapped Jules on the shoulder. "Remember, Jules? You promised to teach me how to scat."

"Okay, Di, let's have a go of it!" He smiled broadly. "This is a little hard for white folks."

Blessed with a great sense of rhythm, to Jules' surprise, she caught on immediately.

"Oooh, Di, I can't keep up with you!" He sat down on the front porch steps when the music ended, patting his forehead with his hanky. "I'm not as young as I used to be."

"I got another doll and note today." She sat down on the steps beside him. "He was sorry he couldn't make Easter, but promised to spend Thanksgiving with us."

"Please tell me you can play with this one." Jules was disheartened and exasperated with Bob's futile attempts at fatherhood.

"No, it's too fragile. I put it on the shelf." The child asked, curious, "Am I like my father, Jules? Is he tall? Is he skinny like me?"

Jules answered soberly. "No, Di. You're nothing like your father."

"*You* look like you could use another cool one." Virgel handed Jules a third drink. "I make a pretty good Manhattan, but my brother-in-law Hank makes the best."

Jules stood up, politely refusing. "Three drinks makes the walk home in the dark too long."

"Let me give you a lift in the car." Louise suggested, teetering ever so slightly as she descended the front porch steps.

"No thanks, Lu."

"Vait a minute!" Zabel pointed his gnarled finger into the air with an idea, "You should go vit us to the ranch!"

"Yes, please say you'll come with us to Uncle Hanks!" Diana pleaded.

"I really don't want to be any bother," Jules declared.

"Oh for pity sakes!" Louise crowed. "Come onnn! Bea's a pretty good cook. Not as good as me, huh Virg? But you'll still have a wonderful time. Everybody does!"

Chapter 17

On an unusually humid Saturday morning, Alfred, in well-worn bib overalls, maneuvered his shining green and yellow John Deere into the garage. As he bent to wipe a clump of wet grass from the tractor's bumper, he noticed something odd — the nearby chicken coop was quiet — too quiet.

A few yards away, the kettle moraine's stillness exploded with dogs barking energetically and terrified chickens squawking.

"Blasted!" Alfred was exasperated. "Second time this week!" He ran through the woods into a clearing to watch helplessly as the dachshunds chased his chickens down the road and into The Depot.

He yelled for Ben and, together, the men frantically gathered each pampered chicken. Within the hour the roosters were also penned and the hens were again clucking contentedly in their coop. Each hen was named with Hattie's flair for jollity after Henry VIII's beheaded wives.

Out of breath, Alfred placed the last hen, a banty, Hattie's favorite she'd named Marie Antoinette, into the coop. "Get the Buick ready, Benny." Wheezing slightly, he took off his straw hat, pulled his large red bandana from around his neck and wiped his face and hands. "We're late to pick up Noël. It's too late for me to change."

"When our fashionable Mr. Coward sees you," Ben crowed, "won't he have a laugh!"

"I can't be bothered." Alfred tucked the bandana into his front bib pocket, "I would much rather listen to my hens clucking, any-time."

An hour later, as expected, Noël quipped smugly as the two strolled to the waiting Buick from the Milwaukee train station. "Love your gentleman farmer's get-up." Climbing into the backseat of the car, he caught a whiff of Alfred's downdraft and chuckled, "A bit gamy today, aren't we, old pal?"

Alfred sat down in the back seat and patted the perspiration off the back of his neck and forehead with his soiled bandana. "I know I look like a weary old hack. But, had I stopped to shower and change, the eggs for your Benedict tomorrow morning would be all over The Depot! On top of it all, Lynn's god-damned goose thinks my pool's a bird bath! I had to clean droppings and feathers from an overflowing filter before the pool's motor burned up!"

The conspicuous black Buick pulled into Delafield, a picturesque town of red brick federal-style structures near Nagawicka Lake. A half-way stop to Ten Chimneys, it was Alfred's favorite lunch spot.

At lakeside, while Mr. Lunt laid a blanket under a shade tree, Ben retrieved their basket lunch. Their picnic fare was chicken salad sandwiches on homemade white bread, sweet pickles and assorted fruit from the orchards. A last minute indulgence for today's luncheon was a fine bottle of Courvoisier.

Mr. Lunt took great pleasure in serving freshly baked breads for his meals at Ten Chimneys. At midnight, he could often be found kneading dough in the kitchen for next morning's breakfast.

Noël stretched out his thin, six-foot frame and gluttonously devoured a sandwich.

Studying Noël's bony face and slicked back hair, Alfred admonished, "Don't they feed you in Jamaica? You always appear starved to death when you come home, Sonny Boy!"

Coward was a worldly, intelligent, sophisticated wit, a voracious reader and a prolific lyricist, writer and entertainer. But he always appeared only moments away from a great sadness.

He was penniless with a suitcase full of plays, when Alfred and Lynn first met him upon his arrival in New York City, but the three best friends optimistically agreed to work together. Noël was to write for them and they were to act for him. This pact was later to become a storyline for Noël's hit play 'Design for Living'.

After a full lunch, Alfred sprawled out on the blanket, sated. He rolled onto his side and lazily propped his head up with an elbow.

Noël was in the midst of a rant. "...those fucking flickies..." Oblivious, Alfred's eyes wandered and fixed upon an attractive woman in a two piece sunsuit, sunbathing nearby. "...Laughton, Donat, even our beloved Oliviers! All money-grubbing traitors!" Noël became more agitated. "Goddamn it, Alfred! You're not listening to a word I'm saying!"

"Look, Noëllie! Aren't they the most perfect, luscious orbs?" Still staring at the woman, Alfred slowly bit into a ripe, juicy peach.

Coward glanced briefly at the woman and turned away, disdainfully. "Her tit's are hanging out, for Christ's sake!" His words were scathing. "Women's breasts remind me of cow utters. They should be swaddled and hidden!"

"It's getting awfully hot out here." Alfred patted the sweat from his brow with his hanky, "Sonny Boy, let's pack it up and head home. I miss my Lynnie." He got up, brushed off his overalls and began to fold the blanket. "You are wickedly irritable today, Noël. I know just the ticket. A cool swim in our pool."

"You're right, I'm just a miserable old sod," Noël lamented. "You and Lynn are the happiest married couple I know. But I don't know many, my friend."

Ben followed behind them, taking the blanket and basket, and loading the trunk.

Walking to the car, however, Noël again exploded in a fresh burst of rage. "Times are changing, dear friend! These young mewling pups of the cinema who dare call themselves actors! They clamor to steal the limelight from great theatre talent. Bastard studio executives!" He spat the words. "Out to steal for the cinema. Wolves, I tell you!"

"I have not regretted Lynn and I refusing to sign MGM's million dollar contract." Alfred lit a cigarette and offered one to Noël. "The studios, those sons of bitches, would not allow us enough creative control. Our burgeoning young stage actors will most definitely be plucked with the promise of big money."

At the car, Noël paused and intently fixed his eyes on Alfred with great gravity. "Quite right! We — everyone in theatre — are in quick sand up to our dicks you know."

In the backseat, through venting for the moment, Noël poured himself and Alfred a glass of cognac. "How is it you don't drive, ol chap?"

"Did once," Alfred confided. "Truth is, my curiosity got the best of me. You know I seriously aspired to becoming an acrobat in a circus as a lad. Some years back, I spotted a marvelous old circus billboard, and cut across three lanes of traffic to give it a good look. Lynnie insisted "Never again!"

"God knows I adore Lynnie to death — but Alfred, could you be more quinney-whipped!" Noël smirked, slapped his friend on the back and tossed down the liqueur. He thought for a moment, then said glumly, "We are to be swallowed up and replaced by a throng of fresh bun boys!"

"The theater as we know it will surely cease to exist." Lunt took a large gulp of cognac and shook his head, "Old friend, we are ruined."

CHAPTER 18

The blacktop was melting under Diana's sandaled feet as she stopped her bike on Depot Road in front of her grandparent's house. Martin, the Perkins brothers — and Butch — followed her up the hill.

The first house up the road from the Herrold's belonged to Ben Perkins' brother, Chet and his wife Marie, and their two children. Saturday mornings, Diana and the Perkins brothers huddled around their ten-inch black and white Philco watching Hopalong Cassidy, Roy Rogers and Dale Evans. The brothers lived on top of a hill engulfed in woods, the perfect location for Hide-and-Seek or Cowboys-and-Indians. The children all loved to play, but no one ever wanted to be an Indian.

Butch had attached an ace of spades and clubs to the spokes of his old bike with clothes pins and was pedaling in circles around Nippy. The whirring sound was scaring the poor, hapless creature who was barking incessantly, chasing and biting at the bicycle tires.

"I told you letting Butch play with us was a bad idea!" Diana yelled at the three boys.

"Yeah," Martin scowled, "even if he said he'd be an Indian and we could tie him up!"

Hanging clothes in the back yard, Louise heard Nippy's agitated barking. She immediately threw an armload of wet bed linens on the grass and, loudly talking to herself, charged around the house.

"Shut up, you old flea bag!" Butch shouted and kicked the dog with the heel of his foot.

Nippy yelped in pain and ran up the stone driveway into Louise's arms.

"What's your name?" she fumed.

Butch didn't answer.

The group of kids parted quickly as Louise marched down the driveway toward Butch, crunching gravel with every step. Martin fell backward over his bike.

"I know you — you're Frederick Miller's boy, aren't you?" She glared at him thinking to herself Butch would look just like his old man when he got older.

"Fred, Junior." Butch was openly belligerent.

Louise gritted her teeth menacingly, her face flushed as red as her hair. "I'll tell you what —" she was only inches from Butch's face. "If you ever touch my dog again, I'll kick you so hard, your old man will have to call you Frieda instead of Fred, you little son of a bitch!"

"I'm getting the hell out of here!" Butch jumped on his bike. "You're one crazy old lady!" he yelled back at her as he raced down the hill toward The Depot.

"You can't hide from me. I'll find you, you little shit!" She shrieked and raised her fist. "Don't think I won't!" Nippy wriggled and fell out of her grasp.

In stunned silence Martin and the Perkins boys climbed onto their bikes and pedaled away.

"Oh, my sheets! Diana, grab Nippy for me, put him in the house, and don't forget to hook the screen!" Louise disappeared around the house. "They're gonna get ruined with grass stains! U-u-u-mpf!" Her nervous tic appeared.

As Diana chased Nippy down the driveway toward the road, the Lunt's black Buick sped around a blind curve, and the small dog darted in front of it. The car veered off the road, bumping and weaving, grazing a tree trunk, and, in a cloud of dust, landed in a graveled ditch.

The rare bottle of French Napoleon Courvoisier had upended,

spilling out and over everything in the back seat. Angry, Alfred rolled down his car window, coughing and waving away the dust. "You best keep that mutt away from the road! A dog that's not afraid of cars is a dead dog!"

Dumfounded, the child could only nod her head up and down, foolishly, and straighten the cowboy hat on her head. Noël instantly defended the young girl, "Don't be such a bastard, ol' man!" he scolded. "What would you do if one of your precious German mini-turds romped in front of a car?" The Lunts now had four dachshunds Lynn took everywhere, even on their theater tours.

Diana watched in rapt silence as the three men got out of the car, rolled up their sleeves, and strained and pushed the luxury auto back onto the road.

As the Buick sped away, Noel leaned out the opened window and threw the girl a stick of chewing gum, "Cheers darling!"

CHAPTER 19

When Alfred and Noël arrived at Ten Chimneys on this hot spring afternoon, Noël didn't wait for Jules to unpack his personal items in his guest room. He marched to the bathhouse, put on only a white robe and paraded out to the pool where a group of playwrights and thespians were sunbathing. Some lucky members of the Lunt's Chicago theater company had been invited to the estate for the day.

"I'm an enormously talented man, and there's no use pretending I'm not!" Noël threw off his robe and, with great aplomb, exposed his skinny lily white frame — top to bottom. "Lads, don't be shy to show off your witches!" he shouted and dove into the cool water.

The theater entourage of mostly young men chortled and twittered amongst themselves. A middle-aged gentleman, a Chicago playwright new to Ten Chimneys, enormous and fleshy in tight swim trunks, grasped and patted his adolescent male companion's leg in hilarity as they lounged at poolside. But Alfred's mother who was having a late lunch in her kitchen, witnessed Noël's indiscretion through her cottage window, and was not amused.

In her brightly-colored housedress, red lipstick and high heels, Hattie marched down the grassy knoll, her hair tied-up in a scarf with two knotted ends at the crown bobbing up and down like rabbit ears.

Jules watched her approach from the open kitchen window of the main house. "Oh — my — Gawd!" he whispered under his breath.

She entered the kitchen waving her ten-inch cigarette holder — fuming. "*Whilst* I was trying to enjoy my bratwurst, Noël suddenly dashes in front of my kitchen window sporting nothing more than his pecker! *Shocking*! He *smacks* of nouveau riche!" Hattie loved to drop French phrases — made her feel more cosmopolitan.

Continuing to prepare supper, Jules nodded his head sagely.

"And do you know what that bony bastard did next? The nerve of him! He smiled in all his glory and wished me a good day! Jules, you *must* have a talk with Alfred." Hattie finished her tirade, exhausted.

Lynn strolled into the kitchen wearing a wide-brimmed black hat and strapless white bathing suit. "Jules, we must go out at once," she mocked, "and summon the local vicar!" She poured herself a cup of coffee, snuck a small bite of Jules' pastry, still hot in the baking pan, and popped it into her mouth.

"Well, I *never*!" Hattie was speechless.

Sipping her coffee, Lynn calmly walked back outside to join her guests at poolside.

Respectfully, Jules fought to mask his merriment. He was to be Hattie's caregiver and confidant in her later years. Other than Alfred, Harriet Sederholm would tolerate no one else.

"I'll speak to Mr. Lunt my first opportunity. Please sit down, Mrs. Sederholm, and we'll enjoy some of my fresh coffee and Danish."

Later, after Jules served the other guests at poolside, he walked into the empty foyer and took Mr. Coward's luggage upstairs to unpack.

Noël Coward's room was one of the most comfortable rooms in the house. A white chenille reading chair and matching bedspread gave the room an inviting charm. Jules immediately opened the windows to create a cool cross breeze during the heat of the day.

With quick efficiency Ten Chimneys' major domo hung Mr. Coward's assorted silk ties, dress shirts, an off-white linen suit, argyle vest, and set his two-tone spectators in the closet. In the dresser drawers, he carefully placed folded Bermuda shorts, polo shirts and underwear. Lastly, he hung a lavender cheesecloth ball in the wardrobe, and arranged Noël's personal toiletries near a neat stack of Turkish hand towels in the adjoining bath.

He placed a pack of Lucky Strikes and a lighter on the desk along with Coward's writing materials, making a mental note to return to the room after dinner to close the windows and start a fire in the corner fireplace. On a small table next to the reading chair, he set a decanter of brandy and cordial glass near a short stack of books. To complete the room's ambience, on the desk he placed an old 'Private Lives' program, one of Mr. Coward's most acclaimed plays.

As Jules gathered the now empty suitcases, Noël bounded up the spiral staircase, wrapped only in a towel at his waist.

"So glad Lorn had the divine insight to pack my books in my valet," Coward observed gratefully. "Absolutely couldn't manage without my salty secretary, you know. She keeps my whole world in order. Much like you and Mr. Lunt, eh old chap?"

He reached for a cigarette on the desk and noticed the 'Private Lives' program. "Oh, how thoughtful, Jules. Haven't seen one of these in years. I was on holiday in Singapore, I believe it was 1929, and had an extraordinary dream of Gertrude Lawrence in a white gown. Sat down immediately and penned it, you know. Starred myself, Gertrude and Larry Olivier, and we packed houses on two continents."

Making himself comfortable in the reading chair, Noël lit his cigarette. "Somewhat ruined the farce for me when 'American Spectator' published Nathan's parody." He poured himself a cordial and opened the old program.

"Will there be anything else, sir?"

"No thank you, Jules. Everything is perfect as usual."

Jules softly closed the door behind himself.

As he walked down the hall, sounds of a squirmish, a bumping, groaning and a muted scream, came from the Olivier bedroom.

Shaken, Jules knocked on the door. "May I be of assistance?" At no response, he knocked again, adamantly.

Their newest guest, the playwright, dressed slatternly in a smoking jacket, answered the door. "Perhaps a refreshment, Jules."

Concerned, Jules looked past the large man breathing unsteadily, standing in the doorway. Behind him, a young man was lying on the bed, disheveled.

"Yes, of course," Jules murmured. "Right away." Thinking he must find Alfred immediately, he reeled and quickly ran down the spiral stairs.

Shortly, over cordials in the library, Alfred had a serious discussion with the perpetrator.

"Mr. Lunt, how must theater survive? It is common knowledge the earnest man dies either from a bullet or overwork. But is it not the prodigal who is rewarded? And the strayed sheep? Tell me, sir, what must a fellow do?"

Quickly understanding this man was a tortured soul, Alfred responded with cool restraint.

"Tell me, sir, what must a host do when a felony occurs under his roof?"

The playwright and his companion left Genesee Depot, preferring not to stay for dinner.

At Alfred and Lynn's insistence, Mr. Coward remained at Ten Chimneys the entire summer. As the hot season came and went, though, Noël's shocking behavior was escalating — and he still hadn't finished a play for the Lunt's next theater tour.

Somewhat nervous, Alfred suggested actually locking Noël in The Studio. Alfred had fallen in love with the 18th century Swedish hunting lodge during his travels and had dismantled, shipped and reassembled it at Ten Chimneys. Surrounded by acres of woodland, Mr. Lunt hoped to perhaps embolden the playwright's creative thought. Something magical always happened to those who spent time in The Studio. Differences of opinion, heated contentions, even the Lunts' infrequent arguments were resolved there. They sometimes danced, sometimes slept problems away in the loft, but conflicts always seemed to melt away in The Studio.

Noël Coward, Bob Sherwood and comedy specialist, S.N. Behrman who wrote 'The Pirate' and 'I Know My Love', all complained of arduous, endless rewrites when working at Ten Chimneys, but always praised Alfred and Lynn for vetting a better, more excellent play.

Without a Coward satire to launch their theater season that year, the Lunts chose a Behrman play. 'I Know My Love' was dubbed their least enterprising property, however, they enacted brilliant performances. They were rewarded with a generous Broadway run and, to Lynn's joy, Alfred bought a chic four-story New York brownstone "chock full of fireplaces".

CHAPTER 20

For Diana and Martin the hot humid summer days seemed to last forever. Bordering the Herrold's property, a neighboring farmer's corn field grown for animal fodder, became their favorite place to play. Tired and sweaty after a rousing Hide-and-Seek, they rested under the nearest shade tree and gobbled down ears of raw sweet white corn.

"Owww!" Covered with mosquitoes, Diana swatted her legs and arms. "Come on, Martin!" They jumped on their bikes and headed toward the neighbor's large granite watering trough. She plunged into the cool dampness.

"What are you waiting for?" she teased him.

"I don't know how to swim!" Martin squashed some pests on his neck and forehead.

"Are you kidding me?" she splashed him. "You can't drown in here! It's only up to our knees!"

She pulled him in after her. "Eweeee! You have blood on your face!" She rinsed the mosquito remains from his face.

While they idly floated, belly up, relaxing from the sweltering heat, Diana observed dreamily how fast the clouds were moving above the trees.

A train whistled in the distance.

"I'll beat you!" Martin hollered. Dunking her to get a head start, he jumped out of the trough and onto his bike.

Sputtering and gasping for breath, she leaped out of the water and followed close behind.

"Over my — great-grama's dead body!" she spouted.

They raced down the three small hills toward The Depot with the shuffling sound of cards clothes-pinned to their bicycle spokes. The wind on her soaking wet skin was refreshing as she quickly caught up to Martin. When she slowed down to peek at Ten Chimneys through the trees, though, he zoomed past her.

"Last time we made it in three minutes!" Martin screamed.

The summer before, as the Milwaukee 'Galloping Goose' passenger train slowly approached the small village, blowing its whistle, Diana had waved at the friendly conductor. He immediately tipped his hat and threw her a taffy. The next day a gaggle of kids gathered in the same place.

Good-naturedly, he threw a handful of Tootsie Rolls. Every summer day from then on, he had continued with different treats like Bit o' Honey and Bazooka bubble gum.

This summer day was no different. As a handful of kids raced their bikes to The Depot just seconds before 'The Goose' passed through, Butch deliberately cut in front of Diana. Forced to brake suddenly, she tumbled off her bike into a ditch, scraping her leg on the gravel.

Unaware of her plight, Martin waited at the train tracks with the other kids and screamed with delight when the conductor threw handfuls of Bazooka gum. He scrambled in the dirt to claim every brightly-colored wrapper he could find.

A few yards down the tracks, the kindly conductor noticed Diana struggling with her bike and a bloody knee, and threw another handful of gum to land near her.

Immediately, Butch pedaled past, pushing her into the ditch again, taunting, "You can't blow bubbles with your gap-tooth, anyways!" Joe Bazooka was his favorite, so he quickly grabbed all of her gum, jamming it into his already bulging pockets.

She watched him pedal away and, for a moment, started to cry. Then, despite the pain and with new resolve, she leaped onto her bike and chased Butch home — with Martin following close behind.

Approaching his house near the railroad tracks, Butch maneuvered his bike around broken beer bottles and squawking chickens. He threw it down near the porch and ran inside, with a torn screen door slamming behind him.

Diana hobbled after, pedaling straight through the Miller junkyard. She pounded on the screen door. Fred Miller Senior answered the door holding a beer, his big belly bulging out from under a dirty t-shirt.

"Butch stole my candy!" Diana screamed angrily.

Martin joined her on the porch, "And he pushed her down!" He yelled, "Look at her knee, she's hurt!"

Butch's dad gazed at the blood running down her leg and yelled back into the house, "Give it back, shit-for-brains!"

He could hear Butch frantically unload his cache into a bedroom dresser drawer.

"You heard me, give it back!" Fred hollered over the crack of a baseball bat and the roar of an ardent crowd on the television. "Hurry up! You're making me miss my game! The Cubs are down three to two!"

Struggling with the broken wooden drawer Butch shrieked back, "Hell no! She's just a dumb Gap-face!"

"Don't make me come in there and get you, boy!" His old man bellowed, his face purpling.

In the recesses of the dilapidated house, it grew quiet. Moments later, Butch reluctantly stepped up to the front door and threw the bubble gum at Diana.

"Goddammit, you're gonna get a whuppin for that! Pull down them pants!" Butch's dad slipped his huge belt out of its pant loops and snapped it like a whip.

"I ain't gonna do it!" Butch looked at Diana, defiantly.

"You get over here, boy! I'm already pissed off!" Fred yelled. "Without that God-damned Jackie Robinson the Cubs just lost! And I'm in no mood to put up with your shit!"

Painfully, Diana picked up the handful of Bazookas and limped back to her bike, where Martin was waiting.

She ripped the cards off of her bike spokes. "This was a dumb idea, anyway!" Wincing, she hopped back onto her bike, then looked at Martin expectantly.

"Yeah, a really dumb idea!" Martin ripped the cards off of his bike, too.

As the two pedaled away, they could hear Fred Miller's belt crack each time Butch howled. "We got our ass kicked!" *Whap!* "In front of the largest crowd!" *Whap-whap!* "Ever! At Wrigley Field!" *Whap-whap-whap!*

While Butch bawled with each snap, crowing in victory, Diana and Martin popped the bright pink gum into their mouths, tasting its gooey sweetness.

She put out her hand, "Give it up."

"Wha?" Martin's cheeks were full to bursting as he chewed.

Under a shade tree, she stopped her bike and held out her hand resolutely. "All your gum, Martin."

Her best friend spit the mushy lump into her palm and Diana jammed it into her mouth. Carefully, with childish concentration, she blew a gigantic bubble that encircled her head.

Martin let out a long, low whistle. "Wow! You musta beat your own record!"

When it burst, Diana's triumphant smile was profiled in pink-gummed relief. Proud she had stood up for herself, she plucked the sticky mass from her face and whispered, "Yeah, a personal record!"

Chapter 21

With the front toe of a scuffed tennis shoe, Diana winced as she flipped the kickstand of her bicycle with her injured leg. Martin joined her as she painfully stepped onto the old boardwalk in front of the Genesee Depot post office. Every summer afternoon the youngsters picked up their family mail and brought it home.

From behind the old worn postal counter, perched on a high stool, Agnes Pronold readjusted her bifocals and peered at them. "Hi there, kids!"

A tiny kindly lady, Aggy and her brother Gibby were the 'miracle babies' of The Depot. The Gibson twin's story was well-known. Each barely a pound-and-a-half at birth and not expected to live, their mother had kept them warm in cotton-lined cigar boxes placed near her woodburning stove.

To the town children's delight, the grown adult twins stood shoulder to shoulder with most of them.

When Aggy's only son left his position as postmaster years before, she had purposefully stepped up to the task. Across the street from the post office she lived in a small turn-of-the-century dwelling with Jim Pronold, her husband, The Depot's train station agent, and her brother Gibby, who never married. The children never knew what Gibby did for a living, but he could often be seen at Stags and his friendship with Zabel Luckert ran deep after many years of story telling over cold beers.

Barely able to reach across the postal counter, with a broad friendly smile Aggy handed each child a bundle of mail tied with string. She loved people, especially children, always hiding an ever-present heartache, the loss of an infant boy, now buried in St. Paul's cemetery.

"Thanks, Aggy!" The children waved goodbye and walked their bikes across the street to Torhorst's General Store. They often stopped there for a cold root beer before the heated uphill bike ride home.

Eyeing her favorites, Diana stood in front of the candy bin. Harry Torhorst, the store's owner, had painstakingly grouped the confections in order. Necco wafers, cigar-shaped bubble gum, candy cigarettes, Smarties candy pills, waxed root beer barrels, large red waxed lips and Smith Brothers cherry cough drops were all displayed in neat rows.

"Don't touch the candy! I worked all morning on that!" Harry was a cranky middle-aged man who didn't trust the children and rarely smiled when they came in.

While Harry watched suspiciously, Diana dumped all the pennies in her pockets onto his counter near the register and began to count — slowly. Realizing she didn't have enough money to buy her favorites, Martin emptied his pockets, too, which started their laborious count all over again.

"There! That's just enough for one of each if we don't get root beer." Diana was disappointed.

"I have more at home!" Martin shouted excitedly as he darted out the door.

"Hurry up, there's someone waiting behind you." Harry spoke impatiently through pursed lips, watching Diana closely as she walked back toward the candy bins. "Gotta watch the local kids — sticky fingers, you know." He confided to a woman customer.

The petite, pleasant-looking, middle-aged woman with some supplies in her arms stepped up to the register. She pulled out a credit card.

Obsequiously, he apologized. "I'm so sorry, Miss Hayes, I'm not set-up for credit cards. But I'd be happy to start a tab for you during your stay at Ten Chimneys."

"Do you have any children, Mister, uh..." Helen Hayes turned around to read the gold letters on his store front window, "Mr. Torhorst?" She didn't wait for him to reply. "That little boy just gave her his last pennies so she could buy candy. Is that someone who would steal from you?"

Diana 's eyes got big and round as she listened to the adult exchange.

Minutes later, she felt very stylish as she stood in the middle of Torhorst's General Store wearing her newly-bought bright red wax lips and candy necklace — a gift from her anonymous benefactor.

"Kindly add some iodine and band-aids to my tab, won't you?" Helen Hayes called to Harry, "I'll also have two cold root beers, please!"

Helen bandaged the scrapped knee and whispered to Diana. "Does Mr. Torhorst always look like he just ate a sour ball?"

Giggling, Diana quickly looked at Harry and stopped. She'd been taught it wasn't nice to laugh at grown-ups.

Once outside, sitting on Harry's front steps, Diana laughed some more with this nice lady while finishing their root beers.

Butch pedaled by on his bicycle, "I see England, I see France, I see Diana's ..."

"... And I saw your little willie!" Diana stood up and shouted.

Helen exploded into laughter and gently patted the child's sore knee. "My dear, how did this happen?"

She told Miss Hayes about Butch and his whooping.

"Don't you worry, honey," Helen said sagely. "Mark my word, Butch will always meet his match. By the way, my name is Miss Hayes." She held out her hand to shake. "What's yours?"

"I'm Diana." She smiled brightly and shook Helen's hand firmly. "Thanks so much for the root beer."

That evening Diana told her grandmother about the nice lady she met at Harry's.

"What was her name?" Louise asked.

"I don't remember," Diana answered. "But she's staying with the Lunts."

"Oh, my God, what did she look like?" Louise pressed.

"Like a nice little lady," Diana said matter-of-factly.

"I bet you met Helen Hayes! Jules said she was visiting," Louise gushed. "How come I never get to meet anyone important in The Depot!"

The following day, Louise Herrold marched into Harry's. "My Diana would never steal from your cheap-sorry-ass store! From now on we buy at Russell's! You'll see only the Herrolds' backsides from this day forward, Mr. Harry '*Tortoise*'!"

Chapter 22

"Come on up, Di." Jules waved to her from an open upstairs kitchen window.

Wearily, she gimped up the Ten Chimneys' stairs.

"Oh child, how did you get so sweaty?" Then he noticed her bandages. "And what happened to your knee?"

"All day," she sighed, "I've been delivering Nana's pies on my bike in this heat."

"Come wash your hands. Sit here next to me and take a little rest." On the table he placed a bowl of vanilla ice cream in front of the child, which she quickly consumed. Amused, Jules cautioned, "Hold on, Di. You're gonna get a brain-freeze!"

In a sunsuit, Miss Hayes popped into the kitchen momentarily for an iced tea. "Well, well — here's our little Genesee neighbor! Is your knee better today, Diana?"

"I see you've already met my godchild, Miss Hayes." Jules beamed.

"Are you going swimming in the pool, dear?" Helen asked.

Diana looked troubled, "I don't know how to swim."

Helen took a sip of her cold drink. "Oh, not to worry. It's as natural as breathing," she reassured. "Perhaps in a few days, after your knee heals, I could teach you."

After Helen went upstairs to her room for a nap, Jules sat down at the table with a bucket of corn.

"My bathing suit doesn't fit any more," Diana complained as she helped him shuck an ear of corn.

"Oh, I'm sure Lu will take care of that!" Jules laughed.

While they separated the golden threads, she spoke, "Nana says my hair looks like corn silk. Do you think it does, Jules? I hate my fine, thin hair! It gets all tangled."

He patted his thick nappy head, "I wouldn't know about such things!" They both smiled. "God made us all unique, didn't he! See this?" He held up a gnarled, arthritic thumb. "Alfred calls it my 'pickle-pusher'!" Jules grinned, widely. "It's from years of pushing the last pickle tightly into a jar."

"But my Nana doesn't have a pickle thumb!" They both chuckled.

"I hear a child's laughter..." Lynn Fontanne entered the kitchen.

"Miss Fontanne, Diana just delivered another pie from Mrs. Herrold in this heat," Jules stated. "I suggested she clean up and have something cool to drink before she returns home."

"How lovely. We must send you home with a thank-you note." Lynn took Diana's small hand, "Come upstairs with me first and let's give your face a proper cleansing. Oh, Jules, our old friend Edna Ferber will be arriving for dinner this evening. Have you arranged for Ben to pick her up at the train station?"

"Ben is washing down the car in the garage as we speak, Miss Fontanne." Always efficient, Jules backed away and returned to his work.

Miss Fontanne led Diana through the Flirtation Room toward the library, where Alfred was lounging in a comfortable down-filled chair reading a book next to the fireplace. A lazy thread of smoke rose from the cigarette in his hand. He slowly lifted it to his mouth and took a long drag, then closed the lid of his silver cigarette box with a click.

The library was paneled in Wisconsin limed, golden oak, and on the wall behind the desk was a particularly handsome portrait of Alfred. On the opposite wall above the hearth was a portrait of Lynn in her late teens entitled 'The Blue Coat' by de Glehn, a member of the British Royal Academy. De Glehn's portrait of Miss Fontanne, 'The Spanish Mantilla' hung in the Academy for many years. She had been a favorite model of Jane and Wilfred de Glehn, both famed English artists. Another de Glehn oil of Lynn was to hang in Washington D.C.'s Smithsonian.

Mr. Lunt was an avid reader with a wide range of literary interests and a vast collection including a 'History of England' and a complete set of Dickens. On his desk were disparate contemporary Pulitzer-tomes, Edna Ferber's 'Giant' and Capote's 'In Cold Blood'. Also born and raised in Wisconsin, Ferber had inscribed in Alfred's first edition:

September and a new play for you in London
September and a new book for me in New York
A hardworking three.
God Bless us all.
You, dear Lynn.
You, dear Alfred.
And me.
Edna,
New York
September 3, 1952

As Miss Fontanne and Diana passed the library, the child, unaware of Alfred's proximity behind her, looked up into Lynn's face. "I'm really sorry I made Mr. Lunt so angry."

"What could you possibly do to upset Mr. Lunt, dear?" Lynn gazed, pointedly, past Diana into the library at Alfred.

"I'm not sure, but when he shot at those squirrels," Diana admitted, "I really got scared!"

Lynn's eyes blazed in alarm, then narrowed to slits. So *that's* what those rifle shots were, she thought. "How close to the squirrels were you, Diana? You could have been hurt!"

"No, I dove out of the way."

"My dear, you could have been sitting in a patch of poison ivy!"

The child was uncomfortably quiet.

As they ascended the spiral stairs, prisms of color reflecting from the large crystal chandelier above, danced all around them. Diana was again struck by the mistress of Ten Chimneys' beauty. Dressed for dinner in a smart tailored black suit with padded shoulders and matching heels, Lynn's dark, shining hair was fashioned in a chignon.

Hand in hand they entered the bedroom where the young girl was fascinated by the huge bed, the English rose wallpaper and the large adjoining sunroom. She sat on the side of the bed, then bounced up and down. "Do just the two of you sleep in this great big bed?" she asked innocently.

"That could perhaps change!" Lynn whispered vehemently under her breath.

"In the winter when Opa visits, three of us sleep in one little bed." Diana admitted. "That's how we all stay warm."

Lynn smiled, "I remember doing the same with my sisters during cold English winters."

She lead Diana to a vanity illuminated by a window framed with floral glass lights and porcelain flowers. Lynn sat her down in the chair and knelt at the child's height.

Miss Fontanne studied Diana's face in the mirror. "Would you like me to teach you my beauty secrets?"

"Oh yes, please! You're so beautiful." Diana avoided looking at her own reflection. "I wish I had your eyes."

"I'm not beautiful, *dah-h-h-ling*." Lynn stared at her own image. "Even though Mr. Lunt often flatters me to the contrary."

Lynn began the beauty ritual by pulling Diana's hair away from her face. "Let's bind up your hairs." Lynn smiled at the child's puzzled expression. "That's *Shakespeare*, dah-ling."

She wound her hair tightly, and held it in place on the crown of her head with two jeweled Asian-style hair picks.

Diana giggled, "Chopsticks!"

From a jar Lynn palmed a small mound of facial cream and massaged it into Diana's face.

"Here's the first secret," she coached her. "Always stroke your face and neck in an upward motion. Audrey Hepburn's smooth neck is highly underrated."

"Whipped cream!" Diana smiled brightly as Lynn gently tissued the fragrant lotion off her face.

"Now child, close your eyes." She gently patted her false eyelashes onto the top of Diana's eyelids.

Wrapping a long flowing silk scarf around both of them, cheek-to-cheek, they looked into the mirror. "Raise your chin. Open your eyes — half way — just — like — *that*!"

For a moment, Diana had Lynn Fontanne eyes.

Self-consciously she smiled, trying to hide the wide gap between her front teeth with her upper lip.

Amused at the child's facial contortions, Miss Fontanne spoke in her most authoritative dramatic whisper. "With infinite care, I contrive to look smart, Diana. You have big, beautiful front teeth. You'll see. When you grow into them, your smile is going to be your best asset!"

"For years I have dreamed of the house that lies behind the trees — and here I am!" Diana rejoiced.

Touched, Lynn gave her a big hug and whispered, "What would you think if you were to..."

There was a movement behind them. Alfred was standing in the bedroom doorway, brooding, petulant.

"It's getting late," he stated. "Edna should be arriving shortly and Jules needs our assistance in the kitchen. And we have much to do before Larry and Viv's visit in a few days."

"Very well, then, enough for today, Diana."

After the young girl's footsteps sounded down the hall, Alfred shut the door.

"Splendid! What every displaced child needs! A doting older woman with illusions of motherhood!" He could cut deep when he wanted.

"Just what I expected from you," Lynn seethed. An older man who acts like a spoiled mummy's boy. How *dare* you call me doting, when Hattie's living only a few hundred yards away! Just because I'm devoted to stage, doesn't mean I can't have a fulfilled life!"

"*Mummy's* boy?" Alfred screeched furiously in his high-pitched nasal. "Fulfilled life? How could our life here not be fulfilling! So, what does fulfilled mean to you, Lynn?"

She took a deep breath and closed her eyes for a moment. "Alfred, I came here to Wisconsin to be with you. My God, she's even arranged to have you buried between us! I must not only share you in life with Hattie, but even in death?"

"Don't be ridiculous!" Alfred shrieked. "What-the-devil does my mother have to do with this? Truth is, I remember when I first met you, Lynn. Your confidence was unshakeable, or so I thought." He was confused. "You stunned me with your independence. You didn't need anyone!"

Incensed, she moaned into the mirror at his reflection. "I want a *chiiild*, Alfred!"

Wild-eyed and red in the face, he opened the bedroom door and stomped down the stairs.

Lynn ran to the landing and mimicked his peevish bawling, "Go ahead, call for your *Muthuh! Muthuh*!" She screamed at his back, "And I know you shot my squirrels — you God-damn-son-of-a-bitch!" She ran back into her room and slammed the door.

She could hear his clipped, angry steps proceed down the hall as he muttered to himself, "I knew that child was trouble."

A moment later the library door banged shut.

Innocent of the turmoil she'd caused, Diana blissfully walked her bicycle down Ten Chimneys' driveway toward home and waved back to Jules, who was standing at his apartment window.

"Close the gates, Di!" he called to her.

As she pedaled home, she remembered the burning question she had wanted to ask Jules.

Who were Larry and Viv?

Chapter 23

"Laurence Olivier? Vivien Leigh? In The Depot?" Louise chortled and fanned herself as she sipped her highball. In the humidity of the late afternoon she sat in her lawn chair with her head wrapped in a scarf and a thick layer of white cold cream on her face. This was her time to pamper herself. Her pork roast was in the oven and Virgel was repairing the ringer washing machine in the basement.

"I'm over the moon, Di! If I'm lucky, maybe I'll meet them!" Her fleshy underarm flapped like a wing as she fanned herself with the most recent 'Confidential', one of the first published magazines sensationalizing the plight of celebrity.

Diana had something else on her mind. School was about to start. She had picked up a brown parcel from Sears and Roebuck at the post office that afternoon, and was excited to open it and model her new school clothes for her grandparents.

Virgel, wanting to instill a strong sense of work ethic, had suggested she sell raspberries to earn money. Diana couldn't wait to erect a fruit stand at the intersection just past St. Paul's outside of town.

Nana suggested she set-up her table in the late afternoons when the men were coming home from work. The locals were eager to buy Diana's berries, the best deal around for 35 cents in overflowing quart baskets. She always sold out in less than an hour. Diana earned seventy dollars and proudly handed it to her Nana to help pay for a new school wardrobe.

"Check if I have enough lard in the cellar, Di." Louise admired her freshly-painted red nails. "We must make two pies for Saturday!"

Dutifully, Diana went inside the house. "And bring Virgel a cool drink!" Louise yelled after her. "The dear man's probably sweating bullets down there!"

It was suffocatingly hot in the basement as Diana walked down the steps with a tall, iced glass of cherry Kool-Aid. Virgel grunted, trying to tighten some pipes with a wrench. Nana was right, he was sweating profusely.

"Thanks, my little Di," he said affectionately. The ring finger on his left hand was noticeably missing as he accepted the cold drink and swallowed it down in one long gulp.

"You want me to get you more, Virgel?" she asked.

"No, darlin'. You go keep your Nana company. I'm almost done here, anyways." He was not one to think of himself first. "Mmmm, it sure smells good up in the kitchen."

"Nana says the roast will be done in about a half hour." She smiled at him, retrieved the empty glass and went obediently upstairs.

Virgel Herrold worked long, erratic hours. At Pet Milk Company the dairy products were closely monitored, with cultures taken every other hour and evaluated under his microscope in his lab. The plant equipment also had to be dismantled and thoroughly cleaned every day. He also inspected the pasteurizers, washers, tanks, vats, and unassembled bottle machines.

To Louise's irritation, in addition to Virgel's managerial duties, he was repeatedly called for mechanical repairs. Without complaint in the middle of the night and early mornings, he often drove to the milk plant to resolve sudden equipment and delivery truck breakdowns.

It was one of those emergencies that cost Virgel the ring finger on his left hand. Tired and bleary-eyed late one night, he caught it in machinery gears all the way up to the knuckle. He was compensated seven hundred dollars for the appendage loss, a sizable sum in those days. He did not spend the money, but placed it in safekeeping.

At day's end when her grandmother picked Virgel up from work, Diana couldn't wait to run into his lab. He always greeted her as if he hadn't seen her in years, lifting her up in his arms, placing his 'Pet Milk' paper hat on her head and swinging her around lovingly.

Self-educated and blessed with innate intelligence, Virgel Herrold invented a milk formula he called Sweet Acidophilus. Without the funds to market the formula, his patent was placed on hold. Shortly after his death, the twenty-year patent expired, and was immediately bought by a conglomerate and approved by the FDA.

A wise man, Virgel knew loving Jesus was very important to his wife and he encouraged her faith. It kept Louise's fragile sensibilities stabilized. Both Virgel and Diana had learned if Louise was excited or angered, she had to talk it out with herself first. It was rumored Louise Herrold had a nervous breakdown in her mid-twenties. She was actually diagnosed with tuberculosis, the side effects having since proven to include symptoms of bi-polar depression.

That afternoon while Louise rested in the shade, Jules strolled past the hedges and onto the Herrold's front lawn. With great ceremony, he cleared his throat and presented her with an envelope of fine white linen.

"On behalf of the Lunts, may I extend this invitation. We look forward to the pleasure of your company for tea at four this Saturday." He chuckled and bowed, formally. "Good afternoon, Mrs. Herrold."

The antithetic whimsy of Lu's Jazz Singer whitened face was not lost on him. Shaking his head with mirth, he walked back down the hill and into the dense kettle moraine.

Her mouth agape, Louise sat in the lawn chair studying Ten Chimneys' engraved envelope for a long moment. Finally deciding not to rip it open with her fingers, she called loudly, "Di?"

Licking an orange Kool-Aid Popsicle, her granddaughter opened the front porch screen door and peered outside.

"Get me my letter opener, would ya, doll?" Louise asked her. The child looked confused. "Inside the linen closet, Di, in the hallway. It's still in a gift box."

With trembling hands, Louise opened the invitation with her seldom-used letter opener and read it excitedly. “Miss Fontanne has invited us to tea and the movies! Isn’t that wonderful?”

As Diana went back inside the house, she could hear Louise talking to herself. “Miss Fontanne, I always use your Pacquin cold cream... No. I love your Pacquin advertisements in the magazines... No, no. Lynn...Oh, my *God*, no! Miss Fontanne, I love your cold cream...No! No! No!”

For years Louise proudly displayed the Ten Chimneys’ invitation on a glass shelf in her living room.

After dinner Diana modeled her new wardrobe on the Herrold’s front porch.

“Virgel, doesn’t Di look cultured? Get the Brownie!” Louise shouted. “Hurry!”

Louise thought for a moment, then followed Virgel into the house. In her bedroom at the foot of her bed, she dipped into a small cedar chest and lifted up a silk bridal peignoir, yellowed with age, and a tattered, hand-me-down mink stole.

Returning to the front porch, Louise declared eagerly, “Now, let’s make you a movie star, Di!” The lanky pre-teen slipped into her Nana’s finery and a pair of her highest pumps. “Oooh! You look just like Jean Harlow!”

In front of Virgel’s camera Louise struck a pose with one arm behind her head and one arm on her hip. “Like this, Di! Just follow your Nana!” she cooed, batting her eyelashes and hoisting her dress above her knees as she strutted down her front sidewalk.

As Diana walked down the cement cat walk, their terrier barked happily, darting in and out of her legs.

Virgel boasted, “I’m a lucky man, aren’t I, Nippy?”

CHAPTER 24

Anxious, Louise hadn't slept well last night. Humming her and Virgel's favorite, 'Melody of Love', in a loud mezzo vibrato, she rhythmically sliced bacon, broke eggs to scramble and dropped them into a cast iron frying pan. As the food on the stove sizzled, she pulled butter and homemade strawberry jam out of the refrigerator and popped some bread into her Sunbeam toaster.

"Oh, my God, the milk!" She hurried to the front porch, relieved to find her Pet Milk dairy order still cool in its wooden crate.

The humid temperatues had already climbed into the 90s and the heat over her stove was oppressive — but Louise was oblivious. She was wearing her best satin petticoat and still had her hair in pin curls. Her cheeks, already rouged a bit too much, were flushed with the heat.

Virgel entered the kitchen, washed his hands at the sink as usual and sat down at the table.

"Oh my man I love him so..." she sang as she poured his coffee. "When he takes me in his arms..." she dipped close to him.

"'Mmmm," he smelled her Avon cologne. 'Here's my Heart'. My favorite," he whispered in her ear. "Come on over here, Toots!"

Virgel chased her around the kitchen table, grabbing her ample waist and pulling her to him.

When their granddaughter entered the room, Louise giggled, swatted him away and handed Diana a breakfast plate.

"I can't believe after all these years," Louise was overjoyed. "I'm actually invited to Ten Chimneys to meet Miss Fontanne!"

Later in her bedroom with her imagination still soaring, Louise donned a pink off-the-shoulder floral dress with cupped sleeves. This was the biggest day of her social life, she thought. She added a rhinestone ring to the Sarah Coventry matching set, a crystal three-tier necklace, bracelet and earrings, then studied herself in the mirror.

"Let's face it," she mumbled at herself, her confidence dropping to her ankles. In addition to the dark circles under her eyes from lack of sleep, she was plump and matronly, with extra flesh under her chin, under her arms, around her tummy and hips, below her buttocks — everywhere — except maybe her ankles. Louise looked down at her new shoes. She had thought they looked so smart when she purchased them. Now they looked — frumpish. She began to cry.

The old German clock down the hall struck three chimes.

"Di, go and brush your teeth!"

With her nose in a favorite Nancy Drew mystery, 'The Hidden Staircase', Diana shuffled in and peeked up over the book. Her grandmother's face was tearstained with black mascara running down her cheeks.

Taking her hand, Diana led her to their full-length wall mirror in the living room. The young girl tissued the dark stains off her Nana's cheeks and hugged her. "Look at you, the most beautiful woman in the world."

"Not quite a duchess yet, but close." Louise looked in the mirror and laughed. Her face softened and a confident spark reappeared in her eyes. She turned around and looked herself up and down. Actually, she thought, her dress looked pretty good.

She rushed into the bathroom, pulled out a small red mascara box, wet the tiny Maybelline brush and reapplied her mascara.

"Is this ring too much, doll?" Louise reconsidered. As Diana brushed her teeth, her grandmother quietly removed the ring and the three-tiered necklace. She re-entered her bedroom, placing them back in their original box, all the while talking to herself. "My Virgel says my neck is too pretty to hide..."

At precisely 3:50 p.m., Louise drove the Herrold's old Chevy down Depot Road toward Ten Chimneys' gate.

Lynn Fontanne and Alfred Lunt were renowned for expecting Ten Chimneys' guests to be prompt. In a throaty, theatrical voice, Lynn would say, "The gate will remain open between 3:45 and 4 p.m., *dah-h-h-ling*." The implication was if one arrived for tea at 4:01 p.m., the gate would be closed. The Lunts did not tolerate a missed curtain call.

"What's that?" Louise pointed to a little black suitcase in the car's front seat.

Diana held it up excitedly, "Our bathing suits, Nana! Remember, Miss Fontanne invited us to swim after tea!"

Louise's confidence dropped down around her ankles again. Her face contorted and her head jerked involuntarily as her old foe returned. "U-u-u-mpf!"

She steered the car down the long winding driveway, braking with a jerk in the front courtyard.

"*That* old thing! I haven't worn it in twenty years! When I was fifty pounds lighter! That's all I need right now..."

"...And what's tea at four, Nana?" Diana interrupted.

"Something poor people never do..." Louise yanked the emergency brake.

"U-u-u-mpf!" There it was again.

CHAPTER 25

"Do you take milk with your tea, Mrs. Herrold?" Lynn Fontanne asked, seated at a table under a quaint red and white canopy near the Ten Chimneys' pool.

"Yes, please." Louise brought herself back to the conversation. She had been admiring the Lunt's vast flowered gardens.

Miss Fontanne poured from her two silver servers, one filled with warm milk, the other with hot English tea. "Do you take sugar as well, Mrs. Herrold?"

"What a beautiful tea service!" Heaping the tiny sterling spoon with sugar from the bowl at center table, Louise stirred her tea and placed it on her saucer. Realizing her faux passé, she awkwardly dried the spoon under the table with her napkin and returned it to its bowl.

As she sipped her tea, struggling to keep her nervous tick at bay, her hand trembled, rattling the fine bone English china.

Dying inside, Diana watched her Nana helplessly.

"Have you ladies seen 'Gone With The Wind'?" Lynn asked.

"Oh yes!" Louise answered too quickly.

"This lovely silver service," Lynn continued, "is a treasured gift from our dear friends Laurence Olivier and his wife, Vivien Leigh, who portrayed Scarlett in the film."

Lynn compassionately focused on something other than Mrs. Herrold. Pouring more tea, she spoke soothingly. "Taking tea is an

English family tradition. For an hour or so, sip by sip, the world becomes simpler and uncomplicated, almost genteel, don't you think? Quarreling couples can talk things out civilly. It brings out the best of judgment naturally. It is the most pleasant way to calm my poor Alfred, I assure you. Why, Mr. Lunt and I have had tea in almost every room of Ten Chimneys except the loo!" The three ladies laughed together.

"Will I have the pleasure of meeting Mr. Lunt today?" Louise tittered, immediately star struck.

"Miss Fontanne?" Diana changed the subject, "Nana and I were wondering why tea is served at four. That's almost supper time."

"Why we English have tea at four..." Lynn pondered. "That's a very good question, dear. Well, let me see. Oh, yes. A long time ago in the 1800s there was a duchess. Her official title was Anna the Duchess of Bedford. That being over a century ago, the English had only two meals a day. Breakfast and a very late supper."

Miss Fontanne broke a scone and scattered crumbs at her feet where, to Louise and Diana's delight, a waiting squirrel gathered the biscuit and hurriedly ran up a nearby tree. She continued, "The Duchess became extremely hungry between meals and instructed servants to serve tea with light sandwiches and desserts at four o'clock. She started inviting friends to tea to share in conversation. Tea at four was destined to become..."

"Can this old dame join you for tea?" A few yards away, Hattie in a house gown with her hair wrapped in a scarf, yelled down from her cottage balcony.

"...the social event of all England." Lynn responded, edgily. "Of course, dear Mother!"

"I've always wanted to look like a duchess," Louise admitted, lightheartedly. "The only thing Duchess Anna and I have in common is our love of food and to be with friends."

Hattie disappeared in the recesses of the cottage only to strut out the door minutes later in her bright red lipstick and high heels. Her hair was pulled up in a smart chignon and she was dressed in a bold floral cotton sundress.

"Louise and Diana," Lynn spoke tensely, "may I introduce you to Harriet Sederholm, Mr. Lunt's mother."

"Oh, I'm much more informal than my very English daughter-in-law. You call me Hattie — if I can call you Lu! Mmm — What delectables has Jules stirred up for tea this afternoon?" Hattie drew up a chair, lit a cigarette in her long holder. "Of course my Alfred prefers a good strong Swedish brew," she chided. "Good Lord! I don't see you eating, Lu."

Quickly Hattie and Louise piled their plates.

Biting into a scone, Louise could not swallow the hard, dry lump. Jules must have forgotten the lard, she thought. It was the worst biscuit she had ever tasted.

"Let me show you," Hattie spooned fresh juicy raspberry preserves on the scone and smothered it with Devonshire cream. "I was just like you, Lu, when I first started having tea. This'll soften it up for you."

While the two older women devoured their mounds of food, Lynn delicately ate two finger sandwiches. Hattie pointed to Lynn's plate. "She must stay svelte, you know, for when the Royals call her to knighthood. That's why Dame Lynnie's a stick, and we are... Well, you know, Lu!"

Together the ladies laughed affectionately.

"Not completely true!" Lynn interrupted their gaiety. "Ever since I was a teen, I've always had a little tum-tum." She patted her stomach.

Finally after a third tasty scone, Louise gained enough confidence to speak with ease. "How could anyone have troubles living here? This must be the closest to heaven possible!"

Noticing Ben a few yards away, carrying a weekly stack of newspapers to the shed, Lynn got an idea. "Diana, I should like to design something especially for you!"

When Jules arrived with a dessert tray, Lynn asked, "Jules, would you be a dear and bring me several newspapers and my sewing basket? And, oh yes," she winked at Louise, "perhaps you could find Mr. Lunt and ask him to please bring the Bell & Howell? He adores taking home movies!"

With all her sewing tools at hand, Lynn expertly cut and fashioned nips and tucks. Soon Diana donned a chic newspaper dress. When Alfred appeared, to Louise's great joy, he was unable to resist his artistic impulse and begrudgingly directed Diana in a pirouette for his camera lens.

Mr. Lunt soon turned the lens on his mother who immediately shunned the camera. "No, Alfred dear, I'm not at my best."

"Oh Mother, you must smile for the camera, my joie le vivre!"

To which Lynn whispered tersely, "*My* pain in the arse!"

Before Alfred could say anything, Lynn pecked him on the cheek. "Alfred, you must go now — continue with what you were doing." She then called to the women, "To the courtyard, ladies! Where Ben is waiting!"

Louise took Hattie's arm, secretly relieved the swim was forgotten. "Oh, Hattie, how wonderful! You're coming too?"

"Lu, I sense you and I could really have some fun together!" Hattie laughed and patted her hand. "Let's bon mots in the backseat!"

"What?" Louise was confused.

"It means to dish, Lu!" Hattie hooted stridently. "You do love to gossip, don't you?"

While Hattie and Louise climbed into the Buick in the courtyard, Lynn gently tore off the newspaper dress and disposed of it in the garage. Diana saddened instantly, "I wish we could have saved it somehow."

"You'll have many pretty dresses as you become a lady," Lynn declared, guiding her out of the garage and into the courtyard.

Surprised, Diana noticed Lynn's mature breasts jiggling under her light cotton dress and whispered, "Miss Fontanne, you forgot to put your brassiere on today!"

"Oh my dear little one!" Lynn chuckled, "When you're older I hope you enjoy this freedom!"

"I hope I never grow breasts. They're too much trouble. I don't want a husband chasing me around the kitchen table like Virgel does to Nana, either." Diana was disgusted. "Does Mr. Lunt do that to you?" Laughing raucously, Miss Fontanne helped Diana climb into the waiting Buick.

Alfred stepped through the Flirtation Room's French doors and shouted down into the courtyard. "Lynn, where are you going?" In his hands he held a long narrow piece of paper with pen poised. All day he had been immersed in noting the wattage of every light fixture on the estate, his instructions to Jules for replacement bulbs.

Lynn leisurely waved through the Buick's open window. "Why, we're going to the *cinema, dah-h-h-ling*!"

As the ladies departed, the lace curtains above them closed abruptly. Alfred stood in his crow's nest behind the lace, puffing on a pipe, mumbling to himself. "So, she has joined forces with the enemy!" Inflamed, his imagination turned to mockery.

❧ ✻ ☙

FADE IN: Flickering black and white Chaplin-esque silent film images...

INTERIOR - A 1930s STUDIO EXECUTIVE's OFFICE - DAY

ALFRED and NÖEL enter with their hats in hand. A young JACKIE COOPER look-alike sits behind a huge desk with his feet propped up reading a newspaper. He rudely ignores the men as they stand, sweating about why they've been called to the big man's office. He finally puts his paper down and seems surprised the men are still there.

SUBTITLES:

COOPER

(barks)

Sit!

Like dogs, both men cower and sit.

COOPER

(condescending)

So! What was so wrong with my contract that you couldn't sign?

ALFRED

(wringing his hands)

Control. I needed control.

COOPER

(angry)

Control? Don't you know?
NO ONE is in control!
Not you, not me! NO ONE!

Cooper laughs, grabs the men by their lapels and physically kicks them out the open door of his office. Alfred and Noël, tumble and fall over each other (Keystone Cops-style) down the stairs.

FADE OUT

FADE IN:

INTERIOR - STUDIO EXECUTIVE's OFFICE - NEXT DAY

LYNN and HELEN HAYES enter. Cooper slavishly admires them and presents them with a film contract, which they both immediately sign with a flourish.

COOPER

You dames have to see the new backlot I just bought!

Laughing excitedly, Cooper, Lynn and Helen exit.

FADE TO BLACK

FADE IN:

EXTERIOR - STREET SCENE ONE YEAR LATER

Lynn and Helen, dressed in costumed finery, walk their diamond-collared dachshunds on the streets of Hollywood. They pass Alfred and Noël who are now bums, huddled together on a street corner. The ladies throw some coins into their alms cup. The two derelicts scramble, fighting each other for the pittance.

SUBTITLES:

NÖEL
(pleads)
Lynnie! Helen! You made a wrong decision! You must know that, don't you?

ALFRED
(frantic)
Wait! Dearest! What about Ten Chimneys? Our summers...your flowers...your teas
(agonizes)
My dinners!
Where are you going?

LYNN
(laughs)
Why, to the cinema, dah-h-h-ling! Where else?

As the women strut off stage with their dogs, the men chase after them.

FADE OUT

⁂

Startled, Jules appeared from his apartment to find Mr. Lunt in the kitchen heatedly pounding a tack on the inside of a cupboard door, muttering. "All this effort to make Miss Fontanne look perfect and profound... So she can go off to the cinema... *Dah-h-h-ling*!" He punctuated his words by slamming the cupboard door shut.

In the late afternoon, under the lit marquee of The National Theater in Milwaukee, the black luxury Buick pulled up to curbside.

While Ben helped Hattie from the car to the sidewalk, she reminisced. "Years ago tuxedoed doormen actually used to open our car doors... And when it rained, they sheltered us with an umbrella... When it snowed, they lightly brushed us off..."

Taking their place in line near the island box office, Hattie continued, "...There used to be over a half-dozen movie palaces for three blocks, right on this avenue. We called it 'The Great White Way'. Alfred's and my favorite was the glorious Butterfly."

Staring with eyes full of wonder at The National's patinaed copper dome and heavily draped, arched window, Diana asked Hattie, "Why did they call it the Butterfly?"

"There was an enormous butterfly lit by thousands of light bulbs. Broke my Alfred's heart when it was torn down before the Depression..."

Lynn approached the ticket window. "Three adults and one child, thank you very much."

An inquisitive matron in line whispered, "I'm *sure* that's Miss Fontanne!"

Preening herself and deliberately adjusting her sweater, Louise collected Diana who had wandered over to admire a large Snow White poster framed in glass. "Come along now, Diana. Miss Fontanne is waiting. Pardon me."

The line politely parted to allow the two to pass. Louise smiled proudly at the other theater patrons. "Have a lovely day."

The lobby was flooded with ebbing daylight when the women entered the old grand movie palace and passed the elaborate white-marbeled staircase.

Once inside the darkened auditorium, Lynn selected a perfect place to sit. Above them, hundreds of starlights floated over a Spanish courtyard. On the walls surrounding them, water from lion's head fountains dripped into shell bowls.

Hattied continued to reminisce, "...Tuxedoed ushers escorted us to our seats..."

When the points of starlight dimmed and the Barton organ began to play, a heavily-tassled velvet curtain lifted and Diana was transported into an animated technicolor dream.

As Snow White gazed at her reflection in a wishing well and sang 'Someday My Prince Will Come', the enraptured child whispered to Lynn, adoringly. "Snow White looks just like you!"

Pleased, Lynn gave her a kiss on the cheek. While the animated heroine arranged a freshly-picked bouquet of flowers on the dwarfs' dining table, Miss Fontanne whispered back. "Is that something you would enjoy learning? With your grandmother's permission, perhaps you could join me in my garden tomorrow."

Seated in the row behind them, Hattie patted Lynn on the shoulder offering a napkin and a bag of popcorn.

"No, thank you." Lynn raised her hand in quick refusal.

"No, of course not," Hattie groused as she passed the popcorn to Louise. "Did you read in 'Confidential' that Robert Mitchum went to a fancy party in the buff?"

"Yes!" Louise gushed as she breathed in the irresistible buttery aroma and helped herself to another enormous handful. "He said he wore ketchup and went as a hog dog!"

As the movie ended, the music swelled to a crescendo, drowning out their muffled laughter.

In the enveloping silence Louise heard the faint sound of trickling water from the walled fountains and stopped chewing her popcorn. The power of suggestion had grown too strong. She leaped out of her seat.

"Excuse me." She stepped awkwardly around knees and elbows of seated patrons and hurried down the aisle to the ladies' room.

CHAPTER 26

The next day with a peach cobbler in her bicycle basket, Diana pedaled down Ten Chimneys' now familiar drive.

Stopping just short of the scrolled iron gate, she parked in a stand of trees, carefully balancing Nana's cobbler in both hands and praying not to have another encounter with Mr. Lunt.

Hunching down under the neatly-trimmed hedges, she peeked up through the underbrush, taking in every detail of the red exterior of Hattie's cottage. She admired the Scandinavian architecture with the broad expanse of lawn and flowers planted everywhere.

Lost in reverie, she didn't notice Jules approaching from a knoll behind her. He smiled to himself as he watched his godchild. Her rapt interest was touching.

He cleared his throat.

Jumping to her feet, Diana mutely dusted the earth from her sunsuit and bandaged knee.

"Oh, Lu outdid herself this time." Jules smelled the fresh peach aroma and collected the dessert from Diana. "Thank you!"

"Miss Fontanne invited me to pick flowers in the garden with her today," the child frowned. "But I'm afraid I'm going to run into Mr. Lunt."

"Come with me," Jules said with resolve. "It's high time I formally introduced you to someone."

He led Diana up the path to the cottage. Inside, Alfred Lunt was intently positioning his Dala folk art atop the Swedish hearth's terraced brick steps in the corner of the great room. He placed an angelic delft blue, golden-haired icon on the top terraced step. From his years living in Scandinavia, Alfred had acquired sagacious insight into their folklore traditions.

Surrounding him in his mother's great room was a wall canvas brightly-painted in Old English script 'Jesu + Model' penned in Lynn's hand. Also tacked to the walls, floor to ceiling, were his hand-painted canvases of The Ten Commandments and, across the ceiling beam, a Christmas tree banner from the set of 'There Shall Be No Night' that read 'Peace, Goodwill To Men' in Finnish.

Mr. Lunt was intently reciting lines for Sherwood's newest. Using flawless diction, he was testing inflections and phrasing.

The Lunt technique of stage banter and over-lapping dialogue was world famous. Their stage manager often ran back and forth prompting Alfred and Lynn separately as they recited and memorized their lines. Then, once they were 'off the book', they would begin perfecting their timing together.

Alfred scowled at the interruption when Jules and Diana entered. "A visitor, Jules?"

Eyes wide at the sight of Alfred Lunt, the child looked around the room for a means of escape.

"Diana, I would like to introduce you to Mr. Lunt," Jules announced. "Diana has brought another dessert, sir, from Mrs. Herrold."

"Oh, yummy. What flavor this time?" Alfred growled, "Blackberry? To match the dent in the Buick?"

Jules hid his alarm, wondering how Diana could possibly be involved in the Buick's mishap.

Puzzled, the child stared at the simplistic wall figures of Adam and Eve. Their faces appeared the same. She was to later learn Lynn had posed for both.

Resignedly, Mr. Lunt looked directly at Diana, "So, what shall we have for dessert this evening?"

Withering under his gaze, she whispered, "My grandmother's peach cobbler, sir."

"Speak up, child," he grimaced. "People won't hear you in the front row, let alone in the balcony. What flavor again?"

She cleared her throat and spoke as loudly as she was able, "Peach, sir!"

"Much better." Satisfied, Mr. Lunt turned his back once again to face the hearth. "That will be all, thank you. Run along, child."

On the brick step just below the Dala angel, he strategically placed three pigs in a row. "Jules, where-the-devil did we put the cleaning solvent? These are in desperate need of a good washing." He turned around and scowled at her. "Why are you still here?"

"I've been invited to pick flowers today." The frightened girl responded.

From outside the cottage, Lynn could be heard, "Walter, *dah-h-h-ling*, look at these roses." As she entered the room, Walter her pet goose waddled in behind her. "First of the season. Always the best!"

The Toulouse goose, upon seeing Alfred, began aggressively pecking at his pant leg.

"Must you let that wretched creature in here?" Alfred eyed Lynn's pet disdainfully. Walter adored Lynn and rarely allowed anyone near her. He particularly loathed Mr. Lunt.

Ignoring Alfred, "We must have mixed bouquets in every room when Larry and Viv arrive." Lynn glanced down at her overflowing basket of red roses, "But for the Oliviers' bedroom, only these American Beauties will do." She declared, "Viv, with her five hundred Notley Abbey rosebushes will surely die of envy!"

Lynn noticed her young ward, "Well, hello there, dear neighbor!" She pulled her gardening gloves off to reveal small, flawlessly manicured hands. "I see you already met my grumpy husband."

Stooping down to the little girl's level, Lynn gently touched her chin. "When one tends a rose, my little friend, a thistle cannot grow."

Mr. Lunt raised an eyebrow. Disheartened, he watched Lynn and Diana leave the cottage. The crowning insult was Walter, honking contentedly behind them, obviously pleased to share Lynn with the child.

Loudly, through the open window for Lynn to hear, Alfred shouted to Jules who stood only inches from him. "Walter appears to fatten up every time I see him." He added, threateningly, "Larry especially adores goose pate."

Still ignoring Alfred, Lynn handed Diana a pair of gardening gloves from her basket. "Now then, let's find you a hat..."

While pulling on a glove, Diana noticed a tag on the inside. "What's Saks?"

Lynn looked back at Alfred and laughed. "Something Mr. Lunt *hates*, dah-ling."

As Miss Fontanne and the child strolled down the path, Alfred bawled through the open windows, "Oh, go pick your lovely flowers and put them in your little baskets. But remember..." he shook his index finger in the air, "...it was I who seeded, cultivated, weeded on my hands and knees, sweating bullets in the hot sun on my John Deere! While *you* in your beautiful straw sun hat with Italian leather gloved hands — pick the flowers, put them in a vase and *get all the credit*!"

"Forgive me, Diana, dear, I forgot something." Lynn smiled pleasantly at the child. "I'll be back in a moment."

She marched back toward the cottage.

Alfred had resumed reciting his lines and was startled when she swung the door open menacingly.

"I've grown dreadfully tired of your immature mockery, Alfred!" Lynn rasped under her breath. "You think you're being ever so amusing. But truth is you've become such a bore! I should like to advise you and your best friend, Mr. John Deere, to go fuck yourselves!"

Stunned, both Alfred and Jules stood speechless as she coolly turned and exited the cottage, hissing back at Alfred. "And if you touch one feather — I'll shoot you myself!"

CHAPTER 27

Clicking her heels to the beat of a familiar jitterbug tune, Diana's taps struck the field stone steps winding past Hattie's cottage. She approached The Studio door and knocked timidly. The music, several decibels louder, floated over her as Jules immediately opened the door and drew her into the room to scat dance with him.

As the child and her godfather gyrated and tapped their heels in rhythm, Lynn sat down in front of them, captivated.

"Why, we have before our very eyes another Fred and Ginger!" Lynn patted the chair next to her, "Come, sit here beside me, Alfred. I've invited Diana to honor us with a private dance recital today."

Miffed, Alfred spoke in hushed tones, "If I must. Jules, a tray of martinis, please." Then, raising his eyebrows, "A stiff one for me and a light one for Lynnie." Conceding, he sat down.

Backing away, Jules quietly slipped out of the door. Diana, now conscious the Lunts were watching her, stopped to shore up her courage. She began the tap dance routine learned in her class in Waukesha and, within a few minutes, finished with an awkward bow.

Lynn rose with enthusiastic cheers and clapping.

Unexpectedly, Alfred followed, "Bravo! Bravo! Bravo!" His loud clamoring scared Diana and she fell forward — striking her head on a coffee table and landing in a heap on the floor.

As the child held back tears, Miss Fontanne studied her forehead.

She spat at Alfred, *"A bump as big as a young cock'rel's stone..."* Stroking Diana's hair, she sympathized, whispering, *"Thou wilt fall backward when thou has more wit. Wilt thou not, Jule?"*

"Is that your best effort Diana?" Alfred chided. "First nighters pay up to a hundred a seat! I must teach you the correct way to bow to your adoring masses." Lifting both sides of his jacket with thumb and index, he planted his left foot behind himself, slowly curtsying.

Her head throbbing, Diana stood next to him and managed to follow his example.

Alfred looked at the embarrassed little girl, then to Lynn. "Much better! Don't you agree, my dear?"

"A most apt pupil. Right, *dah-h-ling*?" Pleased, Lynn smiled. "Alfred, you must show Diana what we found in your trunk!"

She sat the child down in front of the coffee table and Alfred opened a nearby chest. "I recently retrieved from storage some childhood items that are most dear to me." Gently, with his large hands, he lifted a pile of old theater programs and playbills, placing them on the table. "This cherished program is handsigned by Sarah Bernhardt! Are you familiar with her, Diana?"

Not giving her time to respond, he exclaimed, "Oh, my God, look Lynnie! Remember this?" Out of the chest he lifted Giraudoux's Amphitron 38 playbill. On the cover was a picture of an obviously ill-at-ease Alfred wearing long, flowing Greek robes with a wig and beard of tightly-wound curls and ringlets. "I look like I swallowed Shirley Temple, don't I?"

Diana laughed, giddily, "I don't know Sarah — but I know Shirley Temple!" She tried to read the playbill. "What's Am — fit —?"

Lynn rescued Diana quickly by teasing Alfred, "It's an intellectual's play about an immortal god and a mortal woman who bests him! My darling Alfred was so dismayed with the interpretation of his character, he closed down the company. I reassured everyone to take a long break, knowing the show would indeed continue."

"Yes!" Alfred confessed. "I came to my senses and found the green umbrella — but it took a four- to five-hour brisk walk!"

"Thank God!" Lynn patted his cheek affectionately. "Mr. Lunt was brilliant as usual and the show was a smash! Alfred, dear, won't you show Diana your miniature theatres?"

"Quite right, Lynnie! It is to die!" Alfred proclaimed as he picked up a three-foot, intricately-decorated, multi-dimensional stage set. "This is one of which I am most proud! One of my favorites." He studied the Greek-inspired design for 'Parsifal', one of the sixty sets he had designed over the years since childhood. "I worked my God — uh — head off over it! Up to my neck in glue and spit for weeks! Weeks!" Then he announced, pleased with himself. "The Museum of the City of New York will soon exhibit twenty-five of my collection."

"Oh, they're beautiful, Mr. Lunt!" Diana gushed. "Could I help you make...?"

Again, Lynn intercepted, rescuing the child. "Poor Alfred is working night and day to illuminate and place glass fronts on them. I don't know why he troubles himself."

"I don't know why either..." he shrugged his shoulders. "Perhaps to maximize the audiences' viewing pleasure," he admitted. "Truth is, it's out and out pure theater, the very essence of theater."

When Jules returned with a tray of martinis, tucked under his arm was a mysterious white package.

"Ahhh! Perfect timing, Jules." Alfred rubbed his hands together, gleefully, and immediately tossed down what he thought was a martini. "What-the-devil is this! Jules?" Abruptly, he set aside the water and olive in a martini glass. "So you two actually thought you could get away with this!"

"May I have your olive?" Diana asked. "That is, if you're not going to eat it, Mr. Lunt." Alfred raised his eyebrows without comment.

"Dr. Bigg's orders, *dah-h-h-ling*!" Lynn's voice rippled with laughter.

"Orders? Bad enough I just got out of his hospital! Which, incidentally, should be renamed Dachau! I'm in the hands of the Gustapo! The son-of-a-bitch is trying to kill me with his bland diet! And now this! It's the God's truth, Lynnie, I might as well get it over with right now! Jules, where's my rifle?"

Deliberately disregarding Alfred's rant, Lynn looked at Jules expectantly. "Diana, Jules and I have a special surprise for you!"

Triumphantly, Diana's godfather presented the package wrapped in white tissue with a rose Lynn had picked for the occasion, tied in place by a pink bow.

Ecstatic, the child unwrapped her gift with great care. It was a rag doll, lovingly made by Lynn with bright blue button eyes, brown yarn hair secured by a cheerful floral scarf with matching dirndl and white apron.

Jules beamed, "Something you can play with and love."

"Oh, thank you so much!" She hugged them both. "I can't wait to show Nana and Hattie."

As she reached for Alfred, he piped up, "Good idea! Run along now!"

A booming, stage-trained baritone was heard at The Studio door. "*Good morrow, brother Clarence! God Almighty! There is some soul of goodness in things evil, Would men observingly distil it out — For our bad neighbor makes us early stirrers, Which is both healthful and good husbandry.*"

Laurence Olivier stepped into the room and his adoring wife, Vivien Leigh followed behind with a delicate hand placed possessively on his arm.

In awe, Diana watched the stunning couple's aura engulf the room. Their deep love for each other was obvious to anyone who saw them together, even a child.

"Mr. and Mrs. Olivier, this is Jules' godchild. She was just about to show Mother her new doll," Alfred announced quickly. "Isn't that right, Diana?"

Lynn patted her hand and together they strolled to the door. Joining them, Jules winked, opening his hand to reveal a few olives. "Miss Fontanne, now that the Oliviers have arrived, I'll bring up sandwiches and strawberries to be served with chilled champagne."

The child grabbed the olives, and as she ran past the pool and up the stairs to the cottage, she stuffed them contentedly into her mouth.

From the doorway, Jules called to her, "Ask Mrs. Sederholm if she'd like to join us for sandwiches in the kitchen, Di."

Alfred crowed gleefully from across the room. "And Jules, how about some goose pate for Mr. Olivier, compliments of Lynnie!"

Lynn gave Alfred a scathing look.

"Marvelous idea, Alfred." Olivier lit a cigarette. "I'm famished!" he exhaled.

Minutes later, out of breath, Diana opened Hattie's kitchen door and shouted excitedly. "Mr. and Mrs. Larry Olive have arrived!"

Chapter 28

Back in The Studio in his dark suit and fedora, Olivier's stunning good looks and animal magnetism was palpable. *"Faith, I must leave thee, love, and shortly too. My operant powers their functions leave to do, And, thou shalt live in this fair world behind,"* He took his hat off and struck it to his chest. *"Honoured, beloved; and haply one as —"*

"O, confound the rest!" Vivian was only five foot three inches tall and exquisite in a slim, form-fitting linen suit, wide-brimmed hat, gloves and heels. *"Such love must needs be treason in my breast." In third husband let me be accurst."*

She began to slowly peel off her gloves. "None wed the third, but who killed the first." She looked knowingly at Larry and giggled, having switched the bard's words to suit her purpose. Vivien Leigh was considered by many world-wide to be the most beautiful, well-spoken creature ever to grace this earth.

"Wormwood. Wormwood." Alfred hooted.

Laurence gazed at his wife and laughed wickedly. "I pray I shan't rue the day when I first set eyes upon the possessor of this wonderous, unimagined beauty."

Years ago, Olivier was unaware when he was on stage at Theatre Royal, Vivien had become obsessed with him — returning to see his performances again and again. On one of those occasions she told a girlfriend, "that's the man I'm going to marry," sententiously aware they were both already married. The couple was destined, with Vivien's determination, to finally meet during the filming of 'Fire Over London'.

Privately quick to admit she couldn't get enough of Larry, Viv was high-spirited, keenly fun, but elegantly reserved with impeccable manners and great poise. Although she said Larry aroused a passion in her she had never felt before, her doctor had already secretly diagnosed her with tuberculosis; a condition of which heightened, uncontrollable sexuality was unfortunately a common disorder. The sickness also contributed to other health issues, including manic depressive symptoms. Larry had implored Alfred and Lynn to tell no one, as few people were aware of her illness.

Olivier's Hollywood agent, Myron Selznick was the legendary David O's brother. When Myron introduced Viv, he simply announced, "David, meet your Scarlett O'Hara!" Selznick was already filming his 'Burning of Atlanta' scene for 'Gone with the Wind'. But he immediately declared to the press that after two and a half years, he had finally found his perfect Scarlett, Vivien Leigh, "the wife of a London barrister".

Because Leigh and Olivier were married but not to each other, David Selznick insisted they not be seen together in public, knowing it would ruin his picture — and their careers. They did, however, immediately marry the year their estranged spouses granted them divorces.

Although the Oliviers desperately desired to be the next Lunts in the new cinema, it was not to be. Immensely popular individually, their teaming together on screen and stage was never well-received by the masses.

During this visit with the Lunts, Larry was very pleased with himself. It was rumored he was to finally be knighted. "Alfred, wouldn't it be spectacular if Lynn and I were bestowed our knighthood together at Buckingham Palace?"

"Here! Here! Her Majesty's accolades are long overdue!" Lifting his glass to toast, Alfred eyed his 'martini' noting, in addition to missing its alcohol, it was now sans an olive. The absent child must have taken it, he mussed. Refusing to allow anything to spoil these golden moments, he slapped his old friend on the back. "It's been more than two years since your last visit to Ten Chimneys. So glad you've come. I've missed our 'bard banter', good ally. How about some 'Hamlet'."

"Oh, Alfred must you steal Larry so soon after his arrival?" Lynn directed Vivien to a comfortable couch by the window. "Very well then, Viv and I have much to talk about. Don't we, dear?"

Always anticipating, Jules arrived with a steaming pot of Earl Grey. "I thought you and Miss Leigh might enjoy some hot tea and crumpets. I'll return shortly with the iced champagne."

"So wonderful to see you again, Jules," Vivien smiled at him as she sipped the strong tea. "Are you doing well, I hope."

"I'm doing very well, indeed. Thank you very much, Miss Leigh," Jules bowed his head slightly.

"Hello old chap!" Olivier patted him on the shoulder as he was leaving The Studio.

"Welcome to Ten Chimneys, sir." Always discreet, Jules left The Studio and disappeared over the knoll.

"You lucky bloke — to have found Jules," Olivier complimented.

"He has never given Alfred a moment's worry," Lynn commented.

"*Speak the speech, I pray you, as I pronounced it to you — trippingly on the tongue...*" Alfred blustered, plunging headlong into a soliloquy. "*... Do not saw the air too much with your hand, thus...*" Alfred, worked his arms like a windmill, imitating one in the throes of emotion, "*...for in the very torrent, tempest, and as I may say the whirlwind of your passion, you must acquire... smoothness.*"

Both men laughed, uproariously.

"*O, it offends me to the soul,*" Olivier continued, "*to hear a robustious, periwig-pated fellow tear a passion to tatters... I would have such a fellow whipped for o'erdoing Termagant. It out-Herods Herod. Pray you avoid it.*"

Their writer-friend, S. N. Behrman publicly admitted years later, "In only two actors was genius suggested the moment they stepped on stage: Alfred Lunt and Laurence Olivier."

As Jules came and went with a tray of champagne and strawberries, the two women still at tea and deep in discussion, were enveloped in a warm ray of sunlight near The Studio's window. Alfred looked across the room at them. "My God, Larry, how did two weary hacks like us end up with such ravishing English roses?"

Taking the champagne bottle in hand and popping the cork, Laurence immediately sobered. "For more than a year now Viv has been recuperating at home, you know. She refuses to go to a sanitarium," he confided to his old friend, pouring a glass for both of them.

"Let your own discretion be your tutor. Suit the action to the word, the word to the action, with this special observance: that you o'erstep not the modesty of nature..." Alfred lifted his glass and drank the bubbly.

Olivier looked down into his glass at his eye's reflection. *"...to hold as 'twere the mirror up to nature, to show virtue her own feature, scorn her own image, and the very age and body of the time his form and pressure."*

Much later Alfred would realize Olivier was unknowingly presaging his wife's impending collapse.

Bursting with excitement, Lynn leaned over and whispered into Vivien's ear. "So, dear friend, do you have good news? Is there a doctor's confirmation?"

"Yes, it's true! Larry's over the moon!" Vivien's face was illuminated with an inner beauty. "In a short seven months I shall be most gloriously up to my neck in dirtied nappies!"

Delirious, the women hugged tightly. "Imagine how beautiful your and Larry's child will be!" Lynn cooed, "I'll design the most heavenly christening gown."

"You and Alfred will travel abroad for the ceremony, I trust?" Vivien glowed.

"Of course, we'll not miss it for the world!" She called to the men across the room, "Alfred dear, you and Larry must join us! I should like to propose a toast!" Lynn replenished the men's flutes with the sparkling celebrant and holding her glass high, beamed. "To we women who are still awaiting our best of arrivals!"

After the hugging and kissing, including Alfred's stiff-lipped perfunctories, the women sat down once again to continue their gossip.

"You're so terribly thin, Viv darling." Lynn spooned some large strawberries on a plate. "You must eat and sleep well to strengthen your body. That, along with loving kindness and patience from your wonderful husband, will be all that wee little cherub in your tum-tum needs."

"Yes, you are right, Lynn dear," Viv spoke with a twinkle in her eye. "You know I don't get enough sleep."

"Tons of hugs and kisses doesn't hurt either! That reminds me," Lynn fluffed a pillow and placed it at the small of Vivien's back. "There's something I'm dying to know," she asked mischievously. "How was it kissing the great Mr. Gable?"

"Utterly repulsive," Vivien retorted, raising a coy eyebrow. "He had bad breath!" She whispered, dramatically, "His false teeth, you know."

The women erupted in delicious laughter.

"So, what are you doing now?" Lynn inquired.

"Well, Brando has signed to play Stanley opposite my Blanche in 'Streetcar'," she confided. "Yes, yes, I know what you're thinking, Lynn. He's a risk. But Kazan wants him and he did study under Strasberg."

Some hours later the Oliviers chose to remain in The Studio when Alfred and Lynn left for the main house to dress for dinner.

"Well, *happiness to their sheets*!" Alfred looked at Lynn knowingly as he closed The Studio door.

Deliberately walking ahead, Lynn spat, "Perhaps Larry prefers not to threaten his wife's guiltless dalliances with cruelty." Lynn could not forgive Alfred's treatment of their young, innocent neighbor. "He's obviously a far brighter bard than some fusty old dullard I know!"

No longer hiding behind their afternoon's performance, the Lunts walked back to their manor house in obstinate silence. Neither husband nor wife were willing to compromise their deeply personal differences.

Inside The Studio, Laurence poured both he and Vivien another glass of champagne. *"Therefore, queen of all, Catherine, break thy mind to me in broken English: wilt thou have me?"*

"Dat is as it shall please de roi mon pere." Fluent in French, Vivien was ripe to play the role of King Harry's Catherine in Henry V. For years well-coached by Olivier for stage, Vivien now spoke forcefully, a full octave lower than her normal, reedy voice.

"Nay, it will please him well, Kate," Laurence downed his glass of champagne in one long swallow. *"It shall please him, Kate."*

"Den it sall also content me," Vivien tried to match his entrain, but gasped on the bubbles. She covered her mouth and belched, delicately. "Mousser, excusez-moi."

Amused, Laurence tenderly kissed her hand. *"Upon that I kiss your hand, and I call you my queen."*

"Laissez, mon seigneur!" She asked her lord to refrain from kissing her, but flattered him with a curtsy.

He pulled her close, whispered in her ear, his mouth lingered near hers. *"Then I will kiss your lips, Kate."*

"Le dames et demoiselles pour etre baisees devant leurs noces, il n'est pas la coutume de France." Decorously, she stated French ladies did not kiss before marriage, a brazen understatement Shakespeare knew would tickle his English audience.

"What say you?" He whispered in her ear. *"No, Kate? I t'would tell thee in French, but t'will hang upon my tongue like a new-married wife about her husband's neck, hardly to be shook off."*

"Dat it is not be de facon pour le ladies of France — I cannot tell vat is "baiser' en Anglish." Vivien's Catherine did not know the English word for 'kiss'.

"To kiss." Whisper-soft, Laurence breathed on her neck.

"Your majeste entend bettre que moi." Viv's Catherine was trusting of her King Harry.

"It is not a fashion for the maids in France to kiss before they are married?" Olivier's deep resonant voice was incredulous.

"Qui, vraiment," Vivien protested, coyly.

Olivier laughed, *"O, Kate, nice customs curtsy to great kings... We are the makers of manners, Kate, and the liberty that follows our places stops the mouth of all find-faults, as I will do yours, for... denying me a kiss. Therefore, patiently and yielding."*

Her lips parted and he kissed his wife, wildly and deeply.

"You have witchcraft in your lips, Kate. There is more eloquence in a sugar touch of them... and they should sooner persuade Harry of England..."

Vivien broke away and spouted lustily, "...En visite privee!" Requesting an unscripted private visit with her king, she took Larry's hand and, giggling, lead him up the rough hewn, precarious ladder to the Lunt's infamous loft.

With Olivier's support, Vivien Leigh had matured into a skilled actress, appearing in more than forty stage productions, many co-starring with or directed by her husband.

But more than anything in the world, Vivien wanted to have Larry's baby. Sadly, during the filming of 'Caesar and Cleopatra' she was to fall on the set and shortly after miscarry. This was to be the first of two miscarriages for the Oliviers.

Back in England when Sir Laurence and Lady Vivien were knighted by their homeland, Noël Coward's letter to the Lunts described the Olivier's royal bliss. "He and she are so beautiful that knighthood, instead of being an absurd and rather dubious honor, seems to come in flower again with them."

At Ten Chimneys, Alfred continued reading Noël's letter and raised his champagne flute to his wife, "Were the honors to have included our beloved Lynnie, our lives would have been complete. Chin up, our darling Dame! Your most sought after entrance is yet to come."

CHAPTER 29

"Diana, do you still like olives?" Cal asked her, a smoldering cigarette hanging loosely from his mouth. She watched the thin, thread of smoke wreathe and rise to the ceiling, and nodded her head. Unnoticed, the ash dropped and scattered onto the bar in front of her.

Leon 'Cal' Pietrowski was a bartender. Every year Virgel insisted Louise take Diana to visit her biological grandfather. Her annual visit usually lasted less than an hour.

The child and her Nana sat on bar stools in the cavernous, smoke-filled room of a seedy bar in downtown Milwaukee. An open door to a back alley created a diffused, dim shaft of light in the hazy interior. Muted city noises of passing traffic, sirens and jack hammers could be heard in the distance.

With yellowed, nicotine-stained fingers, Cal opened a large glass jar of stuffed Spanish olives, placed some in a shot glass and slid it across the bar to Diana. "How old are you now?" He coughed up a glottal spew of tar.

"I'll be eight on April 25th." Diana said matter-of-factly, thinking maybe he might remember and send her a birthday card next year.

"What grade?" he asked.

"Second," she answered with a mouth full of stuffed olives. Diana loved the pimentos, but knew she risked a belly ache later.

"Have you heard from Bobby?" Louise questioned.

"No. Same as last time you asked. He's got better things to do than to call his old man." Cal downed a shot of Jack Daniels. "Want a drink, Lu?"

"No thanks. He remarried, did you know that?" Louise said hopefully. "I think he settled somewhere in Denver." She tried to hide her heartbreak.

"Could I have some more, please?" Diana showed Cal the empty bar glass. He refilled it with more olives.

Louise had little to say to or about her ex-husband. Cal was an alcoholic and adulterer. He had given her little support physically, mentally or financially while young Bobby was stricken with tuberculosis of the bone. Her young boy had endured painful surgeries and braces from hip to heel for years, resulting in lifelong physical and emotional scars. It was during those house bound years, though, when his God-given talent developed into a brilliant self-taught artistic skill.

Among Bob's first professional career-building creations was a freehand drawing of the original Skippy for the canned dog food and several Breck hair shampoo illustrations widely used for merchandising ads. After advertising lost its appeal, he divorced and moved to Southern California. He began to design upscale interiors for restaurants and lounges in the San Diego area. Like his father Cal, Bob was a devout alcoholic and insomniac, and he loved the night life.

"Bob's life is a waste. Just like mine." Cal downed another shot of whiskey. "I really screwed up, didn't I, Lu? How's your life now?"

"Virgel is a good man," Louise reached across the bar and patted his hand. "It's never too late, Cal. You need to talk to a priest."

"I haven't been to confession in more than sixty years." He took a long drag on his cigarette. "Not since my confirmation."

"We can't change the past, Cal. But we can change our future. You have the choice to save yourself." Louise rarely talked about their years together, but Diana was aware that during her marriage to Cal, her grandmother had suffered a nervous breakdown. She was also stricken with tuberculosis a few years later and sent to the Statson Hospital Tuberculosis Sanitarium after their divorce. That was where she met Virgel Herrold, who worked at the nearby Brook Hill Dairy Farm.

As Louise drove out of the city, Diana was struck by the many taverns on every street and the grimy factory chimneys spewing their putrid smoke.

Twenty minutes later, the landscape drastically changed to the green pastures and rolling hills of the kettle moraine as the Chevy sped home. Louise hummed 'Melody of Love' while her granddaughter counted grazing Holsteins.

"Nana," the child asked. "do you think if Grandpa Cal had lived in Genesee Depot, his life would have been happy?"

Turning into their stone drive, Louise answered, "Sometimes we have to make our own happiness, Di."

CHAPTER 30

Hattie was getting her hair dyed at Gertrude's salon. That evening she was to attend a Lunt performance of 'O Mistress Mine' at the Selwyn in Chicago. For the theater she almost exclusively dressed in black with her silver hair fashioned in a smart chignon. Alfred Lunt's mother always radiated sophisticated style at his appearances. She preferred entering a sold-out theater just before curtain call to be escorted to her seat with adulation befitting royalty.

The Lunts were called aristocrats on stage, but in the audience, Harriet Sederholm had no peers.

Those who knew her well said, had Hattie chosen, she herself could have been a great actress.

"That wretched chain-smoking Noël is visiting again." Hattie flourished her long cigarette holder, some ash dropped on Gert's floor. "I hope it doesn't trouble dear Alfred's stomach. I have to tell you, he positively reeks of tobacco! His clothes should be hung out the window. My poor Alfred. He's in agony all the time and never shows it. I won't be surprised if it's ulcers. Thank God for bicarbonate of soda!"

"Well, Miss Diva." Gert twisted Hattie's hair up, admiring it in the mirror. "How about a whisper of palest pink on this glorious white dome for the theater tonight."

Hattie lit another cigarette in her holder, "A diva is not only one who affords luxury, but deserves it!" She took a deep drag, lifted her chin and brazenly exhaled a cloud of smoke, engulfing the ladies. "Good Lord, that *is* me!" Albeit blind to her own shortcomings, she was a true tour-de-force.

"*Phuttt!*" Gert squeezed hair dye onto Hattie's scalp.

"I don't trust Noël around Lynn either," Hat continued, "he's always eyeing her décolletage."

Gert and Louise exchanged looks. Gert wondered how Hattie could not recognize Noël's homosexuality. Louise was unsure what décolletage meant.

It was eleven when Louise checked her watch. Her life was still structured around watching soaps everyday from eleven a.m. to two p.m. She even scheduled her doctor appointments around 'her stories'. Quickly she tuned into 'The Guiding Light' on Gert's television. On the small black and white screen, an abundantly endowed woman and man were wrestling in a bedroom scene.

Returning from her kitchen, Gert balanced a tray of steaming coffee in mugs and generous slices of warm pecan pie smothered with melting vanilla ice cream.

As the ladies devoured the pie, Hattie complained, "Couldn't get Lynn to eat this! Alfred's always trying to fatten her up with his French sauces — but she's still a bag o'bones. Never gains an ounce! The trouble with Lynn is — she's just so *English*. But she still knows how to bake Alfred's biscuits!"

The women exploded in laughter.

Not finished trashing Noël, Hat shouted above the panting and pawing on TV as she puffed on her smoke. "Shockingly, out of nowhere he darts sans bathing suit in front of the Life magazine photographer. Ruined a positively marvelous pose of Alfred and Lynn on the steps leading to The Studio. My son had to choose another photograph for the cover instead. The fellow was sooo disappointed — he wasn't able to catch Noël on film!"

Dramatically, she snuffed out her cigarette. "But I can tell you first hand, there's not much to catch."

Rocking in laughter, Louise shouted, "I can't take much more of this." She ran to the bathroom. "I'm going to pee my pants!"

"Slow down, Lu, I just waxed the floor." Laughing, Gert placed a shower cap over Hattie's hair.

"Alfred rages every time I ask him about a TV." Hattie imitated Alfred's high-pitched bawl. "I'll *not* have one of those damn ugly things in *my* house!"

They giggled and continued to watch Louise's daily drama fix.

Louise quickly sat back down with another slice of pie. "You know Mr. Lunt will do anything for you. Just cry Hattie," she advised. "My Virgel can never say no to that."

"Oh, my angel boy doesn't need me to cry to grant my requests!" Hattie took a long gulp of coffee and smiled knowingly.

"I didn't realize those two were getting married." Gert obviously didn't watch the soaps regularly.

Louise filled her in, "The mother had an illegitimate son who was adopted and now they find out they're brother and sister — on their wedding day!"

Sometime later, weeping into their hankies, the three women watched the intense fictional moment of truth unfold.

"I always feel so much better after a good cry!" Louise howled.

"*Phuttt!*" Gert finished squirting the crimson dye into Louise's hair and placed a cap on her head, too.

"Oh my God, Hattie!" Gert jumped up and pulled Hattie's cap off. "I forgot to time you!"

There was a moment of horrified silence as the women stared into the mirror, then all three shrieked in unbelief! Hattie's hair was a shocking magenta!

That evening at the Selwyn Theater, Hattie wore a stunning floor-length gown, long gloves, fur and a bejeweled black turban.

The following morning, already up at dawn, Alfred had been clearing brush for two hours from the back orchard when he called through the cottage door. "Good morning, Mother! Are you there?"

He washed his hands at the kitchen sink, then shouted up the stairs, "Come down, Mother. I brought some fresh eggs from the coop. I'll make us a wonderful omelet."

Sometime later enjoying their breakfast at poolside, even Alfred was fooled. Hat had wrapped a flowered scarf around her head to match her lounging robe.

"Mother, what you can do with a common scarf!" Alfred cooed. "It's smart, actually."

"Yes, isn't it," Hattie replied uneasily as she sipped her coffee.

CHAPTER 31

Rain clouds were gathering overhead when Diana and Martin hurried home on their bikes from the post office. Waving goodbye, Martin pedaled up his driveway.

In spite of a cold gust of wind, Diana broke into a clammy sweat as she approached her house. The front screen door was ajar and Nippy was out again. Diana had hooked the screen when she left the house and Virgel was at work. So this time Nana was to blame.

The first burst of rain was a windy torrent drenching her to the bone. A flash of light streaked across the sky — revealing Nippy, muddy and shaking, crouched under a nearby tree. Moments later, deafening thunder clapped and rolled across the sky and the frightened, confused dog bolted toward Depot Road.

Motionless, with water dripping from hair and clothes, Diana watched in horror as the familiar black Buick sped through the blinding rain and bumped the dog into a ditch like discarded litter.

Inside the car, Ben turned down the radio. He thought he felt something small, perhaps a rock, hit the fender. Through the wall of water, he could see nothing on the road.

Only inches from her, Nippy's broken body lay in a mud puddle. Devastated, Diana bent down and tenderly picked him up in her arms. His breathing was labored. With his rib cage crushed, his little pink tongue distended, and button eyes half-closed, she wrapped him lovingly in her coat and carried him home in the heavy rain. When she stepped onto the front porch, his shallow breathing stopped.

Louise opened the front door and Diana quickly passed through. "How did he get out again?" her grandmother admonished angrily.

Carrying Nippy through the house, Diana began to cry as she laid his lifeless body on the kitchen table.

"No! He's not dead!" Louise moaned. "He can't be dead!"

Collapsing on a kitchen chair, she cradled him in her arms, rocking him back and forth, sobbing. "Oh dear Jesus! You have the power to bring Nippy back to life!"

Unwrapping his sodden, inert body from the wet coat, Louise cried out, "He's freezing cold, Di, go get a blanket!"

Moments later Louise swathed the blanket around his stilled body. "As soon as he gets warm, he'll wake up. Just a little longer and he'll wake up." She repeated, caressing and kissing his head. "My sweet little boy. You're home now. I'm going to take care of you."

"He's gone, Nana," Diana sobbed as they both dissolved into tears.

"Can't you see? He's getting better, Di." Her grandmother continued to rock their beloved pet, singing softly, 'The Old Rugged Cross', her favorite hymn.

Virgel caught a ride home from work that evening and entered a dark house. He quietly put Louise to bed and cooked he and his granddaughter dinner.

Louise Herrold was far more fragile than her granddaughter ever realized. Perhaps Nippy had become a substitute for her estranged Bobby. But one thing was certain, Diana understood more deeply Virgel's love, patience and caring for his wife.

From the attic dormer window she watched her grandfather bury Nippy in their backyard and mark his tiny grave with a simple wooden cross.

On that fateful rainy evening, the young girl decided never to reveal who killed her Nana's Nippy.

It was to be her secret.

CHAPTER 32

Like many people, Louise Herrold was afraid of death. But her fear was beyond normal. It was, depending on how you viewed it, either paranoid or paranormal. And she, unfortunately, passed her fear on to Diana at a young age.

Before the time of embalming, German folklore spoke of those buried still alive and later, for whatever reason, exhumed. There were tales from the Old Country of bodies that had turned inside their coffins, and other stories of nail marks found inside coffin lids and finger nails that had continued to grow.

But Louise had a different story to tell. When Diana was five, she was shown the picture of Anna Luckert, her great-grandmother. Not the portrait of a smiling matronly woman with babies on her knee, it was the black and white engraving of a young woman in a white lace gown and white satin slippers, laid out in a full-bodied open casket.

At the turn of the century, Louise's mother, a vibrant twenty-five year old, suddenly died — leaving her children behind, with a father too grief-stricken to give comfort to her crying babes.

In those days it was customary to place the deceased in the home parlor where mourners paid their respects. All mirrors were covered and the clock pendulums stopped at the moment of death.

For three days a black satin ribboned wreath shrouded the Luckert front door. Inside, the home was filled with Anna's youthful, inconsolable friends and family.

In the back of the parlor on a small divan, five-year-old Louise and her three-year-old brother, Hank, viewed their dead mother, surrounded by rows and rows of flowers. For hours with red, puffy eyes, they held each other tightly. Louise could not escape the heady, overwhelming florals; the mixture with her mother's freshly lemon-polished wooden floors, created an insufferable headache.

Little Louise was not only heartbroken, but keenly aware she now had to nurture her toddler brother.

On the eve before their mother was to be buried, the Luckert home was finally emptied of guests. Exhausted, Zabel put his children to bed early. Upstairs, Louise and Hank shared a bed to keep warm, and soon her little brother was fast asleep. In the next room she heard her father's hushed crying cease, replaced by soft, deep snores.

In the dark quiet the wooden stairs creaked with the sound of light footsteps approaching. Knowing no one else was in the house, Louise became frightened as the footsteps drew nearer. She hid under the thick down bed covers, but moments later, petrified and soaked in sweat, she felt someone touch her shoulder — patting her — comforting her.

As the footsteps left the room, shaken, the child peeked one eye out from under her blankets. There was a figure standing at the open bedroom door. Louise was convinced it was her mother in the same white dress and slippers in which she was laid out in the parlor below.

CHAPTER 33

At Ten Chimneys, the Lunts were working outside in the garden near their greenhouse. Alfred was raking leaves for mulch, 'tilling the land' he called it, while Lynn pruned her roses. There was still a grudging silence between the couple.

Alfred, unable to take her coldness anymore, burst into a 'Taming of the Shrew' soliloquy.

"I'll attend her here,
And woo her with some spirit when she comes.
Say that she rail, why then I'll tell her plain
She sings as sweetly as a nightingale,
Say that she frown, I'll say she looks as clear
As morning roses newly washed with dew.
Say she be mute and, and will not speak a word,
Then I'll commend her volubility,
And say she uttereth piercing eloquence."

He held his chest as if to say Lynn's long silence had pierced his heart.

A smile tugged at Lynn's lips, but she held her ground as Alfred continued,

"If she do bid me pack, I'll give her thanks
As though she bid me stay by her a week.
If she deny to wed, I'll crave the day
When I shall ask the banns, and when be married.

But here she comes, and now, Petruccio, speak."

In the play, Lynn's Kate was supposed to speak next. Bending, Lynn snipped an errant branch with her shears and smelled a rose, waiting just long enough to make Alfred uncomfortable.

Straightening, in a throaty clear voice she spoke,

"Well have you heard, but something hard of hearing,
They call me Katherine that do talk of me."

Alfred picked a flawless rose and gave it to her,

"You lie, in faith, for you are called plain Kate,
And bonny Kate, and sometimes Kate the curst,
But Kate, the prettiest Kate in Christendom,
Kate of Kate Hall, my super-dainty Kate -
For dainties are all cates, and therefore 'Kate'— Take this of me, Kate of my consolation:
Hearing thy mildness praised in every town,..."

Then, on bended knee, Alfred began to penetrate her cool demeanor,

"Thy virtues spoke of, and thy beauty sounded -
Yet not so deeply as to thee belongs -
Myself am moved to woo thee for my wife."

Lynn began to warm,

"Moved? In good time. Let him that moved you hither
Remove you hence. I knew you at the first
You were a movable."

She was being playful.

Alfred realized he had finally captured her. *"Why, what's a movable?"*

"A joint-stool," Lynn smirked.

"Thou hast hit it." He reached for her waist and drew her to him. *"Come, sit on me."*

"Asses are made to bear, and so are you." Lynn was trying to entrap Alfred, expecting him to say his next line, *"Women are made to bear, and so are you."*

But Alfred was too quick. He skipped to a line further into Act Two. *"Come, come, you wasp,"* he nuzzled her ear, *"i'faith you are too angry."*

"If I be waspish, best beware my sting," she broke away from him.

"My remedy is then to pluck it out," he laughed.

"Ay," she laughed, too, *"if the fool could find it where it lies."*

"Who knows not where a wasp does wear his sting?"

Alfred drew her to him again. *"In his tail."*

Lynn whispered, *"In his tongue,"* beginning to breath heavily.

"Whose tongue?" His mouth nuzzled her hair and neck.

"Yours, if you talk of tales, and so farewell." Lynn's anger had melted.

Alfred fondled her ear and blew softly into it. *"What, with my tongue in your tail? Nay, come again, Good Kate, I am a gentleman."*

Although Petruccio didn't kiss Kate for several more pages, Alfred couldn't wait for the bard's script and kissed Lynn lustily.

"That I'll try." Lynn was actually getting aroused. Teasing Alfred, she began to walk down the path to The Studio. Alfred followed her.

"A herald, Kate?" He grabbed her hand as they approached The Studio door. *"O, put me in thy books."*

She finally smiled at him. *"What is your crest — a coxcomb?"*

"A combless cock, so Kate will be my hen." He kissed her hand as they entered The Studio.

Once inside, Alfred looked at Lynn questioningly, not sure if she was still sensitive about Hattie. *"Now, by my mother's son—and that's myself—It shall be moon, or star, or what I list... ."*

Lynn had forgiven him,

> *"Forward, I pray, since we have come so far,*
> *And be it moon or sun or what you please,*
> *And if you please to call it..."*

Relieved, Alfred interrupted, *"...I say it is the moon,"* he smiled confidently.

"I know it is the moon," she smiled back.

With Alfred at Lynn's heels, they impatiently scrambled up the ladder to the loft.

"Nay then you lie," he thundered, *"it is the blessed sun."*

Lynn whispered,

"Then God be blessed, it is the blessed sun,
But sun it is not when you say it is not,
And the moon changes even as your mind.
What you will have it named, even that it is,
And so it shall be still for Katherine."

They tumbled into the loft together as Alfred breathed into her ear,

"Tell me, sweet Kate, and tell me truly too,
Hast thou beheld a fresher gentlewoman,
Such war of white and red within her cheeks?
What stars do spangle heaven with such beauty
As those two eyes become that heavenly face?
Fair lovely maid, once more good day to thee.
Sweet Kate, embrace her for her beauty's sake."

Lynn giggled, *"Happier the man whom favourable stars/Allots thee for his lovely bedfellow."*

Alfred whispered and stroked her hair, *"Sirrah Grumio, go to your mistress./Say I command her come to me./The fouler fortune mine, and there an end."*

Lynn batted her eyelashes, coyly. *"What is your will, sir that you send for me?"*

Alfred spoke confidently,

"See where she comes, and brings your forward wives
As prisoners to her womanly persuasion.
Katherine, that cap of yours becomes you not."

Lynn alluringly slipped off her scarf.

"Off with that bauble, throw it underfoot." Alfred tossed the scarf from the loft. It landed ten feet below on The Studio floor. *"Katherine, I charge thee tell these headstrong women/What duty they do owe their lords and husband."*

Lynn slid out of her dress.

"My mind hath been as big as one of yours,
My heart as great, my reason haply more,
To bandy word for word and frown for frown,
But now I see our lances are but straws,

Our strength as weak, our weakness past compare,
That seeming to be most which we indeed lease are,
Then veil your stomachs, for it is no boot..."

She helped Alfred rip off his shirt.

"...And place your hands below your husband's foot..." then she took off his belt. *"In token of which duty, if he please, My hand is ready, may it do him ease."*

Lynn slipped her hand below his waist.

Breathing in a lung full of air, Alfred was obviously aroused. *"Why, there's a wench! Come on and kiss me, Kate."*

They kissed, again, heatedly.

"Come, Kate, we'll to bed. Twas I won the wager, though... And being a winner, God give you good night."

In the throes of lovemaking, they were unaware below them Jules had stepped into The Studio with a tray of brandy. Seeing Lynn's head scarf discarded on the floor, hearing noises from the loft, he smiled as he quietly closed the door behind himself.

After many more minutes of foreplay and lovemaking, the lovers were finally quiet and spent.

Lynn stroked his cheek. "You silly little boy! Taking your frustrations out on poor little Diana. When the time is right, you must apologize."

Alfred, with head on her breast, sighed. "Yes, my darling. You're right. You're always right." He had missed her affections.

A few years before, they graced the front cover of Life magazine with the title, "The Lunts, 25 Years with the World's Greatest Acting Team". A poll had also rated them individually, with Alfred Lunt as the number one actor and Lynn Fontanne following close behind at number two. By popular vote the Lunts had no peers.

Chapter 34

It was four-thirty a.m. and still dark outside. A migratory flock of black and white whooping cranes flew low over Lake Michigan in the cold dawn.

Zabel placed a steaming hot washcloth over his face. He ran his pearl-handled razor up and down a long leather strap hanging from the bathroom doorknob, sharpening the instrument. It was a cherished wedding gift of fifty years ago from his Anna. He dipped his horsehair brush in warm water and swirled the soap in his shaving mug into a foam. While softly humming a favorite German tune, he carefully lathered his neck, face and under-nose, then ran his thumb along the razor's edge, testing for sharpness.

In a room across the narrow hallway, already showered and shaved, Hank sat on his neatly-made bed and put on his socks and heavy work boots. Henry Luckert was very tall, slim and handsome. Beatrice, his wife of twenty years, loved to say he looked like Jimmy Stewart.

The Luckert Minkery had grown over the years into one of the largest ranches in Northern Wisconsin, but Hank and Bea's small red brick home remained modest. They were a barren couple who filled their void with the local Elks Club and highbrow trips to New York. Their holidays at home were uneventful. Bea would go to mass by herself on Sundays without Hank. He was a devout man without ceremony, she would say.

With rays of sunlight inching across the horizon, Bea busied herself in the kitchen. In her neatly-pressed housedress and fresh apron, she rubbed her stomach and passed gas while cooking oatmeal over the stove.

"Oooh, Lu's sauerkraut last night!" she grimaced.

In the bathroom at the far end of the house, Zabel crooned, "I hearrrd thaaat, Beatrrrice!"

She set a hearty breakfast on the table for Hank and Zabel as the men entered the kitchen, ready to start their workday.

While the sun was rising over the lake, the men put on barn coats, gloves and caps and Bea handed them a thermos of fresh hot coffee. The minkery had more than four thousand covered cages and the Luckerts worked every day, along with hired hands, feeding, watering and cleaning the cages. Hank and his crew fished Lake Michigan constantly to feed his mink. The animals ate ground fish with mink meal in the mornings and a ladle of porridge laced with vitamins in the afternoons. A large adult mink could eat up to a pound of food daily. By Hank's calculations, that was two tons of food every day.

Into the kitchen their family guests, Virgel, Louise, Diana and Jules, filed in for breakfast.

"Where are Zabel and Hank?" Jules asked as Bea set a bowl of oatmeal in front of him, along with a large side plate of thickly-sliced ham, fried eggs and potatoes.

"They've been out working for hours!" Bea laughed.

"We're always trying to get our men to rest more, aren't we Bea?" Louise admonished, looking at Virgel. "They're going to work themselves into an early grave."

Bea nodded her head sagely. "Hank and I lived with Pa until we saved enough money to build this ranch." She refilled Jules' coffee cup. "Pa works as hard as Hank around here, but at least he makes time when the work day is over to walk down the road to the local tavern for a cold Hamms."

Finishing her oatmeal quickly, Diana asked to be excused, then ran outside looking for her Opa and Uncle Hank.

"May I help? Please, please!" She peered through the chain link fence watching the men clean the mink cages.

"It's way too dangerous!" Hank warned. "They can bite off little fingers."

"Opa, can I watch you?" Diana knew how to get around her uncle and great-grandfather.

"Hank, I'll take care of Di," Zabel conceded.

"Okay, but don't stick your fingers in the cages!" her Uncle Hank warned again.

Virgel and Jules joined Hank, and together the men disappeared into the feed barn to fill their buckets with mink meal.

"Here, Opa, this one needs water," Diana volunteered. Preoccupied, Zabel didn't respond, while she quickly lifted an empty water and food container from the outside of a cage and refilled them.

Without a word, the child was soon working along side her great-grandfather. They progressed up and down the neat rows of cages, feeding and watering the mink for about an hour.

"Opa has to use the toilet, sveetheart!" The old man walked toward the house.

When he was out of sight, Diana decided to find Nana's pet, Rudy. Four years before, Rudy's mother had died giving birth and he was the only survivor from a large litter of six kits.

"Lu, he's never going to make it," Hank shook his head at the time. With the mother gone, he was prepared to destroy the newborn.

He was silenced when Louise gathered the little pink kit from its nest box and held him in the palm of her hand.

"I think I'll call him Rudolph Valentino," she cooed as the kit began to suckle warm skim milk from an eyedropper.

"Impossible!" Hank had exploded. "Minks are untamable and ferocious!" But he began to reconsider when she made a cozy bed in one of Opa's empty cigar boxes and continued to nurse the kit every two hours. Watching her, he remembered his sister's fierce protection after their mother died.

Louise took Rudy home and in the weeks that followed, the kit grew very playful and bonded with her, refusing anyone else's care.

The Herrolds visited often with the Luckerts that spring. When Lu and Bea drank coffee on the screened back porch overlooking the ranch, Rudy curled in her lap contentedly like a kitten and fell asleep.

Now a three-pound adult male, Diana peered at Rudy in his pen at the minkery. He was more than two feet long with an eight-inch tail and a patch of white on chest and under chin. She stooped down and looked nose-to-nose at him through the bars of the cage. With black, beady eyes and button nose wiggling, Rudy stared back at her.

She was surprised to see he had five toes and his pelt was molting. "Oh, you poor thing!" Forgetting her uncle's warning, Diana poked her finger through the grates to pet his head. As all mink do when threatened or stressed, Rudy promptly emitted a horrible stench from his anal gland.

"Phewww! What did you eat, little fella? Are you sick?" She stroked his belly. "Does your tummy hurt?"

Rudy snarled and hissed at her, then clamped his sharp teeth down on what he thought was food.

"Owww!" She muffled a shriek and tried to pull back, but Rudy refused to let go. The weasel shook his head back and forth, trying to tear the fresh meat. Remembering Uncle Hank's warning, Diana feared she was going to lose a finger — like her Virgel!

When the animal finally released his grip, she was bleeding profusely. Trembling, she pulled a sock off of her foot and tightly wrapped her finger.

Stifling cries, she looked around for Uncle Hank, afraid he might have seen what happened. She ran into the house, past Auntie Bea and Nana washing dishes in the kitchen, and into the bathroom where a surprised Opa was zipping up his pants.

"What's wrong, child?" Opa looked on, concerned, as she unwound the bloody sock from her hand.

"Rudy stuck his nose through the cage and bit me!" she whimpered.

"Don't lie to your Opa. Let's get you bandaged up." He cleaned the wound in the sink and wrapped it with gauze and tape.

"Please don't tell Uncle Hank!" Diana begged.

Zabel scolded, "You must promise to never do that again!" His gnarled index finger touched her nose gently.

That evening, everyone gathered on the Luckert's screened porch. Nana held Rudy in her lap as she sipped a high ball.

"Rudy is short for Rudolph, you know," Louise boasted to Jules. "Have you ever seen such a friendly little guy?"

"Oh, Lu. Rudolph Valentino!" Jules laughed and tried to pet the animal. The ill-tempered mink snapped and gassed him. "Oh, my Gawd! That smell! Second thought, he'd make a smart collar on your winter coat, Louise!"

"That's a great idea!" Diana agreed, eyeing her swollen, bandaged finger. Opa tried to hide his amusement, but couldn't help from slapping his knee and laughing with everyone else.

Automatically grabbing a newspaper and fanning the fumes, Hank entered the porch.

Looking at her husband, Bea grew serious. "Hank and I have something important to announce."

Standing proud and tall, Hank cleared his throat. "My bride is going to be a mama!" He bent down and kissed his Bea on her flushed cheek.

"We have decided to adopt a child. Our neighbor's daughter is having a baby out of wedlock. She's due to deliver next month. If it's a girl," Bea glowed maternally, "we'd like to name her Lynn."

"That's *my* middle name!" Diana was jubilant.

Her Auntie Bea whispered and smiled, "I know!"

"Oh, how vunderbar! A little cousin for Di! Ve need a round of schnapps!" Zabel jumped up and hurried to the cupboard.

Hank had expected Louise and Virgel to be pleased for them, but his sister grew strangely silent as her husband hugged his in-laws, elatedly.

"What a lucky child." Jules embraced Bea and pumped Hank's hand. "To have such a beautiful home and loving parents. I couldn't be happier for the two of you!"

That night, as always, loud snores came from Hank and Zabel's bedrooms. Bea slept peacefully cuddled next to Hank's noise. When he was in New York, she found it hard to sleep without his comforting din. But Jules, in his wrapped stocking cap, forced to share Zabel's double bed, tossed and turned amidst the deafening wheezes and snorts.

Frightened on the Luckert living room couch, Diana couldn't sleep either. Not only was her finger throbbing, but Auntie Bea had turned out all the lights! In the enveloping darkness, she found herself alone and scared.

In the only guest room, Virgel wrestled with sleep too. Nana whispered her displeasure late into the night. And the more she spoke, the madder she became.

"Oooh, my brother Hank!" Louise seethed. "I love him so much, but — can you imagine! At their age! I would never complain for myself. But now he's taking from Diana! He washed his hands of Bob years ago — Hank has made no bones about that. But — Virgel — she's the last blood relative, and Hank knows it!"

"I'm happy for them, Lu. You don't know what Hank's going to do with his money," Virgel reassured. "Now go back to sleep, Toots." He kissed her on her lips, rolled over onto his side and, with his back to her, quickly fell asleep.

Still frightened, Diana timorously tip-toed down the hall and climbed into the double bed with her grandparents. She placed her tiny, cold feet in Nana's lap, her German heishka, to warm them.

"Why should the neighbor's daughter become Hank's problem?" Louise fretted. "Do they even know who the baby's father is? And what does he — and his parents — have to say?"

Irritated, Virgel reminded her, sleepily. "Wait a minute, Toots. Just settle down. Think of it. What would our life be without Di? Do you wish that for Hank and Bea?"

"I s'pose not," Louise admitted reluctantly.

"There. That's better, now." Sighing, Virgel hugged both of his girls, tightly, and all three soon fell fast asleep.

Within the month, Bea had turned her former guest room into a nursery for their new daughter, Lynn. For many years without complaint when Diana and her grandparents visited Hank and Bea, they climbed an unsteady drop-down ladder to sleep in the Luckert's converted attic. When Jules visited, he continued to share Zabel's bed and endure his snores until the old beloved gentleman died ten years later in his own bed surrounded by his loving family.

Chapter 35

That Christmas, Ten Chimneys was especially bright and cheerful. While Ben hung white twinkling lights all around the front veranda and entry, smells of holiday baking filled the kitchen and dining hall. Lynn made her specialty dessert — English trifle, and Alfred and Jules prepared their fare of Prague ham, fish balls in sherry lobster sauce and smoked turkey.

Their guest Carol Channing, however, brought her own meat for Jules to prepare. Rattlesnake — packed in dry ice — to make her skin more youthful. When Carol came to visit, she often brought her own cooler of food, and sometimes her own chef. This time Jules wished she had brought her own chef.

Miss Channing was the special friend who brought Jules to Lynn's attention. In a posh New York home years ago, while a young Ferdinand Johnson waited efficiently upon the Lunt's every whim, Carol had said, "Lynn, you should steal him away. He's a jewel!" Lynn and Alfred secretly offered him a job on the spot and within a few days 'Jules' was permanently employed at Ten Chimneys.

Jules remained with the Lunts for thirty-five years. During those years, he became more than a major domo. He was to become the legendary Alfred Lunt's trusted friend and confidant.

Late that evening, Jules gently placed the last crystal stemware and English bone china dish into the glass cupboards in the kitchen. He took off his apron and rolled down his shirt sleeves, then walked room to room through the house turning out lights to the hushed strains of Christmas music. Quietly, he ascended the spiral stairs and stopped by each of the bedrooms, knocking softly at the doors.

"Miss Hayes, is there anything further you'll be needing this evening?" At each door, he repeated the question to Miss Channing, Miss Fontanne and Mr. Lunt.

There were no answers. Everyone was asleep.

In the drawing room fireplace, the embers were now reduced to ash as Jules switched off the Christmas lights on the eight-foot pine. Straightening stockings on the mantle, he took his own off a hook. He lifted out his presents, already unwrapped; a pair of cashmere-lined leather gloves from Lynn and a cashmere Burberry coat scarf from Alfred. Finally, with gifts in hand, he turned off the music as he left the room.

Exhausted, Jules walked back through the dining room and kitchen, then into his apartment. He carefully placed his treasured gloves and scarf in an upper drawer, showered, and returned to his apartment living room to re-read his stack of Christmas cards.

The phone rang. With freshly-shampooed nappy hair and bowed legs, in bathrobe and slippers, he padded out to the kitchen to answer it.

"Wilhelmina! And Merry Christmas to you!" He listened to her for a moment. "I know you're terribly disappointed. So am I, darling. I was so looking forward to being with you tonight!" He was silenced for a full minute as she poured her heart out over the phone. "I promise you just one more week, Wilhelmina. We'll celebrate New Year's in Times Square and have two glorious weeks together in New York." He paused again. "I just didn't have the heart to say no with Miss Channing and Miss Hayes coming and all. I love and miss you, too, my darling Mina."

In the darkened hallway Mr. Lunt listened intently, holding a glass of warm milk he had fetched to calm his stomach. As Jules sadly hung up the phone, Alfred quietly ascended the stair and returned to his bedroom.

Jules was visibly tired. It had been a long, disappointing holiday for him. From a kitchen drawer, he pulled out a pair of scissors and shuffled back to his apartment.

In the privacy of his bedroom, he laid one of Louise's stockings on the bed. Carefully cutting it into four equal sections, he placed three pieces back in a drawer. He stretched the remaining piece, starting at the back of his head, winding it behind his ears around his damp hair. At the top of his forehead, he twisted the ends into a knot, and tucked it under to keep it securely fastened for sleep. This was how he acquired the flat, sleek hair of a gentleman, the convention the Lunts expected of him.

Bone-weary, he crawled into bed and lifted a rosary from a night stand drawer. Clasping the beads tightly to his chest, he turned out the light.

In the early hours of the morning Miss Channing went into the kitchen to prepare a snack. She had taken off her signature wig and replaced it with a scarf.

As she sleepily added lard and sauteed the snake meat over a high flame, a small fire erupted! She tried to fan the blaze, making it worse. Smoke billowing from the stove, set off a fire alarm!

In the dark with stocking-wrapped head, Jules ran into the kitchen. Startled, neither immediately recognized each other. He stood helpless as Carol towered over him, opened her huge legendary mouth and screamed!

Thinking quickly, he routed through a cupboard, grabbed a box of baking soda and managed to extinguish the flames.

When a swarm of fire trucks arrived in a record five minutes, Miss Channing had already vanished into her room.

Alfred awoke to the sound of sirens outside his bedroom window. He ran downstairs in pajamas, fumbling with a silk robe, in time to see the volunteer firefighters stomp up the spiral stairs toward his kitchen with hose and axes over their shoulders.

"My good man!" Alfred shouted to one who seemed to be in charge. "You must save our Ten Chimneys!" He followed them into the kitchen, grabbed a bucket and filled it with water from the tap.

"No! Mr. Lunt don't..." Jules tried to stop him, but Alfred had already splashed water on the stove. The men leaped back as the water re-ignited the smoldering flames into a sizable pyre.

"Jules! How did this happen?" Alfred screamed above the din.

"I have absolutely no idea!" Jules implored.

"Mr. Lunt, excuse me." The fire chief was standing behind Alfred, holding an extinguisher.

"Oh, yes, of course," Alfred stepped aside.

The flames were snuffed out with foam in minutes and the firemen trudged back down the stairs and outside into the courtyard where their red truck was waiting, still flashing yellow.

Alfred and Jules followed them outside while Ten Chimneys' hostess and her women guests, in hastily clad robes, peered through the second-story French doors at the scene below.

Wringing his hands, Alfred shouted, "Marvelous job! You saved our home! I can't thank you enough! Were you able to determine the cause?" Taking the fire chief aside, he whispered, "Did a small saucepan of milk perhaps cause this?"

"I don't think so, Mr. Lunt. I found some blackened bits of meat — I can't identify — in a fry pan on the stove." The fire chief responded as his men climbed back onto the fire truck.

"How can this be?" Mr. Lunt turned to Jules. "Meat — left on the stove?" Alfred was coming undone. "We'll continue this discussion tomorrow Jules! And will you please fix that — *whatever* you call it!" He pointed to the stocking knot ends dangling in front of Jules' nose.

Mr. Lunt continued to follow the fire chief to his own vehicle. "I'll personally handpick a variety of my frozen vegetables and have Ben drop them off at the fire station with a fine Prague ham for all you boys!" Alfred slapped the fire chief on the back. "A Christmas present from Ten Chimneys! Dreadfully sorry you boys had to come out on Christmas Eve!"

"Mr. Lunt, thank you for your generosity." The chief tipped his hat to Alfred. "And thanks, Mr. Johnson." The fire chief shook Jules' hand. "Water doesn't help on grease fires. But baking soda does."

Humbled, Alfred whispered to Jules, "Well done."

The next morning before breakfast, Miss Channing and Jules found themselves in the kitchen alone again. Embarrassed, neither said a word about the incident to each other.

Apparently Carol Channing's quote "Genesee Depot is to performers what the Vatican is to Catholics!" had become an international catch-phrase, but what happened that night at Ten Chimneys was not to have a confessional moment.

CHAPTER 36

It was New Years' Eve in downtown Genesee Depot and lightly snowing outside. Half-a-dozen girls were partying inside Mary Jo Pronold's glass-enclosed front porch. In spite of the noisy celebration, Mary Jo's great-aunt and –uncle, the Gibson twins, slept soundly only three doors away. A busy family activity center, the Pronold front porch had also become a look-out point for the girls to watch The Depot's comings and goings at all hours, not just in spring and summer, but all year 'round. After gossiping about boys, devouring movie magazines, and experimenting with make-up for hours, the boisterous girls finally fell asleep.

Still awake, however, Diana and her friend Colleen were rehearsing dance steps. Taking the lead, Diana counted loudly.

"One-two-three, one-two-three, one – two – three – four!"

Colleen had been invited to join Diana on the S.S. Milwaukee Clipper's seven-hour voyage across Lake Michigan where the ship featured dancing to a live band. Every summer the Herrolds planned a week's vacation to visit relatives and the two friends were eagerly preparing for their first trip together.

It was late when Mrs. Pronold came in to gather empty dishes and take them into the kitchen, "Have you girls thought about your New Year's resolutions?" She looked affectionately at her daughter fast asleep.

"I hope yours, Mary Josephine," she teased, "is to keep your bedroom cleaner!"

By midnight, all was dark and silent inside the Pronold home.

Miss Hayes and Jules, bundled in their winter coats, left St. Paul's Church. Helen had an engagement in Milwaukee and was visiting the Lunts briefly for the holidays. She and Jules had decided to go to midnight mass at the small chapel. On the way home, arm-in-arm, they decided to take a stroll through the quiet picturesque village.

"O Holy Night, the stars are brightly shining..." Helen sang softly, her gloved hand patted Jules' arm. "What a glorious night! I can't remember a more blessed New Year's Eve!"

"It's such a pleasure to spend it with you, Miss Hayes." Jules tried hard to mask his heartbreak of another postponed visit with his Mina.

Across the street, a shadowed movement caught Helen's attention. To investigate, she stealthily steered Jules around a snow drift and onto the Pronold's white-blanketed front yard.

Jules didn't notice Butch, but Helen did. She parted some bushes to find the juvenile pressing his nose against the cold front porch window, trying to spy on the girls in the darkness.

"Willie! Hey, little Willie!" Helen's shout echoed down the empty street. She remembered the troublesome boy. "Are you still trying to get a peek at girls' underpanties?"

"Miss Hayes, we just took communion!" Jules whispered. They both looked at each other and giggled.

"Shit!" Startled, Butch pried his runny nose from the frosted glass and ran to his bike partially-hidden in the neighbor's yard. Humiliated, he quickly sped away.

The first to rise on New Years' Day, Diana peered out of the front porch window. During the night ice crystals had formed on the exterior glass and, marveling, she watched as one ray of light burst into a spectrum of color. There were some unusual tracks in the snow under the porch window, but she didn't have time to think about that. As far back as she could remember, Diana and her Nana awoke early on New Years' Day to watch the Rose Parade from California. She had to wake the girls.

"I love the Queen's float!" Mary Jo squealed as she switched on the television.

"My favorite are the marching bands!" Colleen shrieked.

"Nana and I look for my father in the bleachers!" Diana yelled.

"Father???" In unison, the girls looked at her, bewildered.

Easily distracted, the young partiers returned their attention to the Pronold's new black and white television, 'ooohing' and 'ahhh-ing' at the flowered Rose Parade floats.

"Whatever do you mean, Diana?" Mrs. Pronold sat down with a tray of hot chocolate and muffins.

"My New Year's resolution," Diana declared, "is to no longer look for my father."

CHAPTER 37

Ten Chimneys' vegetable garden was ravaged that spring by heavy rainfall causing Mr. Lunt great anxiety. The unusually wet spring was followed by an extraordinarily hot summer.

In the summer heat, under a shade tree near the pool house, Oona Chaplin rocked a sleeping baby in a carriage. "Don't forget to watch the young one," she cautioned her oldest child who was in the pool. Even after bearing four children, Oona was svelt in her one-piece maillot with shoulder-length satiny black hair.

Sitting at pool's edge with Miss Fontanne, Diana paddled her feet in the cool water. Although Helen Hayes had taught her to swim, she still had two childhood fears: the darkness just before sleep and diving into water. She was determined to overcome one fear.

Placing her toes at the edge of the pool, she leaned her head down between her outstreached arms, and slowly plopped headfirst into the water. Thinking she was totally submerged, but kicking her feet only inches from the surface, she came up gasping for air.

"Did I touch the bottom?"

"Almost," Miss Fontanne laughed. "Darling, very soon you'll be doing a swan dive from the top of the bathhouse."

Shaking water from her eyes, Diana asked, "In California does everyone have pools?"

"Most people we know do," a child answered before diving under water.

While the children frolicked in the water, Lynn joined Alfred and Charlie Chaplin, sunning themselves on lounges near the cabana.

Tanned and trim, Charlie's eyes were a piercing blue under his neatly parted and slicked back graying mane.

He pointed to Lynn's statue in front of the bathhouse. "I've been admiring your young English maiden."

Leaning over, Lynn whispered coyly in his ear. "I buy a statue, Charlie, but you marry them!"

"I marry them young because I don't want them embittered." He patted Oona's thigh as she approached and settled on the lounge next to him. The Chaplins were a robust and striking couple; Charles in his early sixties and Oona, mature far beyond her mid-twenties. Sadly Eugene O'Neill was to shun his only daughter her entire married life until his death in 1953.

Wet and shaking, Diana and the children ran across the grass to them. Lynn wrapped Diana in a towel and hugged her. "I prefer to imagine mine as a little daughter, like Diana, here."

Still shivering, Diana asked Mrs. Chaplin, "Where did you say you were going?"

"Switzerland," Chapin's loyal young wife answered politely.

"Is that near Germany?" Diana bubbled, "My great-grandparents and Nana came from Germany."

Oona helped towel her children dry and kissed Charlie on the cheek. "See you later, love." With carriage in tow, she gathered her other three children for an afternoon nap and, while Diana waved goodbye, they leisurely walked up the fieldstone steps to Hattie's cottage.

"What do you know of Germany, child?" Chaplin asked Diana softly. "Come, have a seat."

"My Opa Zabel was in charge of the American prisoners during the war!" she declared, dulcetly, as she sat down next to him on the lounge.

"Please share more about your Opa in Germany." Chaplin handed her a cool lemonade.

"He used to sneak them gum, chocolates and cigarettes. Opa

could have been shot if he was caught. But God was keeping him safe for me." She became sad. "God took my great-grandmother to heaven, though."

"A kind and brave man, your Opa." Charlie empathized.

"Oh, yes," Diana brightened, "he loves to tell stories of Germany and sing with his friends at Stags." She smiled. "He's probably there right now!"

Charles pondered to himself, "Being sympathetic to the enemy has its consequences." Then he asked Alfred, "What on earth is Stags?"

Alfred had noticed Chaplin was distant and pensive all morning. Glad to finally engross Charlie in conversation, he announced, "Stags is our local tavern down in The Depot where a fascinating array of gents congregate. Tomorrow we'll walk down the hill for a cold pint." He swished the martini pitcher and plopped a fresh olive in Charlie's glass, refreshing his drink. "To the sympathetic of this world!"

"A real pub? Tomorrow?" Charlie was pleased. "Splendid!" He gulped down more of the clear cocktail.

The phone rang inside the house. Momentarily, Jules appeared outside in his chef's apron with the dachshunds barking and bouncing like popcorn at his heels.

"Mr. Chaplin, it's your brother, Syd. Calling from your studio in California, sir."

With his towel Charles patted the sweat from his brow and hurried into the house.

Almost tripping over the rambunctious dogs, Jules apologized as he herded them back into the kitchen. "It's their dinner time."

It was rumored with small substance that hot summer of 1952, Charles had sympathies to the Red Communist Party. Hundreds of people in the entertainment community were being investigated by the House of Representative's Un-American Activities Committee headed by Joseph McCarthy.

Herbert Hoover had taken umbrage with Charlie's film 'The Great Dictator' and aggressively compiled more than two thousand pages of information and innuendo on Chaplin.

The wagging tongues also conjectured why Charles never became an American citizen and his reason for leaving American soil this particular summer. Depending upon who was talking, his timely or untimely cruise to Europe was perceived as a ruse to escape an eventual subpoena to testify at the McCarthy hearings.

Late that afternoon after walking the grounds together, Alfred and Charlie could be seen approaching the estate from over a knoll. While Chaplin talked, Alfred leaned forward, listening intently.

Lynn waited with Diana and the Chaplin's oldest in the courtyard when the Herrolds punctually arrived for their granddaughter in their old Chevrolet.

As the men passed the young ladies and entered the Ten Chimneys' foyer, Chaplin overheard his daughter inquire, "Miss Fontanne, would it be much trouble if Diana stayed for dinner this evening?"

Holding open the front door, Alfred shot a defiant, searing look at Lynn.

Charlie added, "Would you mind, old chap, if the little blonde lass's grandparents stay as well?"

Chapter 38

Checking on dinner, Alfred found Jules in the kitchen fretting over the vegetables.

"If we don't get rid of these pests," Jules shook his head, "there'll be no more fresh vegetables this summer!"

Alfred took a deep, desperate breath. "Are we reduced to buying from the A &P in Waukesha?" Their French cooking was a shared passion and the thought of their Le Cordon Bleu sauces being served over canned vegetables repulsed both of them.

"There will be three more for dinner this evening, Jules. We'll seat them next to Charlie. This was his big idea."

"It's getting late, Mr. Lunt," Jules reminded him. "Your dinner suit is hanging in the bedroom."

Alfred left in a panic.

Later, when Jules was gathering potatoes in the cool garage, he heard a high-pitched female voice, "Yoo-hoo! Anybody home?" It was Louise. "I know we're early but I couldn't stand it any longer. We'll just hide out with you in the kitchen, Jules."

The Herrolds looked their best, Louise, in a pink beaded dress bought several years before for her cousin's wedding in Michigan and Virgel in his one and only double-breasted suit.

Louise pointed to a row of hanging mesh storage bags, spellbound, "Are those Miss Fontanne's furs?"

"Perhaps," Jules was uncomfortable.

"May I peek?" she pried.

"Oh, that won't interest you, Lu." He gently guided her up the stairs to the kitchen. "I bet you get a new mink every Christmas."

"Does Hank give his only sister a mink?" Louise hissed. "The woman who loved and cared for him, washed and dressed and fed him after our mother died? Nooo!"

As they entered the kitchen, Jules offered, "Lu you look absolutely beautiful this evening. Please feel free to use my bathroom to powder your nose."

Entering Jules' tidy three-room apartment, Louise was impressed. Alfred added this addition to the main house shortly after Jules arrived under his employ. The new suite of rooms, built over the garages, was not only convenient to the kitchen, but also allowed his major domo's watchful eye to view Ten Chimneys' grounds from many angles. The living room overlooked the driveway, courtyard and Hattie's cottage. The bedroom viewed The Studio, pool area, barns, green house and creamery. The bathroom window revealed the back of the estate, including the terrace where breakfast, afternoon teas or before-dinner cocktails were frequently served.

Jules was preparing stuffed mushrooms and artichoke hearts when Louise returned to the kitchen, refreshed and relaxed.

"What would Miss Diana like?" he smiled.

"I love Virgel's Shirley Temples!" she answered.

Into a tall glass Jules poured cherry juice, lemon-lime soda and placed a maraschino cherry on top. With everything in order for dinner, he joined the Herrolds briefly at the kitchen table for Manhattans.

"These are simply delicious!" Louise popped another mushroom into her mouth. "Next weekend you come to our house and let me cook for you."

The sounds of a horse outside, neighing and trotting, brought Jules to the kitchen window. Ben was leading Miss Fontanne's horse Franklin to the stables and Lynn would soon be coming in from her afternoon ride. "Excuse me, please," he lifted an elegant silver appetizer tray, "I'll be right back."

CHAPTER 39

Into the Flirtation Room, Jules brought a chilled pitcher with two martini glasses and, anticipating Lynn's arrival, her favorite, a brandy old fashioned. He set the drinks near his appetizer tray on a table and stoked the fire for ambiance.

Noël had locked himself in The Studio all day to write, finding it frightfully difficult to focus with the childrens' poolside clamor. He was agonizing over 'Future Indefinite.' It took him nine years to finish this work, and it would not see print until 1954. With the Chaplin's visit, however frustrated, he was still determined to make an appearance that evening for cocktails and dinner.

Staring out the Flirtation Room's French doors, Noël gasped. "Ye gods! His world is about to come down and he can still get a stiffy!"

"What-the-devil are you looking at?" Alfred walked up beside Noël and, with wide eyes and pursed lips, they both peered out the window. Outside, strolling over a grassy knoll after an obvious marital romp, Charlie zipped up his pants. Oona giggled as he tenderly slapped her on the behind.

"So you caught the Chaplins inflagrante delicto!" Lynn mocked, removing her riding gloves as she entered the room in her English livery. "Don't get your knickers in a twist!"

"Must you keep changing the subject, Noël?" Alfred was jubilant. "He's been asked to star in David Lean's 'The Bridge On The River Kwai', Lynnie! By God, he remembered you! Excellent! Jules, where did we put my tuxedo!" He gleefully rubbed his hands together, "I smell an Oscar cooking!"

"Your tuxedo? Probably in the attic with my gowns! The lord of the manor who designed Ten Chimneys didn't think to include adequate closet space!" Lynn chastised. "And would you please stop that infernal rubbing!"

Alfred ignored the slight, "Good Lord, Noël! This is your chance!"

"Yes, well, it's not David's original work. Everyone who's anyone knows blacklisted Michael Wilson actually wrote it. His second uncredited masterpiece." Noël stared out the window again, "Well, I'll be gobsmacked! The ol' bugga! He's going to bonk her again while I watch!"

Lynn was not going to let Noël sidestep the discussion any longer. "Yes, yes, the dreadful blacklists." She wagged her index finger at him. "So, what will you tell David?"

"This is positively nerve wracking!" Alfred opened his prized silver cigarette case and offered his old friend a smoke.

They both lit up. "Noël, you must take this part!" he pleaded, "It was written for you!"

Noël inhaled deeply, then exhaled. "How many takes do you think David will do when I bloody hell choke in his camera close up? I can't live up to Lean's excellence right now," he admitted. "I simply don't think I can do it, dear friends."

"Enough of that nonsense! *Dah-h-h-ling*, will you kindly stop skalking around this instant! Come sit here by me." Lynn patted the loveseat cushion beside her as she sat down. "The trouble with the world is that it's always one drink behind."

"How many?" Alfred whispered to Jules.

"First one, Mr. Lunt." Jules was to report to Alfred how many brandy old fashioneds Lynn had throughout the evenings. He thought Lynn had gotten a bit too flirtatious with a guest recently after imbibing three.

"Make that her last." Alfred spoke in hushed tones.

Noël, unaware, grabbed the pitcher from Jules' tray and refilled his empty martini glass. "The Academy has brazenly snubbed the Brits for more than two decades. That's how Helen stole your Oscar in '32, Lynnie," he lamented. "Jules! You should know! What's it like to work for a thrifty, relentless ol' bugga who constantly strives for perfection and seldom appreciates the effort?"

Jules almost dropped the tray he was holding.

Alfred's eyes and mouth flew wide open, "Don't take your irritation out on an old friend, Sonny Boy!" he blustered.

"How about a late afternoon scrabble?" Lynn tried to change the subject.

Neither answered.

"Thought not. Well, gentlemen, I'm going to dress for dinner." She drained her highball glass and handed the empty to Jules. "Please deliver another old fashioned to my dressing room — no matter what Alfred says!"

CHAPTER 40

Clad in black tie, Mr. Lunt grandly opened the double doors to the Ten Chimneys' dining hall. Dinner guests that summer evening were Charles and Oona Chaplin, their oldest daughter, Noël Coward, Virgel and Louise Herrold, and Diana.

At the table Louise noticed her place card scripted in Lynn's hand. Next to her name was written Charles Chaplin. She breathed to herself, "Dear Jesus, what will I say?"

Charlie, always the gentleman, helped to seat her. "Do you go to the cinema often, Mrs. Herrold?"

"Oh, yes, Mr. Chaplin, beginning with silent films when I was a teenager," she replied. "That's when I first fell in love with Valentino..."

As Alfred seated Lynn in her customary place, Noël entered the dining room dressed in white dinner jacket. Slipping behind Chaplin, he whispered distastefully, "Ah, the romantic! Did Oona's Valentino win her on the seas of a sonnet? Or was it with ease on the grass today!" The puckish one seated himself at the far end of the table and shouted mockingly, "Next time use the loft, for God's sake!"

Unaware of Coward's barbed wit, Louise now more comfortable, announced to Lynn and Chaplin, "...When Valentino died, I cried my eyes out. So did everybody else. My whole plant where I was a seamstress had to shut down."

Jules placed the first course in front of Louise, a Bombay bisque.

As he served, she whispered in his ear. "I hate that you can't join us." Then, startled to see Virgel, seated across from her, had already inhaled the spicy fish stew, she kicked him in the shin under the table.

"Ohhh, I didn't mean I haven't watched you, Mr. Chaplin!" Realizing her possible slight to the film legend, "I loved...I mean I love your Little Tramp... when he rescues that child..." Fighting an approaching tic, she became helpless for words again.

"Ah, my favorite as well." Chaplin filled her crystal goblet with wine. "There's something about taking in a child. I feel rather inferior to them," he conceded. "They all seem to have a certain assurance, but have not yet been cursed with self-consciousness."

Louise took a few calming sips of wine, "Ohhh, you are sooo right! She eyed Alfred's second entrée, a meager artistic presentation of tiny tomato, flowered radish and asparagus tip atop a modest mound of endive.

Her stomach growled as she noticed helplessly that Virgel's salad plate was, again, already emptied.

"Diana tells me your father was in the German militia." Chaplin asked, "How is it that he came to America?"

"My father was disillusioned with Germany after the war and my mother wanted them to come to America. But they had little money." Louise again sipped her drink. "After being smuggled on trains and a banana boat around South America, my poor mother contracted tuberculosis and only lived a few more years. She was twenty-five when she died." Louise dabbed at her eyes with her napkin. "I was barely six years old and thought Pa would die, too, of a broken heart..." she drifted. "Without a mother, one loses their childhood ..."

Chaplin grew sullen. "I too lost my mother — so to speak — when I was a young lad..." His emotions surfaced easily.

"I should like to propose a toast, Alfred!" Lynn rescued the lagging conversation. "To Charles Chaplin!"

"To *the* seminal film star of our century!" Alfred stood and bowed. "And to whom I'm honored to call friend."

"Excellent!" Coward stood and raised his glass, finally beginning to enjoy the camaraderie.

Chaplin remained seated but raised his glass. "Here's to loyal friends and dear mothers..." He glanced at Louise who flushed to tears in gratitude.

"...Past and present..." Charles looked lovingly at Oona across the table. He couldn't finish, his eyes began to mist.

Oona and her oldest were tearing, too. Everyone at the table realized news from Chaplin's brother Sydney in California must not have been good.

Compassionately, Noël cleared his throat and raised his voice and glass.

"I'm consoled with remembered laughter and tears
And the peace of the changing sea
How happy they are, I cannot know
But happy am I who love them so."

Alfred was deeply moved, "Why — that's beautiful, Noël!"

Reflective, everyone at table sipped their wine.

"You *are* a poet at heart, Noëllie," Lynn began to tear.

To which Coward exploded, "A few sentences hardly make a poem, Lynnie!"

"But it's a hell-of-a-good start!" Alfred retorted.

"Ah, here lies one whose name was writ in water!" Noël lifted his martini glass and took a long, last draught.

Jules entered with his third course, the main entrée, a drizzled sauce over a small medallion of beef and one thinly-sliced, fanned red potato with julienned carrots and French-cut beans.

When all guests were served, he placed Alfred's dinner plate in front of him. Eyeing his plate carefully, Alfred stabbed an inferior bean with his fork and they both exchanged a look.

"Apologies to my guests," Alfred lamented. "The vegetables may not taste as usual. Don't know what-the-devil is to become of my garden."

"Mr. Lunt, have you had your soil tested?" Virgel spoke for the first time.

Alfred looked down at the end of the table where Virgel was seated next to Lynn. "How does one quiz dirt here in The Depot?"

"Ask Charlie!" Noël blurted. "The bloke was testing soil this afternoon!"

"At least mine isn't as limp as Alfred's green bean!" Charlie sparred back.

"Sometimes a simple soil analysis is all that's necessary," Virgel responded.

"How is this done?" Alfred questioned. "What do you do for a living, Mr. Herrold?"

"I'm a bacteriologist. I just need a small sample to take back to my lab at Pet Milk." Virgel answered. "I can have the results to you in a few days."

Alfred grabbed a plate in one hand and a wine glass in the other, hoisted them up over Diana's head, and walked toward Virgel.

"Jules!" he called out, "You need to hear this!" He gently nudged the young lady out of her seat. "You may have my chair, Diana."

Beaming, she picked up her plate and marched to the end of the table. Before she sat down, however, she noticed Alfred's prized Italian bust on a sidetable behind his chair. Embarrassed, she placed her napkin over its bared breast. Lynn and Oona giggled, but Louise was stricken.

Unaware, huddled together at mid-table, Virgel, Jules and Alfred thoughtfully examined the sickly green bean.

"Could be the result of a possible mold microbe," Virgel wondered. "What type of irrigation system did you design?"

Jules volunteered, "Ben and I were worried the drainage wasn't adequate, remember Mr. Lunt?"

Alfred looked sheepish.

Virgel began, "Do you add anything to your manure? Could be a sick cow...acidic soil..."

Gathering his dinner plate, Noël began to feel the stirrings of creative euphoria and decided to finish his meal in The Studio. "Oh, goodie!" he chortled. As he paraded past the seated guests, he hissed into Charlie's ear, "Think I'll take dinner outside. Care to join me, Charlie? While I watch you *piss in the garden*!"

Chaplin poured more wine into his and Louise's glass, "I'll need to down another bottle of this fine vintage, first!"

Noël, his face pinched in exasperation, shouted across the table, "Alfred, ol' man, you know this bores us senseless!"

To Noël's amusement, however, without raising his head, Alfred's hand went up instantly, lifting his middle finger high in protest.

Coward's resentment broke into shrill laughter. "With Valentino's last words, I'll take my pain-in-the-ass leave, old chap." He placed a hand on Chaplin's shoulder, "Don't worry, chief, it will be alright."

With furrowed brow, the three passionately devoted gardeners remained in deep conversation.

While the women chatted happily, only Chaplin remained reflective, pouring himself another glass of wine.

Chapter 41

The next morning after breakfast, while Lynn, Hattie, Oona and baby basked in the sun at poolside, Charlie and the children playfully splashed in the pool.

Alfred and Jules met Virgel in the garden. With latex gloved hands, Virgel walked up and down the neat rows of vegetables, examining Alfred's crop of beans, peas, carrots, several varieties of squash, potatoes and tomatoes. He scooped a handful of dirt and sifted it through his fingers. Removing a few sterilized Mason jars from a bag, he placed a generous sampling of dirt in each for analysis.

"Well, that was painless. I'm insufferably pleased!" Alfred patted Virgel on the shoulder. "How did you come to be a bacteriologist?"

"I was fascinated with science at an early age," Virgel responded. They left the garden and walked up the long path toward the main house. "After my father died, my uncle, Dr. Russell Herrold became my mentor. He was always encouraging and lent me many of his books to read. He helped me land my first job as a lab assistant. That's where I met my bride!"

Before leaving, Virgel handed a folded paper to Alfred. Thinking it was a bill, Alfred quickly crumpled it into his pocket.

A couple hours after Virgel's old Chevy disappeared down the road, Alfred, enjoying Jules' raspberry iced tea with the Chaplins at poolside, pulled the rumpled piece of paper out of his top shirt pocket.

Fully expecting a charge for Mr. Herrold's services, he could not conceal the surprise in his voice as he read,

"A gift to Mr. Lunt! 'An Ode to a Microbe' by Virgel Herrold...?"

Alfred read on,

"Here's to the microbe that swims in the milk
He's a mighty small fellow, but slicker than silk
For years he's been chased through dairy and barn
But he still takes his milk baths without giving a darn..."

Chaplin exploded in laughter. "Excellent! Alfred has under estimated another bloke! Isn't it awfully grand, Oona?"

Alfred continued with great interest,

"Though the lab boys work late with test tube and flask
A careful baby still has to ask
"Now mater, old dear, I don't want to be mean
Has that nipple been squirted with stem or chlorine?'"

Charlie roared, "Better than the doggerel you write!"

Alfred had to admit, ashamedly, "I misjudged Mr. Herrold, didn't I?"

Chapter 42

During the ebbing hours of the day the ladies were still enjoying tea on the garden terrace with the children. This was the Chaplins' last day at Ten Chimneys. They were to leave by train the next morning for New York.

"Just one moment, I need my hat," Alfred ran to the garage and placed an old straw gardening hat on his head.

Noël continued to isolate himself in The Studio, so Alfred and Charles took a shaded stroll down Depot Road.

"Everyone's doing it, Charlie." Lunt was being sensible. "Why not take out a full-page patriotic ad, *insisting* you'll swear on a stack of Bibles you're neither a Communist nor a sympathizer."

Alfred and Charles spied Zabel Luckert, Diana's Opa, strolling down the road with his walking stick and caught up with him. When visiting the Herrolds, each day after his nap, Zabel enjoyed a brisk walk and cold beer at Stags Tavern.

This hot afternoon, Zabel was dressed in a plaid shirt, neatly tucked into his dress trousers, and comfortable shoes. He held a cigar in his gnarled, arthritic fingers.

"Crest gut!" Zabel tipped his hat, showing his thinning gray hair and a hearing aid in both ears.

Together the three men walked past the Town Hall where sometimes on a Friday night, even Alfred could be found square dancing with the locals to country bands. They arrived at The Depot's tavern five minutes later.

"Mr. Lunt! Good to see you!" Stag gave Alfred a hearty handshake. "Who's your friend? Grab your mug." All of Stag's regulars were given their own mug to drink with, then to hang on the wall to await their next visit.

Alfred grabbed his mug from a hook and passed it to Stag, who filled it with draft from his tap.

"I'd like you to meet Stan Phenus — but he likes his friends to call him Stag." Alfred took a long draught of beer. "This is my friend, Charles." Alfred slapped Chaplin on the back in introduction.

A couple doors down, Harry Torhorst closed his store for the evening and entered Stags for a cool drink before heading home.

"Schnapps for everyone – on me!" Zabel puffed on his cigar and pulled up a chair at a nearby table where Gibby was already seated. "How vas your day, mein freund?"

Stag gave Chaplin an honorary mug filled with ale. "When you finish, you must hang it on the wall!"

"To Charles!" Zabel started an Ein Prosit song and toast. Everyone in the tavern joined in, chugging their mugs of beer.

A stranger strolled into the bar, "Could you tell me, sir, where the Lunts live? Their house is supposed to be around here someplace."

Stag smiled and gave the outsider directions back to Milwaukee.

When the man left, Stag looked at Alfred. With his hat low over his face, he was seated at the bar next to his friend, known only as Charles.

"That's the third one this week!" Stag cackled.

They all laughed. Alfred and Charles laughed the loudest.

With numerous shots of Jagermeister and filled mugs of beer, the Ein Prosit rounds became noticeably louder and more passionate.

"Is the goose still roaming the street?" Harry choked back his laughter.

Stag guffawed. "What was his name, again?"

"Whose name?" Alfred hooted. "The man or the goose?"

"Zer gut, Herr Lunt!" Zabel slapped his knee.

"Van Johnson!" Alfred exploded with a fresh burst of mirth. "And the god-damn goose's name is Walter!"

Stag grabbed Zabel's walking stick and pranced around as though he were fencing. "Van Johnson showed us how to swashbuckle like Douglas Fairbanks!"

Alfred continued, "And when Van left here, I swear on my mother's Bible — Walter attacked him! Right outside the tavern. Right there!"

Imitating Van Johnson, Alfred grabbed Zabel's stick comically cowering and poking at Walter, the invisible goose. "Van ran like a little girl while Walter — honking and squealing — chased him all the way home to Lynn!"

Attempting to sit down on the bar stool, Alfred was laughing so hard, he almost fell off the stool, to which the whole tavern roared in drunken laughter.

"Frau Lunt's pet goose!" Zabel threw his head back and chortled. "Your vife vill close the door on her bet for a month ven she finds you let her goose out!"

"Walter must have followed us into town. Lynn *loves* that goose! She actually *confides* to Walter — more than *me*!" Alfred threw his hands up in the air, grabbed one of Stag's large pretzels and took a bite.

"Here's to the vemen in our lives! Who share our joys unt our troubles." Zabel sobered, staring at Charles intently, sensing a sadness in the man.

"May they have the wisdom," Chaplin toasted, "to keep us well-heeled in prosperity and to edify us during difficulty and tragedy!"

"You have your vife living and vell, Charles?" Zabel teared, "I lost mein liebe frau, Anna, a lifetime ago."

"What does an old man know about liebe!" Harry touted.

"You're schpeaking to a man who has lived it, mein freund. Ach, prima," Zabel reminisced. "Mein sveetheart Anna vould take me to heben!"

"To Liebe — Love!" Charles lifted his glass for another Ein Prosit toast. "And to the love of man for his country!"

"Vat about Gott unt country?" Zabel confessed. "As much as I love Deutschland, I could not schtand by unt vatch my homeland lose its soul."

"Show me a Nazi, I'll show you a Communist!" Torhorst leered. "How many Americans did you kill in the war, Zabel?" Helen Hayes was right. Torhorst always looked like he'd just swallowed a sour ball.

"How many Germans did you kill in the war?" Charles exploded. "Or didn't you serve your country! There are no Nazis here! Zabel nor I. And I'm not a Communist...I'm a humanist!"

The tavern's merrymakers were stunned into silence at Charles' overreaction.

Zabel broke the silence. "I joined the vorkers' party. That's *all* I'm guilty ov." He handed his mug to Stag for a refill. "But the day mein bruder...um...shot ...tot schiessen...a Jew, I left Germany. I lost mein family, not just in Var. Ach! Vat do I know? Just an old Deutches glassblower!"

Stag filled the wise German's mug. "This one's on me, Zabel," he offered, compassionately.

The silence grew thick and palpable in the room. Only Zabel and Alfred knew he was sitting next to the great Charlie Chaplin. He also knew humanism, like communism and naziism was a man's belief in himself not his God. And when God was removed, so was man's free will. Yes, Zabel knew.

The old gentleman spoke again. "To freedom! It is like air unt sun, you must lose it to know you can't live without it."

"To Freedom!" Stag shouted and all the men joined in.

It was getting dark as the men drank together one last time. Then, they all bid each other farewell and staggered down Depot Road toward home.

A week later, while onboard an ocean liner bound from New York to Europe, Chaplin received word from the State Department. Herbert Hoover had revoked his automatic re-entry permit into the United States. He could not return to the country where he had lived and prospered his adult life.

America and his United Artists studio had lost Charlie Chaplin. He sent Oona back to the U.S. to settle their business affairs. She sold their home, closed the studios and packed all of his life's work. Deeply devoted Oona returned to Corsier-sur-Vevey, Switzerland, and remained by his side until his death. To Eugene O'Neill's chagrin, the loving couple had eight children. Charles Chaplin died on Christmas Day, 1977, at age eighty-eight.

From a poor, tragic childhood he was inspired to compose the famous musical refrain "Smile, though your heart is breaking...". Chaplin's Little Tramp had emerged from a wardrobe closet with borrowed voluminous trousers from Fatty Arbuckle, a drastically-trimmed moustache of Mack Swain's, Ford Sterling's boat-sized shoes — on the wrong feet — an undersized jacket buttoned tightly, and a tiny derby to crown his glory.

For twenty five years, he was the most popular film personality in the world. Knighted by his Queen in 1975, Sir Charles Chaplin was another English misfit who, like Lynn Fontanne, knew British poverty and American wealth.

Chapter 43

As Diana grew into her pre-teen years, Virgel realized her need for privacy. He decided she was to have her own room with an adjoining bath, an unheard of luxury at the time. He first built a staircase, then converted the entire attic space of the Herrold house into a bedroom. Louise chose a canopied bed, white Priscilla curtains to embrace the room's dormer windows and pink porcelain for her bathroom.

To adorn the room her grandfather built a vanity, of which he was most proud, patterned after Miss Fontanne's white tulle and taffeta in the Syrie Maugham cottage bedroom. Diana's had two hinged arms that opened and closed to reveal hidden drawers. Her grandmother attached a tightly-gathered flounce in a pastel floral around the vanity with matching gathers to frame a large round mirror.

Where the attic roofline pitched to one side, glass-enclosed shelves were built for her doll collection. Through the years she added native American Indian dolls, each one representing a state as the Herrolds traveled on their annual vacations. The third and last extravagant doll from her father, a bridal doll with blonde tresses, now sat with the other two on a high, isolated shelf.

"This looks just like you, Di..." Nana gushed on the day she received it. "...Someday."

"When I get married, I want Virgel to give me away." Diana said matter-of-factly and she immediately, on tip-toe, placed the figurine out of reach.

From the three dormers in her new pink and white haven, Diana could see in all directions. She often observed the comings and goings in front of the Herrold house and Martin's house next door, all the way up to the Perkins brothers' brick house at the end of Depot Road. Another dormer viewed her grandparent's orchard and gardens, as well as acres of Wisconsin farmland. And — on a windy day — the third dormer revealed ten little chimneys peeking through the rustling trees of the kettle moraine.

She cherished her room and everything in it, but most important to her was how her grandparent's loving hands and hearts had built it.

Although the Herrolds had little money, they always managed to finance one memorable vacation every summer and Jules often joined them on their road trips.

One year they visited New York City. Louise stayed in the gift shop while the three climbed steps leading to the Statue of Liberty's crown to enjoy the Manhattan skyline. At Diana's persistence, they opted to continue up the dangerously steep spiral steps of Lady Liberty's arm to the flame's look-out where Ellis Island could be seen. It was a deeply moving experience — especially for Jules — who had passed through there as a child.

Disneyland's grand opening in Southern California in 1955 motivated the Herrolds to embark on their most ambitious vacation sans Jules, who was spending precious time with Wilhelmina that summer. They visited Hollywood, which included a bus tour of movie stars' homes and Valentino's grave where Louise placed some flowers. They also ventured south of the border to Tijuana, Mexico, where the three were captured in an image atop scruffy burros with shopping bags filled to capacity with Louise's souvenirs.

The next summer Jules again joined the Herrolds when they visited Washington, D.C., colonial Williamsburg, Jamestown and the Southern states. It was very important to Virgel that Diana be exposed to American history, but to Louise it was necessary to be 'cultured'.

As they drove on a country road shaded by weeping willows somewhere in the deep South, Louise shouted, "Virgel, stop!" Swaying in the breeze on a roadside vendor's clothesline were a dozen or so chenille bedspreads. A pastel peacock design had caught Louise's eye. It was to be the perfect finishing touch for Diana's new pink bedroom and canopied bed.

Their final destination that summer was the home of the greatest race horses of all time, Calumet Farm, the crown jewel among Kentucky bluegrass horse farms. Eight hundred acres of rolling deep blue grass was enclosed in thirty miles of white plank fencing and the four visitors were allowed to roam at their leisure through the nineteen stables and paddocks. Louise took a snapshot of Diana standing in front of the distinctive red and white barn as she watched the Triple Crown winner, Citation, bask in his paddock. Virgel snapped another picture of the magnificent dark chestnut animal known as "Big Cy". In the sunlight as he walked toward Louise posing in front of his white fence, the champion's shoulders gleamed a deep maroon brown.

Jules took a Calumet trainer aside and asked, "Sir, I would love to treat my dear friends to the most delicious Southern dining you could recommend."

Eyeing Jules, suspiciously, the trainer hesitated for a moment, then gave him directions to a nearby restaurant frequented only by the wealthier locals. Innocently, the Herrolds piled into the car. Giggling, Louise squeezed one last souvenir, a new straw hat, into their already over-crowded Chevy. Between the luggage, bedspread, Indian dolls and other treasures, she decided it had no where else to go — but on Jules' head!

"Be sure to order their Kentucky Derby pie!" the trainer snickered as they pulled onto the main road.

Virgel turned onto a sideroad lined with willows and layered limestone fencing, steering the car up a large circular drive of an old plantation.

Louise quickly dug a compact out of her purse, patted her nose and refreshed her lipstick in the car's rearview mirror. "Isn't this classy!"

A liveried valet parked their car and the four strolled through white pillared columns of a grand portico, into the elegant lobby of a restored Southern mansion.

Amidst the smell of roasted chicken and dumplings and the muted sound of china dishes clattering in a distant kitchen, they waited to be seated.

'White Only' and 'Colored Only' signs were prominently displayed on the restroom doors in the hallway.

"What does that mean?" Diana asked.

"Something that will not apply to Jules!" Louise snapped angrily as she primped and smoothed her hair in the vestibule mirror.

"I want that table over there!" she pointed excitedly across the room to a big picture window overlooking pasturelands dotted with thoroughbreds.

The maitre d' approached and immediately took Virgel aside and murmured. "I will not be able to seat your negro, sir."

"What's the problem, Virgel?" Louise insisted loudly.

Jules overheard, "I have always wanted to take a walk down an old Southern lane." He stepped back, politely, to leave.

"You're not going anywhere, Jules, except with me to that table over there!" Louise grabbed his arm and brusquely they walked past the dumbfounded maitre d'.

Virgel whispered back to the man. "Trust me — you don't want to mess with my wife."

There was a light luncheon crowd that afternoon in the restaurant and the few diners at table were perplexed as a family paraded their black through the main dining hall to be seated at the most desireable table — while the stunned maitre d' trailed behind.

With a dishtowel in hand, wide-eyed, an old stooped black gentleman with closely-cropped gray hair appeared in a doorway of the back kitchen to watch them curiously.

Seated at the table with their menus opened, the Herrolds admired breathtaking views of Kentucky's rolling hills. Intently, Jules kept his eyes fixed on the menu's bill of fare.

A distinguished-looking waiter stood patiently at the table as

Louise unfolded her napkin, placed it in her lap and took a long, deep sip of her mint julep.

"You go first, Jules..." she smiled broadly at her dear friend.

Chapter 44

In the late summer on a day with the possibility of rain, Alfred, disguised in a rain coat, hat and tall black rubber boots, his English 'wellies', marched resolutely along the front path up to the Pet Milk Company building. He entered the plant through a side door.

Inside, huge stainless steel vats churned milk in various processes of cream, buttermilk, butter, ice cream, cottage cheese and sour cream. A handful of white uniformed workers wearing wedged 'Pet Milk' paper hats were engaged in their daily activities, each one performing his assigned task. Clear, sterilized milk bottles with the red 'Pet Milk' logo stood at attention in wooden crates waiting to be filled with the pure white liquid. Alfred observed one man wearing gloves with a glass ladle in hand, placing a culture in a petri dish and quickly covering it.

"Mr. Herrold, please," Alfred spoke with determination.

"He just went into his lab, sir," the man pointed down the hall. "You can't miss it."

"Marvelous plant!" Alfred tipped his hat. "Good day." The man watched as Mr. Lunt's tall distinguished presence walked into the light of a window, then down a long narrow hallway lit by an occasional ceiling bulb.

Virgel, also in white and a paper hat, was working alone when

Alfred knocked lightly on his lab door. Without lifting his head from his microscope, he answered, "It's open."

Alfred entered the small room and noticed a microscope, on a work table, surrounded by a few petri dishes of bacterial samples in various stages of growth. Across the room on a desk was Virgel's lunch box, open, with a partially-eaten sandwich placed on a napkin.

When Virgel accepted the position as head bacteriologist at Pet Milk Company more than two decades before, Hank lent him five hundred dollars to purchase a microscope. Virgel had never borrowed money before and insisted a promissory note be given to his brother-in-law and the sum repaid in installments faithfully every month until paid in full.

With a clean, white handkerchief Mr. Lunt humbly presented a small, sealed Ball mason jar from under his jacket. "Mr. Herrold — your assistant I presume — kindly directed me to your laboratory."

Virgel looked up, "Another sample?"

"Yes, *my* sample this time." Alfred coughed. "I have an urgent request — for myself as well as Miss Fontanne."

Picking up the mason jar, Virgel examined it and looked back at Alfred.

"This looks like..." he was confused.

Alfred interrupted him, "I've been told by my Chicago doctor that my — 'count' is deficient." He was getting agitated, "This must be absolutely incorrect!"

"What may I do for you, Mr. Lunt?" Virgel was not surprised.

"Prove 'em wrong, old friend," Alfred smiled sadly.

Chapter 45

Ben was trimming the lush ivy on the front pillars of the main house. "Mr. Herrold! How are you? Beautiful morning, isn't it?" In the cool air, dew still hung on the bright green leaves and birds were greeting the morning sun with melody.

Virgel parked his car in Ten Chimneys' courtyard and greeted Ben through his open car window. "Your birds sing so sweetly around here! The Good Lord likes to smile on Ten Chimneys. Don't you think?"

"The Lunts love it but cleaning up all the bird shit drives me nuts!" Chuckling, Ben looked up at the opened kitchen windows above. "Mr. Herrold's here, Jules! Is the coffee ready?"

Jules didn't answer, he was in Hattie's cottage. Approaching her ninetieth birthday, she had become imperious of his time, but he loved her company and shamelessly indulged her every whim. Although her hair was now grey, it was swept up in a bright colored scarf and her lips were still painted red.

"More coffee, Mrs. Sederholm?" He wiped and put away the few remaining breakfast dishes.

"No, thank you, I'm quite sure you have much to do back at the house, with Miss Hayes visiting and all. I'll be just fine." She adjusted a blanket about her knees and began to weep. "Please, dear, sit here beside me -- for just a moment?" He pulled up a chair to sit close to her. "I won't be around much longer, Jules. Tell me you will take care of my beloved boy for me when I'm gone?"

Jules patted her hand affectionately, "Be assured. You know I will."

In good spirits, Virgel got out of the car. "Is Mr. Lunt in the house?"

"I believe you can find him in the vegetable garden, near the apple trees." Ben pointed beyond the house and Virgel strolled up the knoll in that direction.

"But what about coffee?"

"Not today, Ben, thank you." Virgel placed his hat neatly on his head.

From a distance Ben could see the men talking. Mr. Lunt placed his hand on his confidante's back, and bent his head toward him in hushed conversation. Shortly, Alfred patted his shoulder, shook his hand and gave him a bushel of fresh-picked apples.

"You're a damned-good man, Virgel. And Mother certainly found her bon mots match in Louise." Both men laughed, as Alfred shook his hand again and walked him back to his car.

"Haven't seen Mrs. Sederholm's smiling face for some time," Virgel acknowledged.

"Honestly, old friend, Mother's doing better than me. She is still very lucid and absolutely ignores the inconveniences of old age." Alfred smiled, helping Virgel into his car. "There's no doubt she'll outlive me and everyone else here at Ten Chimneys!" After shutting the old Chevy's door, Alfred knocked on the window glass.

"Is everything okay, Mr. Lunt?"

"My good man, could you possibly spare a few of those Pet Milk paper hats in your back seat?"

Upstairs Lynn opened the sunroom windows to the crisp morning air. For a few minutes, she and Helen Hayes listened to an annoying woodpecker as they sat in comfortable down-cushioned chairs working on their needlepoint.

"You know, Lynn, Alfred and I were destined for each other until you placed your dainty English hooks into him! I was barely eighteen and heartbroken when Tyler pulled me out of 'Clarence' and tore me from him." Helen tittered, "It was to be the last time I would play a brilliant comedy. The last time I would hear the glorious laughter. The last time I would hear Alfred play the saxophone so terribly." The two old friends laughed together.

"My poor Alfred learned early the consequences of a mother who squandered two wealthy husbands' inheritances... Oh, that damned old bird!"

Jumping up, Lynn shut the window to silence the loud pecking, mimicking her mother-in-law, "Oh, don't worry, my husband Dr. Sederholm wouldn't *dream* of taking your money!"

Lynn sat down and shook her head as she looped a cross-stitch, "Barely seventeen and in college, he was forced to support Hattie and his three half-siblings — 'the Finns'. With a small inheritance he managed to keep from his mother, he financed his schooling and bought the first parcels of our Ten Chimneys."

Helen nodded her head and rubbed her arms. "Lynn, dear, do you have something for me to ward off the chill?"

"Help yourself to anything in my closet, d*ah-h-ling*."" When Helen opened the closet door, to her amusement, Barbara Cartlan paperbacks covertly stacked in a corner tumbled to the floor.

"My dear Helen, you weren't the only one vying for Alfred's attentions." Choosing a bright red embroidery floss and threading it, Lynn continued her narrative. "There were many young actresses proclaiming undying love for my Alfred. Then there were 'the Finns' — and far more dangerous — our Grand Dame! You could never have managed Hattie!"

Lynn continued to concentrate on her embroidery. "The good doctor gambled the rest of Hattie's fortune. Broke, desperate, he was forced to move his family to Finland to cadge off their in-laws. Poor Alfred! Found his stepfather dead in a hotel room! Just between you and me, Helen, I suspect suicide!" She sighed, "So much luggage came with my Alfred."

"We all have our luggage, Lynn," Helen vigorously wrapped a French knot. "Look at my poor drunken Charlie, he never recovered from the death of our daughter. When I first met him, he dropped peanuts in my hand and said 'I wish these were emeralds.' My heart was forever lost. And then there was our..." she paused, sadly, "...my Mary."

"Your Mary was a fine actress and would have been one of theatre's greatest," Lynn bolstered her friend. "Helen, you had an extraordinary daughter for nineteen glorious years."

"You and Alfred and many others have been so generous to the Mary MacArthur Fund. I continue to be humbled by Dr. Salk's efforts. Blessings are a strange thing, Lynn. Jonas is giving me all the credit for funding his polio vaccine! In losing Mary, I found a passion I never knew I had. Do you have regrets, Lynn?" Helen asked. "You and Alfred — for not having children?"

"I was tortured for years. Even briefly considered the idea of adoption," Lynn confided. "When Alfred finally came around, as he always does, I had already decided that's not a t'all what I wanted. A blessing really." She sighed, "We really are two selfish rots, too devoted to theatre to be proper parents."

Chapter 46

Ten Chimneys was in mourning.

While the Lunts were touring their current New York theater run of Noël Coward's 'Quadrille', Harriet Sederholm had broken her arm and, within weeks, dramatically deteriorated. At ninety-three, she held bravely onto life until 'her beloved' returned home.

Alfred was inconsolable as she whispered her last labored breath to him. "Oh, God! Oh, God!"

Only days' later in the Ten Chimneys' kitchen, Jules and Ben were at the table sipping their morning coffee.

Diana had come to visit with Virgel, bringing a sympathy note and a large bouquet of flowers from Louise's garden. Blowing on a cup of hot cocoa, she listened unhappily.

"I'm terribly worried about Mr. Lunt, Jules." Ben lamented, "Have funeral arrangements been made?"

"Mr. Lunt is contemplating a Viking funeral." Jules confessed.

"A what?" Ben asked incredulously.

"A centuries old Scandinavian tradition to put a loved one in a boat and set fire to it," Jules recited.

"My God!" Ben exclaimed. "Surely Miss Fontanne talked him out of it!"

"Fortunately for dear Mrs. Sederholm, she'll rest in peace at the Lunt family plot in Milwaukee. It was a short moment of great concern for all of us." Jules refilled Ben's coffee cup and replenished the plate of fresh baked banana bread. "But now he's adamant about wanting to burn the cottage to the ground! He swears no one shall ever set foot in it again."

Unnoticed, Diana quickly slipped some bread into her already bulging pocket.

At his mother's wake the Lunts and some of their guests had become ill and Lynn was bedridden with a malaise. Worrying it may have originated from his creamery, Alfred summoned his neighbor for advice.

Outside in the creamery, a morose and unshaven Alfred stood nearby, watching while Virgel collected samples from the milking machine for cultures. Ellen (honoring Lynn's mentor, Terry), Lily (whom Hattie had affectionately named after Langtry), Sugar (the bull named after Sir Hugo 'Sugar' de Barthe, Langtry's husband) and Rose (Lynn's English memorializing that Hattie had puzzled over) stared indifferently from their barn stalls, swatting flies with their tails.

The Ten Chimneys' dairy provided exceptional quality milk products for their privileged guests. Taking his cue from Virgel, Alfred fastidiously kept his creamery immaculate and sterile, to the extent of wearing white from toe-to-head and his Pet Milk hat.

"May I give you a suggestion, Mr. Lunt? Feed your farm animals only what you know they will eat," Virgel recommended. "Don't let fodder set — for even an hour — it could contaminate."

As the men left the creamery and walked through the garden, Alfred could see Diana and Jules approaching through the kettle moraine from the main house. With a tender heart he watched as, every few feet, the young girl stopped to pull food from her pocket to feed Lynn's squirrels.

"How is it Diana calls you Virgel, not grandfather?" Alfred asked.

"I'm not her blood relative. But we are bound by something more perfect." He choked back tears. "The child is my life."

"You're a very lucky man, Mr. Herrold," Alfred complimented. "You've raised a delightfully happy child."

"Yes, thank the Good Lord." Virgel smiled and stopped to admire a magnificent eggplant.

Noticing a patch of weeds, Alfred dropped to his knees, and began plucking them by the roots. His eyes followed a low-flying robin across the knoll as it landed on Hattie's cottage and a deep sadness overcame him.

Purposefully, Diana walked into the garden and put her arms around Mr. Lunt. They barely reached across his broad shoulders. His eyes were puffy and bloodshot from sleeplessness and his face, normally impeccably groomed, was stubbled. Even the simple task of shaving that morning had obviously been a burden.

Her heart ached for his visible torment, "I'm sorry you miss your mother so much."

She began to cry and was shocked when Mr. Lunt hugged her back.

"Thank you, child. I know you are."

"Mrs. Sederholm once told me," Jules reminisced tearfully, "you were the happiness of her life and the iron of her soul. She wouldn't want you to torment yourself, Mr. Lunt."

Trying to hide his tears, Alfred quickly collected himself and stood up. "Mr. Herrold if you have time when we're through, I would love for you to join me in the kitchen for some hot coffee and a fresh banana loaf."

At the mention of banana loaf, Diana prayed there was still enough left.

"I must check on Miss Fontanne." Jules backed away, excusing himself.

Running ahead of Jules, Diana ducked back into the main house, through the laundry room, up the stairs and into the kitchen.

The two men walked the garden area in silence, as Virgel continued to take cultures. He pointed to neatly-stacked bales of hay along an outside barn wall. "You should consider some lightning rods on these buildings, Mr. Lunt. That barn could be easy kindling for a lightning strike."

Surrounded by its many trees, the Lunt estate was especially vulnerable during Wisconsin summer storms.

"Thank you. I will seriously consider that."

Just before Hattie's death, lightning had struck a dry tree that split and fell, damaging the outside of the main house near the drawing room. Alfred, like other friends of Virgel's, was becoming dependent upon Mr. Herrold's common sense and wisdom.

Throughout the 1950s, Virgel Herrold became a trusted friend to Alfred. When Ben or Alfred became frustrated in futile attempts to repair broken machinery, they often called their helpful neighbor. This was the era of burgeoning nuclear fears and Virgel also assisted Alfred in determining the need for a bomb shelter.

As trust deepened between the two men, it also slowly blossomed between Louise and Lynn. Unlike Alfred who was very approachable, Miss Fontanne in her quietly-reserved English manner — like England's Queen Mother — stared straight ahead without acknowledging her neighbors when Ben drove her through The Depot.

After Hattie's death, though, Lynn began to rely on Louise's assistance in the employment of locals and on rare occasion, the use of her home. Lola Parton, who had come highly recommended by Louise, continued to do the weekly laundry and ironing for the estate until she retired of old age.

Miss Fontanne's neatly penned notes were many and often, although sometimes brief:

Dear Mrs. Herrold,

Happy Easter and many thanks for recommending Mrs. Pougel. She is wonderful.

With sincere thanks,
Lynn Fontanne

One year when an entire theater company was invited to Ten Chimneys for Christmas Eve dinner, Lynn wanted a particular cast member, Anna, to remain in Genesee even though all their guest rooms were full.

Lynn wrote later from the Selwyn in Chicago:

Dear Mrs. Herrold,

It was sweet of you to be willing to take a guest in your house on that precious Christmas Eve and we appreciate it very, very much indeed.

Anna had such a good time and became so fond of you all. We are both very grateful to you for being so kind to her.

Most sincerely,
Lynn Fontanne

At age seventy, during the winter sold-out performances of 'The Great Sebastian', Lynn wrote from her brownstone in New York:

Dear Mrs. Herrold,

It was very sweet and kind of you to send us a card with your good wishes on our departure from Genesee.

Thank you very much.

With our very best wishes to you also.

Sincerely,
Lynn Fontanne

No matter how small the kindness, Lynn Fontanne always promptly followed with a thoughtful handwritten note of gratitude.

CHAPTER 47

"Have you ever been jealous, Alfred?" Low in spirits, Laurence Olivier suavely smoked a cigarette and downed a Scotch and soda. As a Sinatra ballad played softly in the background, the men stared out of the twelve-foot-high drawing room window onto Ten Chimneys' rain drenched kettle moraine.

The Oliviers had now been married sixteen years, but these were tumultuous times. Vivien had fallen into fits of envy and depression over Larry's blatant affairs.

"Of Lynn? I have never felt any jealousy in my life." Alfred lit a cigarette. "I can't understand a man who trembles at the thought of his wife going downtown."

Across the room, seated at a table, Lynn studied the men's reflections from a tall, gilded wall mirror as they spoke in hushed tones.

She quipped loudly as she shuffled cards for solitaire. "Alfred averaged fifty mash notes a week, Larry! There was always some actress in love with him — even poor Helen."

"Yes, wasn't I wonderful?" Alfred teased. He made a smoke ring and watched it dissolve into Clagg's muraled ceiling. "Truth is, I had to rehearse Lynnie for her hot and sexy role as Linda in Noëllie's 'Point Valaine'!"

"Alfred, you don't rehearse me in *anything*," she rallied. "I usually come through with a perfect performance in *spite* of you!"

Encircling Larry's shoulder with his arm, Alfred whispered

emphatically, "When I soar too high, Lynn always knows precisely how to bring me back down to reality."

"You two do make me laugh!" Olivier said humbly, "But you are an extraordinary couple of many gifts. Everything I know on stage, you taught me, Alfred."

Admittedly, Alfred Lunt was Laurence Olivier's lifelong mentor.

"Larry, *dah-h-h-ling*, where is Viv? Perhaps someone should check on her?" Lynn reminded him. "She hasn't left her room all morning!"

Apathetic, Laurence took another drag on his cigarette. "Do you mind, Lynn? Viv's probably in one of her manics."

Irritated with Larry's indifference, Lynn laid the deck of cards aside. "Excuse me, gentlemen." She took a deep breath and abruptly left the room.

When Lynn was out of ear shot, Olivier confided, "*O Gertrude, Gertrude — When sorrows come, they come not single spies, But in battalions.* Damned the fates! I could have achieved the greatest of heights with Alfred Lunt — The Master — directing me." He gulped another glass of Scotch, this time on the rocks. "Instead, I've only performed on stage three times in the last six years."

"I desperately wanted to direct you in Rattigan's new play," Alfred lamented.

Laurence stared intently through the window at the dark clouds merging above the kettle moraine creating a fresh down pour.

"She just had another miscarriage, you know. She even had a name picked this time — Katherine — with a 'K'." He faced his old friend with tears in his eyes. "She's broken, Alfred. Not even our Notley Abbey with all its finery can make Vivien happy. Neither I, nor the doctor can fix her in body or spirit. She rarely sleeps. One minute she rips off her clothing, clawing at me for sexual attention; the next minute she screams violently at me for some perceived minor indiscretion. The shock treatments, her body on ice for days, the lithium: nothing works." He slurred his words despondently, "I can't help her anymore."

"I love and grieve for you both, Larry," Alfred whispered, sorrowfully.

"So, my friend, one may wonder how-the-devil does she have the energy to have an affair with Finch?" Olivier looked at his now-empty glass.

"Finch?" Alfred was incredulous. "During the 'Elephant Walk'?"

"Yes. She supposedly got delusional off the set and slipped into her Blanche from Streetcar, mistaking Finch for me!" Laurence spat bitterly. "Our life together has become hideous. We are trapped by public acclaim, scratching about in the cold ashes of a passion that burned itself out long ago. We are successful, envied and adored — and most wretchedly unhappy. Sweet Vivien and — dirty me!"

Upstairs, Lynn knocked softly on the guest room door and entered. She particularly loved this room she and Alfred had designed for the Olivier's, patterning it after a grand English garden with walls and matching tie-back drapes in large florals and deep rich rose tones.

Vivien was still in bed, staring disconsolately at the remaining embers of a fire only a few feet away.

"Where is that marvelous picture with the Queen you were going to show me last night?" As she rekindled the fire, Lynn bantered bravely while inside her heart was breaking. "How is it a Lady of the British Empire with two Oscars on her Notley library mantle can't find something to smile about today?"

Lynn stepped to the window and stared through the rain drops at an empty nest on a tree limb almost touching the glass. "Oh, how wonderful! The baby robins have finally left their nest. They must be deliriously happy, flying in and out of the trees."

She studied Vivien who was unresponsive, "I have watched the small lovely blue eggs hatch into tiny pink-skinned bodies as the little babies grew into their down feathers. Just yesterday, they appeared ready to fly."

"Maybe it's not too late," Vivien aroused, "to save them! You must open the window!"

"Save them?" Lynn was confused. "Vivien, dear, what are you talking about?"

Then Lynn noticed something very wrong. The woods were eerily silenced.

Delicate and thin, Vivien still in her long nightgown, rose and guardedly walked to the window. Dazed, she peered at the now-empty nest and spoke with menacing inflection.

"I saw a large black bird glide and land near them. All I could do was stare, helplessly, through the locked glass as he devoured them one by one. I couldn't get the window open in time, Lynnie! I swear, I desperately tried! His huge, dark head bobbed up and down — pecking away at their tiny bodies. In a matter of seconds it was all over — just as quietly as he came, he flew away. Their mum returned to her empty nest moments later with a worm. She dropped the food and began picking and gathering little bits and pieces. She found only one remaining piece of down and held it in her mouth, trying to understand." She broke down, sobbing hysterically.

"A raven just savaged them? Oh my dear, Viv! In front of you?" Lynn held her in her arms and helped her back into bed.

"I tried, Lynnie! I tried to save my baby! But the blood was all over my bedclothes! It wouldn't stop! And the pain! Oh, the unbearable pain!" Vivien wept uncontrollably while Lynn rocked her back and forth, trying to comfort her. "I couldn't reach the phone. I screamed for Larry, but he couldn't hear me. I held her in my hands, just like mummy bird, trying to understand. Larry blames me, I know it!" She clutched at Lynn's arm. "Lynn, promise me, you must convince him — it's not my fault!"

"Of course it's not your fault, dear. You need to rest. I won't be more than a moment!" Lynn ran down the spiral stairs, through the hall and into the dining room. Opening the kitchen door, "Jules?" She cried out for help, "Jules!"

In moments he appeared.

"You and I alone will take care of Miss Leigh," she whispered frantically. "I don't want to involve Larry. And Alfred's the *last* one to cope. You must find her medicine immediately."

Jules returned shortly to the guest room with Vivien's lithium carbonate and a glass of water. "Don't worry, Miss Fontanne. I refreshed the men's Scotch and they are deep in discussion in the drawing room."

"Thank you, Jules." Relieved, Lynn pulled up a chair near her desperate friend, lying exhausted on the bed. She stirred the white powdered salt into the water and gave it to her. Within moments of drinking it, Vivien drifted into a deep, sedated sleep.

Lynn opened a book and began to read softly.

She must have fallen asleep because sometime later, Vivien's voice startled her awake. "My Larryboy is so cold, so frigid with me." Her slender body wracked fitfully, as she coughed. She nervously covered burns at her temples with her hair caused by recent shock treatments. "I can tolerate his romps with men, but this time he's in love with a woman." She dissolved into tears again. "I've tried everything and sexually he's so bored with me. I've lost him, I know it!" She tore at her clothes as claustrophobia, another symptom of her illness set in. "In spite of all of this, I'm still mad for him! I love him so much. It makes me crazy thinking of him with someone else!" Trembling, Vivien shouted, "What shall I do?"

"You must live moment by moment, Viv," Lynn took her by the shoulders and steadied her. "I promise you — each day you'll get a little stronger. My dear, so many people love you." After years of masterfully resolving difficulties at Ten Chimneys, Lynn declared. "We hear you've become quite the artist. Do you know Alfred and I have a surprise for you? We've set up an easel in our garden room."

Jules entered with a luncheon tray and hot tea, placing it on a table near the hearth. He stopped to stoke the fire, not wanting to leave the room until he knew Lynn was in control.

"Oh, how lovely. Look, Viv, Jules made delicious raspberry crepes for us!"

Jules helped Vivien walk from the bed to the table. "Tea is so much more than..." Lynn caught herself, then poured the tea and handed a cup to Vivien. "This is your first *moment, dah-h-ling*. I do hope Ten Chimneys will inspire you to paint while you're here."

"Will that be all, Miss Fontanne?" Jules asked. They both exchanged a look, realizing the danger had passed.

"Yes. Thank you, Jules," she gave him a relieved smile.

Vivien Leigh went on to have many moments while continuing

to work in film and on stage between her bouts with depression. A few years later — another moment — she garnered a Best Actress Tony award for 'Tovarich'.

The Oliviers' professional careers continued to thrive, but Sir Laurence and Lady Vivien's union of twenty-three years disintegrated. After a year of separation, Larry telegrammed her asking for a divorce. Vivien was shattered. She had always believed her Larry would return to her. However, shortly after the divorce was final, he remarried. The ever-practical, sensible and very English Joan Plowright was to become his third and last wife.

In the following years while Laurence blatantly drifted in and out of same-sex affairs, Vivien wandered in and out of sanitariums.

After more than three hundred tortuous Broadway performances and months of filming her mentally-ill Blanche DuBois role, Vivien Leigh succumbed to a nervous breakdown. During her stay in the sanitarium, her home was burglarized and her beloved 'Gone With The Wind' Best Actress Oscar was stolen, along with other valuables.

One evening at Ten Chimneys while Alfred was drifting to sleep, Lynn stepped out of her closet, nude, in a stunning purple hat with yards of netting.

"Dah-h-ling, what do you think of this hat?" Lynn drolled, sitting next to Alfred on the bed, hoping to intrigue her husband.

"Mmmm. Dramatic. Will look smashing with your new suit." He turned over in bed, half asleep.

Lynn leaned over and kissed him. "I was thinking I'd wear this with it!" She started to tickle him awake.

Downstairs in the kitchen the phone was ringing. Only minutes later, Jules knocked softly at their bedroom door. "Miss Fontanne, it's Miss Leigh for you."

Lynn sobered instantly, threw on a dressing gown sans hat and padded down the hall to the phone niche. Vivien was very sick and, of late, she was calling often to talk with her close friend at Ten Chimneys.

"You know I'd rather have lived a short life with Larry than face a long life without him," Viv confided as they said goodbye.

When Lynn returned to the bedroom, Alfred was awake, reading. Full of sorrow she shared her thoughts with her husband. "Our dear Viv's tragedy is that her adoring public has never realized her desperate illness. They just all assumed she was behaving badly. And her poor Larry, so overwhelmed and weary, could simply do no more."

A tubercular patch found on Vivien Leigh's left lung lead to complications and her death at age fifty-three.

Before she died, Larry visited with her at her home in England. They took a long, private walk together at a nearby lake. Vivien never knew he was battling cancer.

In a hospital room, upon hearing news of her looming death, Olivier immediately checked himself out and rushed to her side.

Standing over her deathbed, he whispered to her, "I pray for forgiveness for all the evil that sprang up between us."

Twenty-two years later a visitor to his home found the eighty-year old Olivier sitting alone watching Leigh in an old film on television. "This, this was love," he said in tears. "This was the real thing."

CHAPTER 48

Small white snowflakes drifted down through the trees, their branches stark and barren against the fomenting dark gray of cloud and sky. It was Christmas Eve again in Genesee Depot.

During the long Wisconsin winters, at Alfred's standing invitation, Diana and Virgel often went ice skating on a small pond deep within the Lunt property.

With ice skates over their shoulders, they trudged across Depot Road and hiked a good distance through the drifts into the whitened forest.

Earlier that week, a horrendous blizzard, short thaw, then freezing temperatures had created a thick, crusted snow. With each step, Diana's boots crunched and sank up to mid-calf. Her progress was slow but Nana's hot mulled cider waiting for them at home was a warming thought in the bitter cold.

Nothing, not even the adverse weather, could quell her excitement as she impishly opened her mouth, letting the frozen flakes collect and melt on her tongue. This was her special time with her grandfather and she loved to ice skate with him.

Staring up at the foreboding sky, Virgel thought perhaps they shouldn't have taken this trek. Breathing heavily from a chest cold, he placed his woolen scarf over his frozen nose.

"Hurry up, Virgel!" she called back to him.

Catching a glimpse of the pond, Diana ran ahead, playfully falling forward and tumbling into a snowdrift. Laughing, she flopped on her back, fanning her arms and legs to make a snow angel.

When Virgel caught up to her, she had already laced her skates. She did a few figure eights in the middle of the pond as her grandfather finished his lacing.

"Looks like a storm is brewing." Virgel was worried as he stepped onto the ice and took her hands. They often skated as partners this way, with their arms crossed, so they could talk. "Di, maybe we should head back home."

Diana turned around to face him, skating backwards, and changed the subject, "Do you know what Santa's bringing you?" Now that she was older, Diana had been leaving 'Santa' presents under the Christmas tree for her grandparents. Her sincere thank-you's for all the years they had given her Christmas gifts anonymously.

Still skating backwards facing him, she stepped up the pace.

Slow down a little bit, Di!" her grandfather cautioned.

Before she could heed his warning, she lost her footing and fell backward on the ice. Still holding hands, Virgel fell forward — on top of her — his skate blade piercing deep into her lower right thigh.

She grabbed her leg, moaning in pain as blood gushed and spattered on her clothes and onto the ice.

Terrified, Virgel, aware of these types of deadly accidents with farming machinery, thought the blade might have sliced an artery.

As he struggled to pick her up and carry her across the ice, a blizzard struck with angry force — dumping a heavy, blinding snow that left him disoriented.

While the wind howled, sweeping huge drifts of snow against the tall trees, Virgel fought the fresh slick snow with his skates. Unsteady he lunged forward and fell to his knees, losing grasp of his granddaughter.

Screaming in terror — wheezing, with bloodied, fumbling hands, he tugged at his skates and feverishly untied his laces. Diana was barely conscious as he wound the laces tightly — a makeshift tourniquet — above the deep gash. Placing his jacket around her shoulders, he picked her up again and began to run through the deep snow in his frozen stockinged feet.

Choking back tears of fear he dropped to his knees again and drew a deep, ragged breath, "Dear God, help me find the road and get us to a doctor."

He looked up. Floating above a tree in the darkened sky were glowing embers – it was Ten Chimneys!

In the Lunt's dining room Jules continued stoking the blazing fire. Lynn's traditional raspberry trifle was chilling in the refrigerator next to his uncooked standing rib roast. He was pleased. His dinner was prepared and he had just finished placing two stockings on the mantle, each stuffed with a gift for Alfred and Lynn.

A horrific scream echoed through the kettle moraine and brought Jules, frightened, outside. He knew Virgel and Diana had gone to the ice pond that afternoon. Without thinking to put on a coat, he frantically ran down the driveway and up the hill toward the Herrold house.

Louise didn't answer the front door when he arrived, so Jules ran around back and entered through the kitchen. Her Christmas turkey was setting on the kitchen counter ready to be stuffed, but she wasn't there. He found her in the living room hysterically talking to herself, running from room to room aimlessly, looking for her purse and coat.

"That was Virgel!" She was hyperventilating. "I'd know his voice anywhere!"

"Where are your sedatives, Louise?" Jules clutched his heart, trying to compose himself.

"In my purse." Leaning on her dear friend, she sat down on the divan and looked up at him. "You look like you could use your heart medicine, Jules."

In the bedroom, he finally found her purse and routed through it. With medicine and a glass of water in hand, he watched her swallow. Knowing she couldn't drive in her condition, he took the car keys and promised to call.

Not having driven since he was a young man, he started the

Chevy's ignition. Wth jolting starts and stops, he managed to maneuver the car down the hill.

When Virgel finally reached the road, he was only a few feet from the car. Jules jumped out to help him place Diana in the back seat. While Jules craddled her head in his lap, Virgel slid in behind the steering wheel and gunned the accelerator.

After spending the afternoon tobogganing on the estate, Alfred and Lynn had found a pine to decorate for Christmas Eve and were attempting to load the tree on their sled when they also heard Virgel's scream echo through the woods.

"Di's been hurt!" Virgel idled the car in front of the Lunts standing at the side of the road. "We have to find Doc Simon!"

From the back seat, still in his stained kitchen apron, Jules cried out, "Please look after Mrs. Herrold!"

Dr. Robert Simon was enjoying an early Christmas Eve dinner at home with his family when the Herrold's car screeched into his North Prairie driveway. Virgel pounded on the door, his ravaged feet creating a puddle of blood on the doctor's front porch.

Pale and breathless, both men looked on as the doctor sutured the young teen's wound, on his living room couch, with the only materials he had at home — his wife's sewing needle and cotton thread. Diana would soon forget the pain, but she would always remember her grandfather grabbing her hand tightly and crying with every stitch.

"They're on their way home from Doctor Simon's right now." Lynn hung up the phone in the Herrold kitchen. "Our saucy little neighbor is going to be just fine."

"Thank you, Jesus," Louise whispered.

"Whatever shall we do for Christmas Eve dinner?" Alfred exclaimed. Without further thought, he grabbed Louise's turkey while Lynn quickly picked up three little 'Santa' packages under the Herrold Christmas tree.

Moments later, Alfred, squinting and hunched over the Buick's steering wheel, precariously aimed the vehicle back down the icy hill with his wife and Louise in tow.

Later that evening, Mr. Lunt still dressed in his woolen outdoor clothing, graciously welcomed his neighbors to the Ten Chimneys' dining table.

Humbly, Jules took his seat next to Diana. Instead of eating alone in the kitchen this year, he also would enjoy the holiday fare at the Lunt dining table.

In her bright, red Christmas apron with bells at the hem, Louise sliced her turkey placed center-stage on the table. She scooped her apple-sausage dressing onto Virgel's plate and chortled, "I thought for sure I would end up in the nut house this time!"

Lynn responded solemnly, "We'll not ever let that happen to you, Louise!" Contrary to her usual formal dining attire, she also wore woolen trousers and plaid shirt.

Miss Fontanne had clothed Diana, though, in her warmest dressing gown and had swept her hair up in a knot. "There you are!" Lynn seated her "little injured bird" in her chair at the head of the table — placing the bandaged leg upon a soft pillowed footstool.

After dinner, with great aplomb, Lynn presented her English trifle, laughing. She had noticed Alfred had placed a napkin over the Majolica statue's bare breast.

"What did you say this is called? Trifle?" Louise giggled. "Well, then I'm getting a 'trifle' tight!" To the amusement of all, Louise helped herself to a second large serving of the potent brandy-soaked dessert.

Above the roaring fire on the mantle, Jules noticed three little 'Santa' packages. "Santa?" he inquired.

"Yes! Diana piped up. "One for Virgel, one for Nana, and one for you!"

"Di, where's yours?" he asked her, concerned.

"I already have my gift." she grinned, "Christmas at Ten Chimneys!"

"Merry Christmas!" Jules gave her a big hug.

Eventually Alfred Lunt and Lynn Fontanne gave sixty acres of property, including the pond, to the Genesee township with the understanding it would remain kettle moraine. Joe Garton's Ten

Chimneys Foundation Cultural Center was to be built there, hidden from the road, much like the natural setting of the main house and in keeping with the Lunt's vision.

The small pond eventually dried up, it's location barely visible, as was the scar on Diana's leg.

CHAPTER 49

"To be hauled out of the theater at half-hour is about as low as an actor can get!" Alfred groaned, feverishly. He lay in a hospital bed doubled over with excruciating stomach spasms. Lynn sat beside him on the bed in the small, sterile, white room.

Troubled 'The Visit' was not the right play with which to open their lavish newly-dedicated Lunt-Fontanne Theater, Alfred had ruminated it might close prematurely. Despite his obsessive fretting, it had been running to sold-out audiences on Broadway for two years. But all his worry had taken a toll. He was hospitalized with a severe fever, sinus infection and aggravated ulcer.

When the Lunts had agreed to 'The Visit', their mercurial British director Peter Brook had altered the Durrenmatt drama to a tragic love story. Lynn's Claire was transformed from a dark, hardened troll to a vengeful glamorous lady with everything, who still demanded blood. Albeit brilliant, Brook's changes were terrifyingly immense and exhaustive for Alfred.

An understudy had quickly been found, but Miss Fontanne abhorred acting without Mr. Lunt. The theater suffered a substantial loss of its ticket sales. Obviously the public also hated a play without Alfred Lunt.

On May 5, 1958, after an extravagant renovation and amidst much fanfare, the Lunt-Fontanne Theater had opened on Broadway's 46th Street across from Helen Hayes' bijou. The theater, originally named after Shakespeare's Globe, was built in 1910. It was designed with a grand carriage entrance, a balcony above for patrons to view the theater elites' arrivals and a dome that could be opened in fair weather.

The Lunt-Fontanne had become the most luxurious playhouse on Broadway, seating an audience of fifteen hundred people, complete with the largest ceiling mural in New York. Helen Hayes commissioned an artist rendering of the Broadway street with her catch phrase as a gift to the Lunts: "To be on the street where you live!" was a popular song lyric from 'My Fair Lady', but it also ignited the fancy of avid Broadway patrons.

Opening night a red carpet was laid across the boulevard for theater arrivals. Among those attending the premiere were the Rockefellers, Bette Davis, Mary Martin, Paulette Goddard and Ginger Rogers. Orchids from Laurence Olivier graced Lynn's dressing table before the performance.

The following day another lifelong friend, Edna Ferber, telegraphed her congratulations for their dazzling reviews.

'The Visit' did not close as Alfred had feared, but because it was not a typical Lunt play, they were not sure if it was going to tour the following season. It did — a year later — and went on for another twenty weeks in seventeen cities across the country, breaking all box office records. In London to everyone's surprise, the play booked for eight weeks — and ran for twenty.

The Lunts returned to Broadway to sold-out audiences for two more weeks. They invited the Herrolds to stay with them in New York and attend a Saturday night performance.

In the dressing room Mr. Lunt, wrapped in an old gray robe, slipped into his thrift store costume and into character. Fascinated, Diana watched Jules expertly assist him, applying hair black and eyebrow pencil to his face, then grit and oil to his hair. He was obviously invaluable to Mr. Lunt, on and off the American and European stage.

"I have reserved seats tenth row, center, not too close, so as not to traumatize Diana!" Picking up a small silver pig setting among the many pots and jars on his dressing table, Alfred shook some of the salt shaker's contents over his shoulder. He responded to Diana's confused look. "For good luck. An ancient gift from an old friend." From that moment on, he refused to break out of his Schill character, reciting lines into the mirror, completely trusting Jules' skill.

"*Dah-h-h-ling*, you found our dressing room!" Lynn entered already in full dress and makeup, beckoning to her. "Don't you look elegant and all grown up this evening! Where are your grandparents?"

"They were so excited, they had to go to the bathroom." Diana giggled. "They'll be here soon."

"Come here, dear." Lynn chose a rose bud from one of her many bouquets and placed it behind Diana's ear. "There you are!" she hugged her tightly. "This is a big night for you. Don't let Alfred's death scene rattle you too much. It's our *shocker*!"

Lynn closely examined her eyes and lashes in her dressing mirror, "Did your tea linens arrive safely from Dublin? Jules and I selected what we hope is the perfect gift!"

"Oh, yes, thank you!" Diana answered with a chuckle. "Nana is convinced they were crocheted by an elderly German woman! I'll cherish them my whole life."

Lynn smiled knowingly and asked no questions as she accentuated her lips with more red liner.

There was a brief greeting when Louise and Virgel arrived, but due to time they were quickly escorted to their seats.

Inside the glamorous darkened theater the audience chattered convulsively as the curtain rose. However, the silence was deafening when Lunt — as Schill the grocer — limped onto the stage. Slouched in a tattered shirt, dirty suspenders and worn shoes, Alfred Lunt was The Master of wordless eloquence.

Awestruck, Diana watched as a strangely macabre play unfolded. Lynn entered, stunning, in red gown, cloak and umbrella. Her Claire had arrived in Güllen, a small German town in Europe, with an empty coffin, two American mobsters and two blind musicians. She was prepared to pay a small fortune to murder a man who years before had given her an illegitimate baby.

Diana's Genesee Depot friends were no longer recognizable. Instead, these characters Schill and Claire filled the dark, cavernous theater with a powerful, dramatic presence. Alfred always made the meticulously-planned appear spontaneous and Lynn brilliantly portrayed a woman whose coolness disguised voracity.

Painfully, Alfred's Schill began to understand Claire's entourage was racking up credit purchases, knowing the grocer would not be able to collect because he was to be killed.

In the final act, the terror of Schill's death was palpable as he ran for his life — howling — then whispering, "Is it to be now?"

Alfred at last fell to the ground with back to the audience, pounding his legs on the floorboards of the stage crying, "Oh, God! Oh, God!" as Schill was strangled — the very pitch and words his mother Hattie had spoken to him before she died.

In the play's last scene after having Schill killed, Lynn's intense voice commanded. "Uncover him." Then sighed, "Cover his face." As Claire, dressed in black mourning, followed the coffin and boarded the train, all who watched in the audience and on stage were mesmerized.

Silence filled the theater as the sound of a train pulled away with Claire and Schill's coffin aboard. Then, a collective breath was followed by thunderous applause.

Stunned, Diana remained riveted to her seat long after the clapping and many standing ovations.

In the dark, rimy air while the Herrolds leisurely strolled along the Manhattan boulevard toward the Lunt's East End brownstone, Diana was unusually quiet. Only a few blocks from the bright lights and marquees of the Theater District, they stopped at a small park, Gracie Square, amidst trees and brick buildings. Across the street, the Lunt's brownstone was a stately building, four stories high. Jules arrived shortly and began to prepare a late, light supper as they gathered around the kitchen table. Louise and Virgel enjoyed Manhattans and Diana, a Shirley Temple.

Jules loved the brownstone's state-of-the-art kitchen. It was a gift from 'Ladies Home Journal' for an exclusive article with photographs, to Alfred's tightfisted delight.

"How about some olives for Di?" Jules smiled, retrieving a jar from the pantry.

With his preparations completed for poached salmon, he gave them a brief tour. Alfred had again asked Clagg Wilson to assist in decorating the interior. With inexhaustible energy, the Lunts had haunted many antique shops for just the right objets d'art. The main entry opened to the foyer and kitchen. Huge white chrysanthemums, lilies and pompoms and a large flickering crystal candelabra complemented the boldly-painted second-floor drawing room walls of deep blue. Across the hall was Alfred's favorite, a Swedish dining room. The third floor housed the master bedroom in subdued 18th century yellows and warm grays inspired by Chaney's stage sets in 'I Know My Love' under Alfred's direction.

"Di, you're gonna love this!" Jules opened the fourth- floor guest room window to a breathtaking Hudson River view. "Hear that?" In the distant darkness she could hear a steam ship's funnel toot as it passed another ship.

"Where do you sleep, Jules?" Diana asked. He quickly pulled out a small roll-away from the closet and tucked it in a corner.

"Look here, Lu," he showed Louise a beautifully quilted fabric lining the interior of the closet. "Miss Fontanne lined all the closets herself."

That evening at the dinner table, Alfred as usual, obsessed maddeningly over his latest performance.

"Every time they kill Schill, I must bang my legs on the floorboards. It is the most uncomfortable position. I almost wish I hadn't started it, it's become too physically demanding." When tired, his 'walleye' drifted slightly to the outward corner of his left eye. "But the impact on our audience, Ahhh! they feel it with me!"

"I know I felt it with you, Mr. Lunt." Diana asked, gently, peering at his eye, "Are you all right?"

"No, Diana, I'm not all right. Two nights ago I had to invent a line for Schill to exit hurriedly from stage! My ulcer was acting up again instead of me," he complained. "They'll have to take me in a straightjacket before I'll go back to that hospital, though!"

Before dawn on Sunday morning, while everyone was still asleep, Jules carefully laid Schill's black suit flat in a tub of cold water. Because he and Alfred had found the thread-bare clothing in a London second-hand store, he refreshed the suit only once a week to keep it's authenticity. He gently wrapped it in large Turkish towels and squeezed out the excess moisture, then hung it on the back porch to air-dry.

By the time the Herrolds entered the dining room, now bright and sun-drenched, Jules was in the kitchen boiling eggs and taking his braided broiche out of the oven.

"Coffee anyone? Please have a seat at the table." Jules made apologies as he brought in a pot of steaming brew. "You must excuse the Lunts, they have slept in, exhausted from last night's performance."

He hurried back into the kitchen to arrange what he called his 'New York breakfast deli tray' for his guests consisting of lox, bagels, various cheeses and cold cuts.

"Wouldn't it be grand to make the twelve noon mass at St. Patrick's Cathedral?" he suggested.

"I hear Tiffany's is a short walk down the street," Louise poked Virgel in the ribs.

"Is that so, Toots!" Virg chuckled.

"Di and I just want to look around," Louise smiled dreamily.

"More coffee?" As Jules poured refills, he realized he was the only one who needed to change for their Manhattan outing. "I can be ready in a half-hour." He excused himself and returned to the kitchen to quickly clean up.

While the Herrolds sipped coffee at the dining room table, Louise admired the colorful reflections dancing from tiny glass fruits hanging from the chandelier.

"Everything is so classy and elegant here!" Louise sighed, chewing the last of her brioche. "Some people are just born with class. Like the Lunts or an English Lady, or a Duchess. But I don't need any class," she popped the last small bite into her mouth, "you have enough for both of us, Diana."

After mass, everyone walked the few blocks along Madison Avenue to the world premier jeweler. To Louise's heartbreak and Virgel's relief, Tiffany's the epitome of dignity, was closed on Sundays.

CHAPTER 50

"Dear God, Hank, how bad is it?" Not wanting to startle Louise, Virgel whispered into the phone. "What can we do?" He looked at his wife, who was still eating breakfast at their kitchen table.

Over the phone Hank's voice was desperate, "We've lost over a thousand furred-out mink in the last five hours. The vets determined it was food poisoning, clostridium botulinum, from frozen fish. Ranchers from all over the Northeast, including New York and Canada, have been arriving all night. Poor Bea has been up for more than twenty-four hours cooking and setting up cots with blankets and pillows down in the basement. We might lose everything, Virgel. Please pray for us."

Hank's news had come only weeks after the Herrolds' New York City visit, at the peak of pelting season when the minks' furs were thickest. Only days away from being sent to a fleshing company, Hank Luckert always chose the most humane but expensive way to pelt, an injection with nicotine, so the animals died instantly. Having already arranged a privately-chartered plane that year, he had planned to personally deliver his pelts to the New York Fur Auction House.

In Marinette, a dozen women rustled in and out of Bea's small kitchen. Every couple of hours a new shift of freezing men quickly grabbed a bite of food and hot coffee, before rushing back to the thousands of deathly-ill animals.

"Lu can help Bea with the cooking. I'll bring as much as we can spare from the freezer. How many mouths to feed?" Virgel asked.

"There's no telling. Right now at least sixty or more are outside working the ranch. About ten ranchers and their employees are inoculating the sick with the antitoxin. A half-dozen vets are flying in with more. They've promised to come within the next few hours. Each mink must be injected within twenty-four hours or they will all die. I gotta go, Virg," Hank sighed. "I need to get back out there right away."

"Expect us this afternoon," Virgel cradled the phone.

"What's happening?" Louise was becoming frantic.

"Get your nerve pills, Toots. Pack a suitcase full of warm clothes, especially scarves and gloves. We're in for a long night." Virgel dialed the phone number at Ten Chimneys.

Minutes later Alfred loudly knocked on Jules' apartment door. "Jules, the Herrolds are in trouble. Call Ben at home and tell him we need help to empty our freezer into the Buick immediately. And be sure to pack lots of coffee!"

When Alfred ran upstairs to pack a suitcase, Lynn insisted he not go. He had been suffering from severe stomach pains for several days. Reluctantly he agreed, realizing he could be of little help with the inoculations due to his poor eyesight.

It was bitter cold a half hour later as Alfred, Jules and Ben drove up to the Herrold house. They emptied the Buick, loading the Chevy with their frozen food and a large stainless-steel coffee urn while, in the cellar, the Herrolds collected more food, pillows and blankets. Covering her face with a wool scarf to breathe so her nose and throat wouldn't hurt, Diana climbed into the back seat of the Chevy with Jules and Louise.

"You want me to drive?" Ben offered.

"No thanks." Virgel climbed in behind the steering wheel. "I know the way like the back of my hand."

Standing beside the Chevy, Alfred waved farewell.

"Mr. Lunt...All this food!" Virgel choked with tears. "How can we thank you."

"Lynn and I send all our thoughts of strength to your brother-in-law in his desperate situation," Alfred responded compassionately.

With Alfred driving, the Buick awkwardly plowed through snowdrifts, making a path for the Herrolds' old Chevy to follow.

Once both vehicles were side-by-side on Depot Road, Ben asked, "Are you sure you'll be all right, Mr. Lunt?"

Alfred retorted, his warm breath forming clouds of white in the frozen air between them. "If I can't steer a car a few feet down Depot Road, then I better cash it in right now!"

Mr. Lunt slowly maneuvered the Buick back through Ten Chimneys' wooden gate, while Virgel steered the Chevy toward Marinette.

Hours later, Virgel drove past the frozen shores of Lake Michigan and turned into the driveway of the Luckert house. Long lines of cars were parked on both sides of the narrow drive. The Marinette community of neighbors, vets, other mink ranchers and even strangers had turned out in full force. Tired and cold, the volunteers walked past the Herrold car with heaping wheelbarrows of dead animals. Virgel parked near the barn and garages where huge mounds of carcasses lay. Jules and Diana began unloading their supplies from the car onto a wooden wagon.

"Calm down, Toots!" Virgel put his arm around his distraught wife as they walked with Ben in the snow toward the cages. "Hank needs us to save what's left of his ranch. You can't fall apart. We don't have time."

During the next six hours, Diana kept her cousin, Lynn, distracted from the mêlée outside the toddler's bedroom. Jules rolled up his white shirt sleeves and never left the kitchen while, in a long wool coat, snow boots and woolen babushka tied under her chin, Louise worked shoulder-to-shoulder with her father, Zabel. Through tears and prayer, she methodically injected row after row of mink, along with over a hundred other volunteers.

The next morning, Hank, with only a couple hours of sleep, trudged wearily outside to his pens. He watched, stricken, as trucks filed in and out to dispose of the thousands of dead animals for incineration. In more than twenty-five years of mink ranching, tragically, this was to be his only uninsured loss.

Back in the kitchen while Bea poured him another cup of coffee, Hank read "The Marinette" morning newspaper headlines: "Luckert Minkery Loses Over 4,000 Mink". With tears in his eyes, he lowered the paper and announced to his family. "Pa, Bea and I began the ranch with only two mink. Thank God this time we start with five hundred."

Chapter 51

"I'm not going to California!" Maxine was adamant.

"Well then, where do you think you're going to live?" Eileen retorted.

"I'll stay with grandma and grandpa on the farm," Maxine, Eileen's eldest, responded. Her mother didn't disagree. Knowing she would be safe with her parents, Eileen had no apprehension about leaving her high school-aged daughter behind. She got into her old gray Chevy and drove to the Herrold home in Southern Wisconsin.

When Diana was at her mother's apartment in Neenah, she was introduced to Jack, a truck driver of whom she and her sister had become very fond. The girls hoped he would marry their mother, not knowing he was already married. For more than a year-and-a-half the couple had kept their secret. But once it was exposed in the small farming community, Eileen found she could no longer deal with the gossip. Jack was a Catholic who could not leave his wife and family.

Finishing her lunch dishes, Louise heard the crunch of a car's tires turn into her stone drive. She looked out her kitchen window, shocked to see Eileen's car and quickly ran outside as it came to a gravelly stop.

"Bob owes me back child support and I'm going to get it!" Eileen announced, forcefully slamming the car door. "I'm going to California to find him and I'm taking Diana with me."

"How do you expect Bob to give you money if you throw him in jail? Besides, you don't need any money for Diana!" Louise shouted, barring her former daughter-in-law from the front door. "Virgel and I have always taken care of all her needs."

For years the Herrolds had worried this might happen. As grandparents, they knew they could not challenge Eileen's custody in court.

Crouched in the stairwell of her attic bedroom listening to her mother and grandmother argue on the front porch, Diana inched down the steps to watch the ensuing battle.

"Diana needs to get a suitcase together. We need to hurry," Eileen protested. "Will you please move so I can come in and help her."

"No you won't!" Louise shrieked. "You're not setting foot in this house!" She ran into the kitchen to call Virgel at work.

"Oh, I'm Diana's mother and I'm not welcome!" Eileen lashed vengefully. "But the stray Bob dragged in that you knocked yourself out for *is* welcome!"

"Who told you that?" Louise shot back spitefully.

"Oh, the ears of a child..." Diana's mother stepped inside the house and grabbed the young girl as she ran back up the stairs to hide. "Looks like you'll have to go to California without any clothes."

Struggling to free herself, Diana was pulled down the drive and into the car by her determined mother.

Hysterical, Louise peered out the window and screamed into the phone. "Hurry, Virgel, as fast as you can!" But she knew her resistance was to no avail.

Running outside with a caged parakeet, Diana's grandmother wept, "You call me collect so I know everything is okay." Nana handed her the bird cage through the moving car's open window. "Let me know where to send your clothes, all right sweetheart?" Too distraught to speak more, Louise grasped her hand for the last time as the car pulled away.

"Tell Virgel, Jules and the Lunts," Diana whimpered, "and all my friends goodbye for me."

Helpless, Louise watched the car disappear over the hill. She walked back to the house and collapsed, sobbing, on her front steps where Virgel found her and took her inside.

As Eileen's old Chevy sped through downtown Genessee Depot past the Pronold house with its glass-enclosed porch, none of the sisters inside noticed their young neighbor's desperate waves.

In the early evening hours, Eileen pulled into a truck stop near the interstate. It was suppertime and the parking lot was filled with big rigs. Inside, the small noisy diner was packed with hungry truckers and Jack was patiently waiting for them in a corner booth.

Above the diner's counter on a wall shelf Diana stared at a row of four-foot-tall dolls, identical, except for hair color. "Why don't you pick one out. I'd love to buy it for you." Jack smiled. "You can play with her while you travel."

Gratefully, she chose a doll with black hair. When the waitress gave Jack their bill, he whispered, "I'll take another one just like it."

"Oh, I don't need two dolls," Diana declared innocently, "but thank you anyway!"

Tears began to spill down Eileen's cheeks and she desperately grabbed his hand from across the table. "No one has ever treated me with such kindness. I'll always love you." It was the first time Diana had ever seen her mother cry. "We can start a new life together, Jack. Come with us."

"If you love each other so much, why are we going to California?" Diana could not understand these adults and their world. She pleaded, "Let's just stay here and you two can get married!"

Neither answered. Both were quiet with their own thoughts.

Jack finally spoke with tears in his eyes. "Don't make me choose, Eileen. I can't do that."

He walked them to their car, embraced Diana warmly as she held her new doll and kissed Eileen tenderly one last time.

Eileen's car pulled back onto the interstate as Jack sadly threw them a good-bye kiss and placed the second doll into his truck.

As her mother drove in the dark past the state line, Diana, seated in the backseat between the huge doll and bird cage, broke their silence. "What did Jack mean by choosing? And when are we going to pick up Maxine?"

To which her mother curtly replied, "That bird's never going to make it through the desert."

Her mother's inability to resolve her relationships with men would cause a lifelong disparaging attitude and a permanent indifference toward her two daughters.

Chapter 52

"Petey's thirsty, Mother." Diana peered at her blue and white parakeet through the grates of his cage. His heart was pounding erratically in his chest and his water dish was empty. "His towel's dry again, too."

They were all drooping in the hundred-degree Southwest desert heat. The car windows were rolled down and the torrid, sandy air whipped her long hair into her eyes. Frustrated, she pulled it back, twisted it into a knot and secured it in place with a pencil. "Bind up my hairs," she sighed, remembering what Miss Fontanne had taught her.

"There should be another gas station soon. I need to gas up this time." Eileen stopped every couple of hours on the interstate to rest and to keep the car's engine from overheating.

They pulled into a Phillips 66 just outside of Prescott, Arizona.

"There, Petey. You're good for another hundred miles." Diana cooed as she slid his filled water dish into place and set the cold, saturated muslin dish towel over his cage.

She asked excitedly, "Most everyone has a pool in California. Do you think we will?"

Eileen slid in behind the steering wheel.

"Who told you that?"

"The Chaplins."

Annoyed, Eileen revved the car's motor.

Although her mother made no promises, when they arrived in California, their apartment building did have a community pool and, to Diana's delight, she was able to swim every day that summer.

On rare occasions, her mother joined her at the pool to sunbathe in shorts. Deathly afraid of water and never desiring to learn how to swim, Eileen dangled her legs in the water at pool's edge.

One weekend, wearing her first bathing suit, an orange one-piece, Eileen decided to climb into the shallow end of the pool where she could touch bottom. Then, clasping the side of the pool, she shored up her courage and ventured into the deeper water. "I'm getting too...!" She whispered to herself. In panic, she lost her grasp and silently, without a ripple, her body dropped to the bottom of the pool.

Returning from a vending machine with a Coca-Cola in hand, Diana looked around. "Mom?" Her mother's towel was still on the lounge, so she knew she must be nearby.

Horrified, she saw a patch of orange under the water near the pool drain. With heart racing, Diana dove to the bottom, grabbed her mother's arms and tried to raise her lifeless body.

Clawing, Eileen opened her eyes and pulled Diana toward her. She clutched her daughter in a deadly embrace and wouldn't release her.

For a brief moment Diana thought they were both going to die. Then, kicking, she broke away and turned onto her back. In a burst of strength, with her legs and feet, she pushed Eileen's unconscious, weighted body up to the water's surface. Exhausted, she lunged for air herself, struggling to keep her mother's head above water.

Miraculously, their neighbor Mr. Thompson appeared and heaved Eileen out of the pool. After he administered a few tense minutes of CPR, Eileen coughed up a stomach full of chlorinated water. When she regained consciousness, she showed no emotion or panic as her daughter helped her walk unsteadily back to their apartment.

Diana, however, was very emotional. That evening in the kitchen she tried to break her mother's silence. "Mom, thank God I learned to swim at Ten Chimneys!"

"You and Mr. Thompson saved my life, whatever it's good for," Eileen responded, placing a plate of spaghetti on the table in front of her daughter.

"I put every ounce of life into saving you," Diana wept, staring at the food, unable to eat.

"I'm not afraid to die," Eileen stated as she sat down at the far end of the table.

"Well, I sure am — I'm going to go down fighting like a maniac!" Diana sobbed, "I know God has plans for you, Mother. You just can't see them." She leaped up from the table and stomped out of the apartment.

"Maybe it was my time and you interfered with His plans!" her mother shouted at her back. "Maybe He was supposed to take me just like He took Emma!"

During Eileen's first year of employment on the assembly-line at Hughes Aircraft Company in Fullerton, she had become best friends with Emma, a female co-worker. Their close friendship was cut short, however, when Emma tragically died of cancer. Emma was engaged to a guy named Ed who, within months after her death, began pestering Eileen for a date. He seemed to be a nice enough fellow, so the next Saturday after her near-drowning incident, she finally decided to accept his advances.

Six months later, Eileen and Ed were married unceremoniously in a nearby courthouse. When the newlyweds returned from a weekend honeymoon in Las Vegas, Ed moved into their small two-bedroom apartment with only his clothes.

"Diana, when this door is closed," Eileen pointed to her bedroom door, "it stays closed!" Even the smallest show of affection embarrassed her mother.

That summer, anxious to introduce her new husband to her family, Eileen planned a visit to Neenah. The Lemons who had recently moved to Southern California, invited Diana to join them on what was to become an annual road trip to Wisconsin. At summer's end, the newly weds were to pick Diana up at the Herrolds' home and return to California.

In Diana's attic bedroom, sadly, Louise packed the last of her granddaughter's new school clothes and placed a sealed letter on top before locking the suitcase.

Virgel yelled up the stairs, "Toots, they're pulling into the driveway. Where's Di?"

There was a knock at the Herrold front door and finally the two feuding women stood face-to-face.

"You might as well come in, stay for supper." Louise stated, resigned. "Di's down in The Depot at the Pronolds saying her goodbyes. She'll need to eat too before you leave."

Virgel broke the awkward silence by offering to make some highballs for Eileen and Ed. Joining him in the kitchen Ed stated he'd prefer scotch on the rocks.

After an hour or so, the Herrold's car pulled into the driveway and a few moments later Diana opened the back screen door. She said a quick hello to her mom and Ed and joined them all at the kitchen table for supper.

Ed quickly downed his fourth drink and complained, "God-damn it! Is it always this humid here in Wisconsin in the summer?" Then he glared at Diana. "Good of you to be here to welcome us when we arrived!"

Rising from the table, Louise spoke sternly, "Diana has a lot of friends in The Depot and Ten Chimneys she needed to call on. You'll soon have her all to yourself. You better take good care of her..."

Overcome with loss, she began to cry and went into her bedroom.

Diana followed, tearfully shutting the bedroom door after her. "Nana, I'll be back in just three months for the Holidays."

"I know, child." Louise hugged her tightly. "But that doesn't mean I won't miss you any less."

Later that night at a motel near the Wisconsin-Iowa border, Diana opened her grandmother's sealed envelope. Enclosed was a roundtrip plane ticket along with Nana's words of love and encouragement.

The road trip to California was uneventful and Diana soon settled into the new school year at Fullerton High School. Weeks later walking home from school one day, she noticed a white Lincoln convertible parked outside her apartment. Turning the latch key on the apartment door, she heard her mother with some other loud voices arguing inside. Eileen was never home from work before five-thirty p.m. so she listened for a moment.

"...what do you want me to say, Bob? My congratulations to you? I'm glad you're remarried? I'm happy you're so prosperous?"

When Diana walked in, the quarrelling stopped. In the living room sat a stranger, a handsome man in an expensive suit, resting his hand on a cane. Next to him on the sofa, an equally meticulously-dressed woman who got up and embraced the confused teen. "I'm Leona and delighted to finally meet you..."

Curtly, Eileen interrupted, "Diana, this is your father." Her mother's eyes were red, her face bloated and she was shaking. She had been crying a long time.

This was the moment, Diana thought, when the pressures brought to bear between her mother's deep resentment toward her father and her grandmother's unwavering prayer for reconciliation had arrived. She was surprised by her own lack of emotion. All she could say was, "Have I changed much?"

"Bob, come on over here," Leona motioned to him. "Don't pay any attention to your dad, Diana, his bark is worse than his bite. I should know, I was brave enough to marry the old coot." Bob didn't speak as his new wife continued. "You'll see how much fun he can be. We are very anxious for you to visit our home in San Diego. Your mother agrees, we'll have a wonderful time. He's quite famous in California, you know. We want to show you all the hotels and restaurants your dad built."

Bob finally spoke up, "I designed them but Leona's the professional interior decorator."

"Here's a couple gifts for you — and your mom, too. Hope you like them," Leona handed her two engraved Saks' boxes. Diana carefully parted the white tissue and thought longingly of Ten Chimneys and Lynn's gardening gloves. The gifts were instead a cashmere sweater for Diana and silk pajamas for both mother and daughter.

"Well, we really must go," Leona apologized. "A boring dinner commitment, you know."

Giving his daughter a quick uncomfortable hug, Bob handed her mother something at the door as they left.

"What the hell are we supposed to do with white silk PJ's?" Eileen groused as Diana followed her mother into the kitchen.

"They're too fine to use, just put them away." Diana tried to reassure her mother, "You know I see through all this, don't you?"

While Eileen nervously rinsed coffee mugs, a roll of bills accidentally fell to the floor. Without mention, she picked them up and stuffed them back into her pocket.

It soon became apparent on Friday afternoons through Sunday nights, Ed drank to excess. His drink of choice was vodka. Overwhelmed, Eileen chose to ignore the reality of his alcoholism for many months.

One Sunday afternoon Ed, drunk and agitated, was out of vodka and still wanting a drink. "I'm out of Smirnoff —" He tried to snuggle with her. "How about driving down to the corner liquor and getting me a bottle?"

Disgusted, Eileen shunned his grasp, "If you need it so bad, drive there yourself."

"Well, maybe I will! What the hell's wrong with you! You've been an ice cube all weekend!" He grabbed the car keys. "Maybe I'll go into the garage right now and drive that car down the street and into a lamp post. How'd you like to live with that? No, maybe I'll go into the garage right now and blow my brains out!" He slammed the door and, minutes later, instead of the sound of the car ignition, a shot rang out.

Imagining a horror in the garage neither wanted to confirm, Diana and her mother waited, terrified and motionless, on the living room sofa. Eventually Ed returned, uninjured, walked into the bedroom and passed out.

It was obvious Eileen's new husband resented her teenage daughter. Diana desperately hoped her stepfather faced his demons, affording her mother a secure and comfortable life, and found excuses to allow the couple time alone.

She began to baby sit for Mr. Thompson, which eventually became a full-time job caring for his three young children. Five days a week after school, she cooked dinner, fed, bathed and put them to bed, until he arrived home around ten p.m. Only then, with Ed soundly asleep, did Diana feel safe returning to the apartment. As a result, her grades began to slide.

Her weekends were spent with neighborhood friends at the apartment complex recreation facility and swimming in the community pool. On a Friday night at the popular Hillcrest Park Teen Center was where she met James.

"Would you like to go to the school dance and dinner at the Ancient Mariner next Saturday?" James was a senior honor student, dressed neatly in a madras shirt, tan pants and cordovan shoes. He also smelled of English Leather, making him all the more attractive.

When James passed by their hall lockers at school, most of the sophomore girls begged to be noticed by the upperclassman already accepted at Stanford.

Diana only hesitated a second. "Sure!" Not interested in her boy-crazy friends' dating obsessions, she preferred to focus on the thought of hot-buttered lobster at the landmark Newport Beach restaurant.

Chapter 53

To avoid introducing her date to a drunken Ed that weekend, Diana watched from her bedroom window, waiting for James to pull up at curbside.

When she ran down the sidewalk, however, Ed yelled from the open front door, slurring his words. "If you're not home by midnight, I'm going to bite your titty off!"

"Who is that?" James politely opened the passenger door as she slipped into his freshly-washed Corvette.

"My step father." Beyond humiliation, she couldn't look at her startled date.

Overlooking the Pacific Ocean, they had a wonderful time at dinner. Afterwards, their enjoyment was captured in their school dance pictures. James was a real gentleman — he asked no questions — but he never called again.

After another drunken episode a few months later, Ed was suddenly gone, along with his meager possessions.

Two weeks later, however, she came home from school to find everything in the apartment in shambles. Furniture was overturned, the lamps in the living room were shattered and kitchen dishes were broken with glass strewn everywhere on the floor. Diana's first thought was they had been robbed.

Eileen was not due home from work for two more hours, so she ran into the hallway to phone her mother at Hughes.

"You little bitch," Ed suddenly appeared, stinking drunk. "This is all your fault."

Dropping the phone, she fled into the small kitchen where he blocked her escape.

She tried to reason with him, "I was so happy when you and mother got married! I really wanted this to work for you," she pleaded. "Mom said you two needed privacy. That's why I stayed away..."

Ed backhanded her. "Why bother! She's frigid!" As she fell to the floor, he hissed back. "Your mother's an icy cunt."

Diana tried to get up, but he kicked her in the chest and she flew across the kitchen. Braced against the wall, unable to breathe, she struggled to get up.

Ed grabbed the bird cage and smashed it into the wall. Still on the floor, helpless, Diana stared at Petey's lifeless body only inches from her.

Menacingly, Ed stood over her and, with a closed fist, slugged her in the face.

"That's right. Your fucking bird is dead and I'm going to kill you, too, you little slut." He opened a kitchen drawer and pulled out a butcher knife.

"I'm not a slut!" She could taste the blood in her mouth.

Trying to defend herself, she kicked him. But he sliced her again — and again — on her legs.

Lunging toward her, he slipped on the blood and broken glass, sprawling onto the floor.

With great effort she got up, limped past him into the bathroom and locked the door.

"I know what you want when you go out on your dates!" He pounded on the door. "You want it now, don't you?"

Dazed, she stared into the bathroom mirror. Her right eye was swollen shut and he had broken her cheek.

Opening a tiny window above the tub, she tried in vain to climb out of the apartment. Weak, she kept slipping on her own blood and falling. Ed rammed the bathroom door.

Shaking, she crouched down behind the shower curtain, fervently praying to die rather than be raped by her stepfather.

The front door slammed. "You get out of here right now!" She heard her mother screaming in the living room.

In the silence that followed, she began to fear Ed had killed her mother and was again at the bathroom door, deciding what to do with her. Sobbing, she grabbed a wet washcloth and pressed it to her mouth to muffle her weeping. After what seemed an eternity, Eileen finally spoke through the locked bathroom door. "Diana, are you in there?"

An overpowering relief began to replace Diana's terror. "Is Ed there?"

"No, he's gone."

Finally, trembling, she crawled out of the tub.

Diana unlocked the bathroom door and peeked out. Eileen took one look at her and said, "We better get you to the hospital."

On the way to the emergency room, Diana secretly vowed, for her mother's sanity, not to repeat Ed's words.

At St. Jude's Hospital in Fullerton, Eileen requested their physician, Dr. Gordon McCoy. Within minutes, young Dr. McCoy arrived in the ER.

Alone with the doctor while Eileen filled out admitting papers, Diana murmured as he cleansed her cuts. "He killed my bird...I have no idea why Ed hates me so much."

"Who is Ed?" Dr. McCoy asked. When she hesitated, he pressed. "You can trust me, Diana. Shall I call a priest?"

Diana shook her head, "Oh, no, Mother would get upset!"

Dr. McCoy was a devout Catholic in his late thirties. A sensible father of many children, he was wise beyond his years. Compassionately, he stitched her wounds, "Is he a boyfriend?"

"My step father, Ed," she whispered. "He was drunk."

"Your mother needs to come in." He didn't say another word until Eileen entered.

"By law I must report this, Eileen. They will find your husband and put him in jail. When Ed has posted bail, he will surely kill her next time." Dr. McCoy knew Eileen was too unstable to challenge her husband and protect her daughter. "The best thing you can do for Diana is send her out of state immediately. Is there somewhere she can go?"

Diana spoke through stitched, swollen lips, "Genesee Depot."

CHAPTER 54

Battered but relieved, Diana boarded a train early the next morning with only her purse and a small suitcase.

The Herrolds were simply told Eileen was having trouble with Ed, she was filing for divorce and Diana was to stay with them awhile. They were not told of her injuries.

Ecstatic her granddaughter was finally coming home, Louise was busy arranging all of Diana's favorites: a pork roast dinner, a new Lanz flannel nightgown and the fragrance of fresh line-dried linens on her attic bed.

"Damn, Toots! The battery's dead!" Virgel blew warm air into his freezing, cupped hands as he entered the kitchen. "We had better call Jules and see if Ben can pick Di up at The Depot."

It was cold and snowing softly when Diana stepped off Genesee Depot's branch train from Milwaukee. She was in blind pain, both eyes mottled purple and one completely shut, as the porter lead her by the arm, careful not to touch her bandaged hand. With stitches inside her mouth and on her cheek, Diana's face was also badly swollen. Just sipping water through a straw had been agonizing. Weakened, she'd had little to eat the last few days.

Freezing and straining to see, she was expecting to be met by her grandparents. Instead, an enormous, elegant hand that could only belong to Alfred Lunt reached for hers.

Alfred's voice trembled, "Oh my God!" The porter gave him her suitcase. "Thank you very much. I'll take care of her now." He quickly removed his coat and carefully wrapped it around her shoulders. "I can't bear to see you in pain," he whispered, "Diana, who would do this dreadful cruelty!"

She turned her head away in shame and bit down on her swollen lip. A trickle of blood ran down her chin.

"Oh no! Just a moment, dear." Feverishly, Alfred collected some snow and wrapped it in his handkerchief, tenderly holding it to her mouth as they walked toward the waiting Buick.

In the muted whiteness only a few yards away Ben, alarmed, opened the car door quickly and helped her ease into the backseat.

Alfred climbed in next to her. "Everything's going to be fine." He again held the reddened hanky to her mouth. "Everything's going to be..." his voice cracked and his eyes began to mist.

As Diana placed her bandaged hand on his arm, he gently picked it up and kissed it to comfort her.

During the short drive, Alfred composed himself. "Genesee-quoi." He pronounced the word with a soft 'G' like the French. "My dear friend Edna Ferber once said Ten Chimneys has that certain 'Genesee-quoi'." He cleared his throat, "You know, when I was a little younger than you, I was desperately ill — truth is, I almost died. My intuitive, dearest mother brought me here to Genesee Depot. It was to be my beauty for ashes. Diana dear, remember this always. That's the miracle of Ten Chimneys. This pastoral countryside — this magnificent kettle moraine — will most assuredly heal you, just like it did me."

Ben cautiously maneuvered the car up Depot Road's icy hills, past Ten Chimneys' gate and slowly stopped in the Herrold drive.

Giddy with excitement, Virgel ran outside and opened the car door. In horror, he looked from Diana's broken face to Mr. Lunt. "Ed did this — didn't he? I knew there was something ..." Virgel could hardly contain his anger. "He drank too much and when he looked at you, we could see evil in his eye! It chilled us to the bone!"

Trembling, he helped Diana out of the car.

"Do you mind, Virgel, if I arrange to have Diana re-examined.

With your permission, I will place a call tomorrow morning to my personal physician Dr. Bigg in Chicago." Alfred sat back in the darkened interior of the car. "And perhaps Lynnie's gynecologist."

"Thank you, Mr. Lunt." Humbled, her grandfather helped her up their front porch steps.

As the black Buick backed out of the driveway, Louise's cries could be heard from inside the Herrold house.

Her grandparents lead her up the stairs to her bedroom. With anger in check and tears in his eyes, Virgel kissed the crown of her head. "My little Di," he whispered softly. She heard him walk heavily down the stairs with the weight of this unexpected tragedy.

Louise helped her into her nightgown and into bed. Still crying, she, too, placed a whisper-soft kiss on Diana's forehead and quietly stepped away.

Pale moonlight enveloped the pink room in her innocent colors of childhood and illuminated her beloved doll collection.

Downstairs, in their bedroom, she could hear her grandparents. Diana was comforted by their nightly ritual, when, for about an hour before they both fell asleep, they always shared their day. From her early childhood, their soft whispers had become her lullaby.

"Don't cry, Lu...Don't cry." In hushed tones, she could hear Virgel. "The Good Lord works in mysterious ways. I love you, Toots. Everything will be okay...Di's home now..."

Curled up under her old chenille bedspread, she watched the snow fall peacefully outside her dormer window and drifted to sleep, knowing at last she was safe.

Chapter 55

After thirty-three years, Pet Milk Company's 75,000 square-foot, red-brick landmark was to close its doors forever.

Devastated with the reality of having to leave their home and friends, Louise and Diana sat side by side at the kitchen table. Quietly they listened as Virgel persuaded them he was "one of the lucky fellas" because he had been offered the opportunity to transfer out of state. Many of the original local employees with retirement looming near had few career options during this nationwide effort by corporate management "to consolidate operations".

Virgel was convinced he must accept an assistant manager's promotion at Pet's dairy operations in Roanoke, Virginia. However, there was a problem. At the time for Diana to attend public school in Virginia, the Herrolds had to either own their home or be her legal guardians. Her grandfather planned to rent rather than settle immediately, so both restrictions applied. Virgel had already considered all of the choices.

While Louise drove him into North Prairie to work the next morning, Virgel stated with conviction. "Toots, you need to find a leasing agent and a private school in Roanoke for Di."

Over the phone, Mrs. Mary Hammond's voice was polite and articulate, with an educated Virginia drawl. "I am so sorry, Mrs. Herrold, Eaton is ovuh-extended this school year."

The Eaton College Preparatory was an expensive, private school with grades seven through twelve in Roanoke. To help pay her tuition, Virgel planned to use the seven-hundred-dollar compensation from the loss of his finger years ago. He had saved the money, knowing Diana would need it someday.

After a heart-wrenching explanation of her granddaughter's desperate predicament, Louise and Mrs. Hammond instantly bonded on the phone. Mary Hammond was a mother of four and, against her better judgment, she agreed to an interview.

With a week's recuperation, Diana accepted an invitation to tea at Ten Chimneys. Her interview at Eaton Preparatory was scheduled the following week.

She joined Jules in the kitchen before meeting Miss Fontanne and Helen Hayes at four o'clock. Covering most of her leg injuries in a wool pantsuit she couldn't, however, completely hide with facial make-up the black and blue around her eyes and the crimson traces on her cheek and hand from newly-removed stitches.

"I've never seen you this angry before! You must be calm, Jules." She tried to soothe her distraught godfather. "This isn't good for your heart."

"If I ever see that man —" Jules took a deep breath. "I'm sorry Di — but I swear — I'll kill him!"

Composing himself, with great care he placed Lynn's fine bone china on a tray and, together, he and his godchild proceeded down the stairs.

Miss Fontanne and Helen were seated in friendly discussion, as the two entered into the Ten Chimneys' garden room. Eyeing Diana's face, the seasoned actresses quickly masked their initial shock, stood up and hugged her warmly.

"My dear, your shoes are soaking wet! Take them off immediately before you catch your death." Lynn placed her woolen shawl over Diana's shoulders. "I must insist you borrow my snow shoes, there by the door."

As Diana slipped into the fur-lined zip-ups, Lynn arranged a third chair at the table for her. "There you are!"

Lynn poured Diana a cup of steaming hot tea, "I have something for you," she smiled sweetly. "This is not Dame Terry's miniature Shakespeare given to me at your age," she handed her young protégé a booklet, "but it has been a wonderful source of inspiration to me over the years."

Tearing, Diana placed Lynn's gift, 'Leaves of Gold' on the table. "Thank you so very much."

The kettle moraine's winter quietness filled their awkward silence as the women drank tea together.

Raising her cup to drink, Diana's hand shook. "I'm so sorry. I can't seem to get my confidence back... What has he done to me?"

"That dreadful man! But there is nothing lost, *dah-h-ling*, that can't be found if sought." Lynn lectured with affection.

"Every human being is born with tragedy, my dear." Helen smiled demurely. "One has to leave the nest, lose everything and fight for a loveliness of one's own making."

Diana looked Helen in the eye. "But what is to happen if Eaton doesn't accept me? They are very wealthy, educated people..."

"I've known you many years," Helen spoke sagely. "Money has nothing to do with it. Why, look at Lynn and I. We grew up dirt poor and uneducated. My dear, when I first met you, you had more tenacity than any little girl I'd ever met. You can do this, Diana."

"*Dah-h-ling*, you must stop wondering what everyone is thinking about you! Concentrate on what you think of them!" Lynn poured more tea. "I was exactly like you! So — when you arrive — have a look! See who's there! Besides, a little fear in the tum-tum keeps you at your best. Mr. Lunt and I always experience great apprehension before our first entrance. Wonderful things will happen for you, Diana. You'll see. Afterall, it's Eton —" Lynn waved her arms in a grand gesture, "— an English school!"

Jules reappeared from the kitchen, placing a petite cream puff on her dish. He whispered in her ear, "They'll love you Diana."

"There is a line I spoke in 'The Guardsman' I wish you to hold in your heart," Lynn took Diana's hand. "Repeat after me, dahling: I come in faith with hope high mounting."

Diana haltingly repeated, "I — come with hope — high..."

Lynn interrupted, "No, no, child — I come in *faith* with hope... Try it again!"

"I come in faith with hope high mounting." Diana beamed.

Lynn patted her hand fondly. "Memorize it, dahling. Make it your own, your robin's song."

Chapter 56

The eight-thirty a.m. bell rang and a flood of high school teenagers streamed up and down the stairs of the private, college preparatory school, a four-story renovated mansion on a large corner lot in an exclusive residential area of Roanoke, Virginia.

Through the window of the school office, Diana carefully observed the Eaton students as they hurried to class. Boys dressed in white shirts, ties, blazers and slacks jostled and teased each other; while girls in sweater sets, pleated-wool skirts and knee-highs watched the boys and giggled self-consciously. They all had one thing in common, brown penny loafers.

Another single bell rang and echoed down the halls. Everyone, now quiet, merged into one hallway and proceeded downstairs into the basement to begin their day prayerfully in Chapel.

"I come in faith with hope high mounting." Diana's face was still bruised as she and her grandparents entered Mrs. Hammond's private office.

From across the room at her desk, Mary Hammond's compassionate eyes met hers. Dressed in a tailored English tweed suit, Eaton's proprietor and head mistress was a petite woman with naturally-curly red hair.

Over the next few days after testing, she found Diana to be three years behind academically. However, Mary Hammond was the wife of a Presbyterian minister and a firm believer of unconditional love.

Taking Diana under wing, she met with the school's board to recommend admittance.

The board, all parents of children attending the elite private school, voted unanimously against Diana's acceptance. After heated discussions, ending only when Mary stated she would personally tutor Diana and take full responsibility, they reluctantly accepted a three-month probation.

A rental house was easily found, a red-brick Georgian two-story on Williamson Road, a respectable Northwest section of Roanoke, some distance from the influential Southwest area where Eaton school and its students resided.

The Herrolds soon realized Roanoke was steeped in centuries-old Southern traditions. A few days before Diana was to start school, Louise decided to take her shopping for an appropriate prep school wardrobe.

The two stood on the sidewalk outside Tiffany's in downtown Roanoke, staring at the many shoppers in hats, gloves and suits. Gazing into the jeweler's window, Louise spoke wistfully, "Do you think we're dressed classy enough to go inside, Di?"

"You're wondering what everyone is thinking about you!" Diana beamed. "Concentrate on what you think of them!"

With renewed spirit, the two ladies boldly walked through Tiffany's grand entrance, nodded to the uniformed guards and casually browsed up and down the aisles.

"May I try this on?" Diana admired an especially attractive platinum-setting diamond ring behind enclosed glass.

"Cert'nly, ma'am, you have ex'lent taste!" With a flourish the male associate behind the counter graciously unlocked the encasement and presented the ring to her on black velvet.

In awe Diana slipped on the one-carat signature Tiffany setting. "Thank you." With a gleeful smile she returned it to the distinguished gentleman.

That afternoon the California teen traded in her make-up for a well-scrubbed deportment, and her pantyhose for white socks and Bass Weejan penny loafers. Her long, blonde hair was cropped at the ears and she purchased several Pendleton wool cardigans and pleated skirts. A classic fox-collared camel coat completed her elite Eaton look.

Concerned she would not be welcomed because she didn't have the blue ribbons of affluent equestrian English riding competitions, black servants and the Southern mannerisms of "ma'am and sir", she was surprised when the privileged school's students immediately accepted her.

Her sweet, dear elders at Ten Chimneys were right, money had nothing to do with it.

That weekend there was to be a school dance following a hayride. The whole school was abuzz and dates had been arranged for weeks.

"Mah son — I know — would love to escort you." Mrs. Hammond announced in her lilting drawl. "His name is Dallas. He's a few years oldah than you. I'd like to ask your gran'parent's permission fuhst. If they agree, then it's up to you, Diana."

During a quick phone call, Louise instantly tittered her enthusiastic blessing.

"Thank you, Mrs. Hammond, for thinking about me but I'm making a lot of friends now, and really..." Diana paused, "I'm doing just fine."

Later over supper, however, Louise was indignant when she learned her granddaughter had turned down the head mistress's invitation. "You're saying no to the boss's son? Are you crazy, Diana? You dassent do that!"

Friday evening most of Eaton's student body, including Diana and a rather out of place hay wagon were waiting in front of the prestigious school. Mrs. Hammond's eldest son was late and Diana was beginning to wonder if he was going to show.

Something screeched around the corner.

"What's that noise?" Diana asked.

"Oh, Diana-dahlin', that's just Dallas!" Her new friend Sandra laughed as a red classic MG convertible halted at the curb.

A handsome Ivy League man in a navy blue cashmere pullover, khaki slacks and Weejan loafers jumped out of the small English sportster.

"How is't that whut takes most people three minutes, can take uthuhs twenty?" Mary Hammond smiled rigidly. In her Southern genteel manner, she admonished her son for delaying her students.

"Takes a long time to get this good lookin', Mothah!" He laughed and kissed her on the cheek.

Blushing, the proprietress clapped her hands, "Awright then! Hurruh along now. I'll meet you at the dance."

The students, in pairs, laughed and joked as they jumped into the truck's flat bed of hay.

Mrs. Hammond rolled down the window of her station wagon as she pulled up to the hay wagon. "Wouldn't it be fun to have a sing-along, puhhaps 'The Sweethaht of Sigma Chi' or 'The Red Red Robin'! Dallas, would you please chap'rone. You know the rules." Pleased, she rolled up her window and sped off.

Within five minutes of departure, the Eaton School hay ride turned into a heavy 'make-out' fest.

After a brief awkward silence, Dallas leaned in, playfully, whispering to Diana, "Ready to break out of the Suth'un conventions of Mothah's school yet?"

From his shirt pocket, he took a lighter and a pack of cigarettes, "Do you smoke?" He offered her a Marlboro.

"Yes," she lied.

Lighting her cigarette, his fingers almost touched her mouth, teasing her.

Dallas' younger brother Bill piped up from behind a bale of hay. "Mothah will nail you to huh chapel door when she finds out you've taken up cig'rettes..." In the darkness his Eaton steady Judy interrupted him with a kiss.

"Hell, no!" Dallas retorted. "Mothah won't be thinkin' about church. Not after she learns her chap'rone burned up her hayride!"

As Dallas lit up his cigarette, in the small flame Diana perceived a sagacious depth in his blue eyes. "And that bruthuh Bill, here, is fornicating in the hay. Shall we all sing 'When the Red Red Robin comes bob, bob, bobbin' along!'

Amidst the explosion of laughter, a rude voice interrupted them, "Keep it down, you two!"

The red embers of Dallas' cigarette brightened for a moment as he inhaled. "Her Eaton isn't Gilman, but it's damn close."

Diana had never met anyone like this preacher's son with his quick wit and irresistible Southern charm. She was instantly captivated.

After the dance that evening in the Herrold living room, the already-smitten couple talked for hours.

"Lu, do you know how late it is?" Virgel's voice drifted down the stairs. "Is that boy still here?"

"Sh-sh-sh!" Louise whispered loudly, "Leave them alone, Virgel."

The floorboards creaked in the upstairs hallway and moments later Virgel passed gas and flushed the toilet.

As Dallas muffled his laughter, Diana's face reddened.

"What's the matter with you, Virgel! I know they heard you — The whole damn neighborhood could hear," Lu scolded in hushed tones. "How could you embarrass us like that!"

"I don't care, Toots! He should be gone by now!" Virgel groused. "Are you gonna tell him or am I?"

Dallas nuzzled the back of Diana's neck. "I'm on my way, Mr. Herrold!" They both giggled. "Good night, Diana."

He leisurely strolled down the Herrold front walk and without opening the driver's door, jumped into his MG and sped away.

The next morning at breakfast Louise wasn't speaking to her husband. "Diana," she huffed, "would you tell your grandfather to pass the salt and pepper!"

Virgel promptly handed Louise the shakers, "That's a fine how-do-you-do. If a man can't get up in the middle of the night in his own house and pass gas, then..."

Louise exploded, "...He's the headmistresses' son, Virgel! They're *cultured*!"

"Cultured!" Virgel grumped. "What are they, buttermilk?"

Louise gave him a scathing look. "I wouldn't be a bit surprised if we never see him again! Thanks to you!"

"Well, he's not worth a grain of salt if he gets upset over something like that!" Virgel argued. "What's the matter with you, Lu? Don't you think rich people ever pass gas?"

The following weekend the lovestruck pair went on a double-date to Roanoke's Candlelight Club with Bill, an Eaton senior, and his date Judy. The club was well-known for catering to a young adult college crowd.

As the two young couples were seated for dinner, Bill whispered smugly, in his most charming Southern accent. "You know my fine bruthuh is head over heels, don't you?"

After dinner the club's band opened their first set with "The Peppermint Twist" and the two Eaton couples danced all night until the band ended the evening with "When I Fall In Love".

As the mild fall night drew to a close, the spirited roadster with its top down raced up the arduous Mill Mountain, stirring crimson leaves in its wake. Dallas parked his car at The Star City of the South's legendary landmark under Roanoke's brightly-lit one-hundred-foot star that could be seen for sixty miles. While Ray Charles' "I Can't Stop Loving You" drifted over the radio, Dallas finally kissed Diana.

The following Monday at school during lunch break, Judy pulled her new friend into the girls' lounge. "You know Dallas has cancer, don't you? He's in remission."

The bell for class rang — but Diana stood transfixed — unable to breathe. She rushed into Mrs. Hammond's office with tears in her eyes, "Is it true? Is he in remission?"

"Diana, please sit down. Dallas had evruh intention of telling you himself veruh soon." Mary Hammond sighed deeply and remained standing at her desk. "Dallas is much more than in remission — he has been cured! Last year we sent him to Johns Hopkins whuh he received eight months of radiation. His Hodgkin's treatment and cure has been published in a well-known medical periodical. Would you like to see it?" She began to rifle through some journals on a shelf.

"No." Diana shook her head. "That's not necessary."

"Our Dallas is a veruh brave young man and an inspiration to us all. By the way, the Rev'rund has asked if you would like to join our family in church this weekend?"

On Sunday morning Diana sat with Mary and her three handsome sons in their front-row pew of Roanoke's First Presbyterian Church. Mary's first born, a daughter, recently married and now with child living in Baltimore, was the only family member absent.

Enraptured, Diana listened as Dallas' father spoke from his pulpit. Like his eldest son, he was a statuesque, eloquent and soft-spoken Southern gentleman.

Immediately after school for three hours on Monday, Wednesday and Thursdays, Diana met with Mary Hammond to study.

"So —" Mrs. Hammond asked, "— when does Pipin realize he and Estella ah friends?"

"In the last paragraph of the story." Diana pondered for a moment, "Do you suppose that's the reason for Dickens' title, "'Great Expectations'"?"

"Why, uh, yes! With determination, Diana, you will have ouah H.G.A.!" Mary Hammond gushed.

"H.G.A.?" Diana asked.

"Highest Gradepoint Av'rage, of couhse!" Eaton's head mistress beamed. "By the way, what are your gran'parents doing for Easter?"

Triumphantly, on Easter Sunday, Louise handed a huge potted lily to Pearl, the Hammond's black middle-aged house servant and cook, as she opened the front entry door.

Soon after the Herrold's arrival, all were engaged in lively chatter in the living room over cocktails. Sitting on a loveseat, Dallas and Diana were absorbed only with each other.

Grandmother Hammond called her favorite grandchild to task. "Ah'm too old to beat 'roun' the bush, my loves. A small int'mate wedding, don't you think? Remembuh, my Kirk and your muthuh eloped!"

"We do have plans, grandmothah," Dallas affectionately hugged the elder Mrs. Hammond, "in a year and a half." Grandmother Hammond, seating herself in a winged chair, read the cover of a small book on a sidetable. "'How To Quit Smoking in Seven Days' —?" She haughtily sniffed, "Disgusting!" and opened the booklet, reading an inscription from her daughter-in-law, "We love you, Dallas Kirk, that's why ah want you to read this! Love, Muthuh and Billy...?"

Shocked, she stared at him, "Why em Ah always the last to know these things!"

"I'm not the only one, Grandmothah!" Dallas eyed his youngest brother, David, an Eaton freshman. "Maybe someone should do a report on it in mothah's literature class!"

"Dallas, don't you dare!" David whispered frantically.

"Leave it be, David!" Bill interrupted. "I didn't have time to get Dallas' birthday gift and mothah said she'd be happy to pick it out!"

Ignoring his brothers, Dallas helped Diana lock the clasp of a brilliant floating opal necklace, his Christmas present to her. "Oh, you smell good," he kissed her neck.

"Christian Dior." She smiled demurely. The perfume was another gift from her Southern beau.

Dallas eyed his gawking younger brothers. "Eat your hearts out, guys!"

Giggling, the couple disappeared into a hallway leading into the kitchen. Embarrassed, they reappeared only moments later.

"Dinnuh will be ready soon," Dallas announced. "But be forewarned, ouah Pearl always has trouble with the gravy for some reason."

Louise excused herself, peeked around the kitchen door, and called to Pearl. "Yoohoo! May I help you?"

"Oooh, Miz Herrold, you go along now. Enjoy your Easter Day!" Pearl had taken care of the Hammonds' home and family since their children were born.

"I make a pretty good turkey gravy," Louise boasted. "And this is your Easter Day too. The sooner we're done here, the sooner you get home to your own family."

The two ladies stood side by side at the stove, "Don know what's a matter wit dat boy!" Pearl was indignant as she vigorously mashed the potatoes. "His clothes smell a smoke. Tol his mama, I did." Pearl let out a deep, earthy laugh. "An I just caught them two love-birds smoochin in my kitchen!"

Louise tasted her gravy and while adding more salt, she admitted, "Virg and I hope they will marry."

"We all hope your gran'daughter marries my precious miracle boy," Pearl confided. "I held that chil' when he was no bigger than that turkey's leg! Yessah. All the Hammond babies never gived their mammy a moment a disrespect. The Rever'nt and Miz Mary haz been real good to ol Pearl."

"You're right, Pearl. Miracles happen," Louise declared. "You would never know to look at her now, but just last year Diana was almost killed. Her drunken step-father beat her to a pulp, I'll tell ya."

"Mmm Hmm..." Pearl understood. "God has a way a puttin' the hurtin' a this world together. He knows they help to heal theyselves. Somethin' that deep keeps a marriage strong when bad times come."

The dinner table was decorated with the eldest Hammond matriarch's heirloom sterling. On a cut-work white linen tablecloth, her crystal centerpiece bowl was filled with jonquils and tulips, surrounded by pastel-colored eggs.

Amidst applause, Pearl carried in a large platter of Virginia ham and Louise grandly followed with a fully-dressed turkey.

Encircling the table, everyone, including Pearl, held hands and bowed their heads.

The Reverend Hammond spoke in his most sincere congregational tenor. "Fahthah, we thank you for blessing ouah family and the Herrold family — particularly this year." He paused for a moment. "Each of us come before you, having recently struggled with a profound grief. Ouah families ah most grateful Dallas and Diana who came so close to death's door, were spared by Your loving hand..." The good Reverend cleared his throat, his words were becoming too personal, too emotional. "...You alone, Lord, undahstand and know the loss we were facing. Today we honuh Your Son's Life and thank you for His Resurrection. In Jesus' name we pray, Amen."

Each day, determined to make the Hammonds proud of her, Diana came home from school, studied until midnight, set her alarm for five a.m. and studied another hour or two before school. When she was tested again at the end of the school year, she had progressed three years.

That spring, Eaton's annual bus tour of Ivy League college campuses was to include a day and night of fun at Myrtle Beach. To earn her fare and avoid financial hardship for the Herrolds, Mrs. Hammond suggested Diana assist her after school as she taught Braille to a small class of deaf children.

Eaton's upperclassmen toured the universities of five Eastern and Southern states that year. Diana's favorites were Duke and William and Mary.

The day at Myrtle Beach was actually a well-planned surprise birthday party for Diana. To her delight, Mary Hammond arranged for her oldest son to join them. That evening as everyone stood around a bonfire in the sand, Dallas presented Diana with a sterling silver charm bracelet and each of her friends gave her a fitting charm.

Diana spent many pleasant summer week-ends with the Hammonds at their Claytor Lake vacation home. Across the water from the Hammond's cottage, boaters moored in a small cove at a lakeside chapel for Sunday services where the Reverend was often asked to preside.

At breakfast one morning Mary Hammond, Dallas and Diana were alone at the table. The young couple, already dressed in swimsuits, quickly finished their pancakes, anxious for their day to begin.

"Well, I bettuh gas up the boat," Dallas grinned. "The first time I taught Diana to ski, the boat ran out of gas before she did!" He kissed both women quickly and walked outside to the dock.

From the window Mary watched her son, reflecting on the virulent year before. Her Dallas was now in love and, with new vitality, planning his future. Even the ordinariness of him preparing the boat for a day of skiing, brought her a new-found joy.

While the morning sun played on the water around his silhouette, she spoke, "I've nevuh known anyone who enjoys the watuh as much as Dallas, until I met you." She gazed at the chapel on the far lake shore and smiled. "Wouldn't it be fitting if you and Dallas got married theah," she announced wistfully. "You could attend William and Mary, Diana, and the two of you could rent a lovely little apartment nearby. Theah, it's all planned!"

For Eaton's June Prom, Diana chose a yellow satin gown, knowing her corsage would be yellow roses, Dallas' favorite flower.

The day of Eaton's commencement ceremony, Mrs. Hammond spoke into the podium microphone and invited Diana to join her on stage. The Herrolds were sitting near the back of the large hall with Dallas because he had been a tad late in picking them up for the festivities. She walked past rows of students and their families and climbed the steps to the platform.

"Heah at Eaton, and personally speaking, it has been a joy and real inspiration to watch this young lady's progress and happiness." Mary Hammond swallowed her emotion and continued. "Her testing scores have risen faster and stronger than any other student. She has ovahcome obstacles most people nevuh have to face in their entire lives. Diana, your motivation and forgiving nature will live on at Eaton as a model of achievement..."

Applauding, the entire commencement audience rose to their feet. Clapping loudest, Louise and Virgel wiped tears of happiness from their cheeks. Mrs. Hammond handed Diana a white box wrapped with yellow ribbon and declared, "...For your charm bracelet."

Inside was a charm which read, 'Achievement Award Eaton School '62' with the initials 'H.G.A.' engraved on the back.

CHAPTER 57

Two weeks before she began her final year at Eaton, Diana and Dallas burst through the Herrolds' front door with good news to share. Mary Hammond followed them, as excited as the young couple. They planned to invite Louise and Virgel to a family weekend at the lake house for summer's end.

"She can't go back!" On the phone, frantic, Virgel couldn't look into his granddaughter's smiling face. "What about Ed?"

Diana grew numb with fear.

"That's taken care of!" Eileen screamed on the other end of the line. "You can't use that as an excuse. Besides, I haven't heard from Ed in almost two years! I'm told he died!" She abruptly hung up.

Virgel looked helplessly at Mary Hammond. "She's threatened to call the police on me — have me arrested for kidnapping — there's nothing I can do! I tried to reason with her, but she wouldn't hear of it." Crying, he embraced his granddaughter, "She's still your legal guardian, Di. I have no choice. You have to go, sweetheart."

Immediately Diana called her mother back.

Mrs. Hammond asked to speak with Eileen. "Your daughter has great potential. Dallas, the Rev'rund Hammond and I wish to provide her with a fine college education which she most assuredly deserves."

"Put Diana on the phone," Eileen responded. To her daughter she shrieked, "Who do you think you are! You have no right living around those people. They're not like us, Diana. You're going to be spoiled and impossible for me to live with. I'm still your mother and I have the last say-so!" Eileen slammed the phone on its cradle.

The next day, consigned to her mother's demands, Diana asked Virgel if she could take a four-day train back to California instead of a quick airline flight. She needed to collect her thoughts, intending to delay her return as long as possible.

Depressed, Eileen called a few days later and spoke with Virgel when Louise was at the grocery. "Maybe Diana should just forget I ever existed and she ever had a mother."

"No! Don't do that to her — you'll break her heart." Virgel quietly hung up the phone.

When Dallas brought Diana home that evening, Virgel, agonizing, decided not to tell his granddaughter about her mother's latest call.

Days later while Dallas and Diana spent their last hours together, he stopped to fill his car with gas enroute to the train station. Complaining of a headache, he went into the men's room. Returning, he eased back behind the steering wheel holding some aspirin and a paper cup filled with water.

"You can buy aspirin in there?" Diana was surprised.

"Yes, they sell everything in theah. They even sell condoms, Di," Dallas looked at her, meaningfully.

"What's a condom?" She asked innocently.

"You ah very naive, Diana. Just a minute." He ran back into the men's room and returned with a package. He blew one of two condoms up like a balloon and released it. They both laughed as it whizzed into the air and landed about a foot away on the pavement. "*That's* a condom!"

Then, soberly, he leaned over. "When you graduate, I'm going to drive to California and bring you back home," he whispered and kissed her tenderly. "I love you."

When they arrived at the station, the Hammonds, the Herrolds and many friends from Eaton including their parents, were gathered to give her a loving send-off.

Helping her onto the train, and wanting to be the last to say goodbye, Dallas walked with her down the narrow passageway to the small sleeping compartment.

Once inside, he gave her a wrapped present. "I'll write every day and we'll meet two or three times a year," he reassured her. "Promise me you'll take good care of yourself."

The train's final departure whistle ended their embrace. Diana asked, "Please, check on my grandparents every now and then?" They kissed once more, then tearfully parted. A priest, seated inside the dining car, witnessed Diana's tearful goodbyes and watched Dallas exit the train and forlornly walk back to his MG.

Through the moving train window, she waved goodbye to the happiness she'd made for herself in Roanoke and, as the train rounded a bend, Dallas, her grandparents and all her friends from Eaton School vanished.

Only then, she opened Dallas' gift. It was a small sterling silver mail box charm. With a tiny message folded tightly inside, he had written, "I Love You, Dallas".

Emotionally drained, Diana lit a cigarette and continued to smoke heavily in the privacy of her cabin for the next four days.

The following evening she finally ventured out into the dining car where the kindly priest asked permission to sit at her table. "You look as though you need a friend to talk to."

Tears immediately spilled over her eyes and down her cheeks. "Father, all my life it seems I've been saying goodbye to those I love most."

"Looks like we may be in for a long night." The priest asked, "Mind if I smoke?"

"Not at all," she replied.

Relieved, they both lit up cigarettes.

As the Super Chief passenger train made its way through the Great Plains and over the Rocky Mountains, they continued their heartfelt conversation.

"My child, soon, very soon you'll be of legal age to make your own decisions." The compassionate cleric looked to heaven. "Remember, in God's eyes an entire lifetime is only the blink of an eye."

Chapter 56

Physically exhausted with a high fever, Diana arrived on the West Coast four days' later. Diagnosed with pneumonia aggravated by excessive smoking, Dr. McCoy immediately placed her in St. Jude's Hospital. While she was hospitalized, Eileen stealthily routed through her purse and found the small package with one remaining condom. In confusion and sadness at their parting, the couple had paid little attention to its whereabouts.

"...So your son raped her!" Eileen hissed into the phone at Mary Hammond. "Diana is under eighteen!"

"There must be an explanation..." Mary pleaded.

Eileen didn't listen but, instead, rudely hung up the phone and from her empty apartment dialed another phone number.

"You must have known!" She shrieked at Louise. "All the while, screwing right under your nose! At least now she's back in California where she belongs!"

"These ah serious accusations, son. I must have the truth." In hushed tones, the Reverend questioned Dallas, holding the family Bible in his hand. "Do you sweah to God?"

"We are in love, Dad. We have been very affectionate toward one anothah and many times it was very difficult for me to abstain! But *that* — never happened!" Without wavering, Dallas placed his hand on the Bible and looked into the Reverend Hammond's eyes. "Trust me, fathah."

Dallas' car roared down Williamson Road and screeched into the Herrolds' driveway where Louise and Virgel met him at the front door.

"You know, I was young once and in love like you," Louise reasoned. "I don't prejudge. There was no one in this world more loving than me and my Virgel when we were dating. Isn't that right, Virg?"

Virgel gazed compassionately at this distressed young man standing on his front porch and invited him inside.

"Mr. and Mrs. Herrold, we nevah had intercourse," Dallas pleaded. "My parents and I think Diana should be spared this humiliation. As a family, we should all agree she is not to know about her mothah's accusations!"

When Virgel left the room, Louise quickly stacked every Bible she could find. "If you did, fine. If you didn't, fine. Just don't bull shit me, Dallas!"

Unwavering, he repeated his testimony.

With the Hammond's intervention, Diana, unaware, began her senior high school year in California. True to his promise, Dallas wrote and called often and provided her with plane tickets so they could spend holidays together in Virginia. With renewed confidence Diana began to regain her joy for life.

That year, her grandmother reunited with her in California. It was Louise's virgin flight on an airplane — nothing — even a lifelong fear of flying was going to keep her away from witnessing her granddaughter's crowning as Fullerton High School's Spring Queen. Upon arrival, she and Eileen were still not speaking. The Lemons who lived nearby in Anaheim, insisted their dear friend stay at their home.

In time for spring break that year, Lynn answered a letter from Diana with an invitation. She and Dallas were to visit that weekend in May at Ten Chimneys in celebration of both Diana's graduation and the Lunts' wedding anniversary.

Now eighteen and feeling very mature, Diana flew in from the West Coast and Dallas drove from Virginia for the occasion. Meeting in Milwaukee, the young couple drove the short distance together into Genesee Depot.

The day of their arrival in the late afternoon, the two strolled into Ten Chimneys' dense back orchards. There, in the privacy of nature, out of sight of Jules' eyre window, Dallas presented her with a two-carat platinum Tiffany setting engagement ring.

Under Alfred's flowering fruit trees of citrus, apple and plum, the couple made plans for their wedding and future together.

"What time is it?" Startled, Diana jumped up realizing it was almost sunset. "We have to get back!"

Dallas nuzzled and kissed her, easing her down into a haystack. "What bettuh place for our first romp," he chided, "than in Mr. Lunt's hay?"

"No one is ever late for dinner at Ten Chimneys!" She was panicking.

"I can see it now in the Genesee paper," Dallas teased. "Suth'un gentleman, son of a preachuhman, dies suddenly at Ten Chimneys — from sperm burst — !"

Giggling, she towed him reluctantly along the path past The Studio and down the steep hill toward the main house as he continued to spout, "Police searching Lunt field — for Confederate's testicles!"

Excited to share their news, the blissful pair entered the main house and approached the spiral stairs.

"...And, Alfred, promise me," they overheard Lynn lecturing her husband above them in the Flirtation Room. "You cannot swear or be cleverly lewd in any manner. Diana's intended is the son of a vicar!"

"Darling Lynnie, you know no one can resist me! I shall be charming and on my best behavior for Christ's sake ..."

Diana quickly placed her hand over Dallas' mouth to quell his laughter.

At dinner, graciously sharing their anniversary cake, the Lunts preened over their young lovebirds.

For her graduation, Alfred and Lynn gifted Diana with a tasteful set of single pearl earrings.

"Remember dah-h-ling," Lynn assured her, "you don't need a lot of fufu. With excellent quality, less is always best."

Visibly graying and now in bifocals, Jules brought in a tray of after dinner liqueurs. Lynn, ever-watchful, noticed Alfred was beginning to tire. "Mr. Lunt's had quite enough. Thank you, Jules."

Slowly, Alfred stood, taking his cue. "Diana, your Ten Chimneys' host is not what he used to be. As much as we would love to, I'm afraid Miss Fontanne and I are just too weary to keep company with you in the drawing room this evening." He politely assisted the bride of his youth out of her chair. "Please, make yourselves comfortable. Enjoy the brandy and the rest of the evening!"

With a flourish he opened the double doors, "Oh, by the way, tell me, will you and your betrothed be resting — I mean — spending the night — Ah, oh, the hell with it! Why don't you two just go shag in Noëllie's room!"

Amidst raucous laughter from the gentlemen, Lynn spoke up, "Goodnight, *dah-h-lings*! My charming husband — however pubescent — and I shall take our leave."

Lynn kissed Diana on the cheek and, arm-in-arm, theater's greatest acting couple slowly ascended the stairs.

Long after the Lunts had retired to their bedroom, laughter could be heard from the Ten Chimneys' kitchen.

"I'm out!" Dallas beamed. "For my reward, Jules, might I have some more of your dumplings!"

"Only if you promise to sleep on the couch in my apartment. And Diana, for you, Miss Hayes' room is already prepared."

Into the early morning hours Dallas, Diana and Jules played Canasta and ate seconds and thirds of her godfather's freshly baked maple syrup dumplings.

Although the Lunt's illustrious guests admired the grandeur of Ten Chimneys, those who visited often soon realized sitting around Jules' kitchen table always felt like coming home — Something Dallas was learning and Diana had always known.

Chapter 59

After graduation, Eileen didn't suggest college to her daughter, but instead scheduled an interview for her at Hughes Aircraft Company in Fullerton. A few months after she was hired, Diana was chosen from a host of nominees to represent the company. Among other duties, she was to conduct private tours for political and foreign visitors, organize employee events and arrange fundraisers. This commitment was to last a year.

Her image was circulated on the front cover of the Hughes Global News the following month. Even the eccentric Howard Hughes helicoptered in for a short visit of congratulations. Already becoming a recluse with long hair and nails, he spoke briefly, "I am confident you can do the job, Diana. I'm depending on you." To her this was a huge responsibility, and she took great pride and satisfaction in her new duties.

That summer, Dallas retired his MG and bought a new navy blue convertible Mustang for the coast-to-coast drive to bring Diana back with him to Roanoke.

Exhausted and not feeling well upon his arrival in California, he quickly tossed his luggage on the hotel room bed in Fullerton, not taking time to unpack. Eileen had refused to permit him to stay at their apartment.

He appeared at Diana's front door that evening in a new suit he'd bought the same afternoon, holding a bouquet of yellow roses from a local florist.

An hour later, while dining at an intimate Italian restaurant, he kissed her ringed finger.

Fatigued, with his throat inflamed, he rasped, "For two long years we've waited for this..." His temperature was climbing and, devastated, he finally conceded he was too ill to continue.

The next morning on her way to work Diana checked on him at his hotel. He was incoherent with fever. Alarmed, she immediately called Dr. McCoy's office. Diagnosed with a highly-contagious streptococcus, the doctor urged him to stay in bed for a week on antibiotics. The following evening after work, Diana arrived at the hotel with an armload of fluids.

"Let's just go home right now, Di." It was his fever talking. "Let's get out of here!"

"You can't drive, Dallas," she tried to calm him. "You're too sick!"

He pressed her in his soft, Southern voice. "If you love me, you'll come home with me!"

"Dallas, be reasonable. I have responsibilities," she rationalized. "A lot of people depend on me at work."

"You sound like Mothah," he was extremely agitated. "I can't bear the thought of having our children raised by nannies."

"Why are you over-reacting, Dallas?" she pleaded.

"I feel like hell — I have a business to run — to make matters worse — Mothah has planned a surprise reception for us," he entreated. "To arrive on time, we must leave tonight."

"What?" Diana was incredulous at his audacity. He hadn't even told her, let alone asked her about her schedule. "My work means nothing to you, does it?"

"I was remiss not to tell you at dinnuh last night." He raked his fingers through his hair, desperate.

"Dallas, you just don't understand," Diana pleaded. "I have a commitment to finish this year at Hughes."

"Look me in the eye and tell me you don't love me anymore, Diana," he was adamant. "That's the only way I'll leave."

Angry and hurt she was required to make such a quick unreasonable choice, Diana took the ring off her finger and handed it to him.

Shattered and flushed with fever, Dallas clasped the ring, grabbed his bag and walked to his car. A broken man, he slowly drove away without a glance.

Stunned, from the hotel's empty parking lot, Diana watched him disappear around the corner. For the first time in her life, she felt utterly alone. Why hadn't she explained her need for a few more months. Dallas and Mrs. Hammond would have understood.

With her mother and stepfather she had been conditioned to suppress her words and actions, and had become very good at hiding her feelings. Now — when it was too late — Diana admitted to herself even though Dallas was being unreasonable, she dearly loved this extraordinary man.

A few months passed and Dallas moved to Atlanta to start another business, a mail order catalog. The Country Store, with imports from all over the world, became quite prosperous. When visiting family in Roanoke, he called on Louise and Virgel, inquiring if Diana was happy.

Diana resolved to fly to Atlanta the following month to make amends.

On an early Saturday evening while she was in the throes of coordinating Disney character costumes and gifts for the children's portion of Hughes' annual Family Spring Celebration, the phone rang. It was a call from her grandmother. Diana immediately sensed dreadful news even before Louise spoke. "Something terrible has happened..."

"Is it Virgel — is he all right?"

"No, Diana." After a long pause, "It's Dallas."

"Dallas!" she gasped. "Is he hurt?"

"He drowned, darling." Louise caught her breath between sobs. "Searchers are still looking for his body."

"I won't believe it..." In the stunned silence, Diana prayed. "Please find him...walking along the shore..."

"You know he died loving you..." her grandmother moaned. Too grief-stricken for more words, both hung up the phone.

Sitting in her living room, indifferent to Diana's suffering, Eileen continued to watch Lawrence Welk on television. Staring ahead she said, "That's too bad," making no attempt to comfort her daughter.

An hour later Louise called back, she had learned Dallas had been scuba diving in a lake with an instructor and they had become separated. It took seven hours for the search team to find his bloated body. It appeared his oxygen hose had been severed.

"...Grandmother Hammond has collapsed," Louise wailed into the phone. "Mary is with her in the hospital right now ..."

Stricken, Diana numbly walked into the bathroom, turned on the shower full blast and stood under the water, sobbing.

Later that evening, barely composed, she placed a call to the Hammond home.

"The family feels Dallas would wish," his mother summoned her courage, "to be buried in the suit he bought in California."

The Reverend offered a round-trip plane ticket for the funeral, but sadly Diana was bedridden and too physically ill to attend.

Dallas' service ended when Mary Hammond graciously chose a perfect yellow rose from Diana's bouquet and placed it in her son's hand.

Chapter 60

Not aware how long her phone had been ringing at her bedside, Diana answered.

"*Dah-h-ling*! We are just devastated to hear of your loss!" Lynn's voice was hoarse with emotion. Over the wires, Diana could hear a commotion in the background. "Very well, then, Alfred!" There was a brief pause. "Diana dear, Mr. Lunt is anxious to talk with you."

Alfred grabbed the phone, "Oh my God, Diana! It's the cruelest of fate. I don't have tragedy's answers. But I do know this. You need to heal. You must come home to Ten Chimneys."

A week later, as Diana drove into the Ten Chimneys' courtyard, Jules was waiting at the front door. She ran to her godfather and clutched him tightly.

"Oh, Di." His hand trembled as he stroked her hair. "You're too young to be burdened with this grief." He could only weep with her and hug her tenderly for many minutes. "But you'll see. There will be joy in the morning."

"It's horrible not to have my grandparents in their home anymore," she wiped her tears. "I couldn't bear to drive by."

"We all miss the Herrolds, but Ten Chimneys is your family, too. I've prepared Miss Hayes' room for you," Jules smiled compassionately, "complete with a bouquet of lilacs arranged by Miss Fontanne. She'll be of great help to you, Di, always a model of reason. Go now, child, they're waiting on the back terrace."

In the late afternoon under the familiar lilac bush, Lynn, Alfred and Diana sat at tea together.

"We must have a heart-to-heart, Diana. You take milk and sugar, right?" Lynn's eyes, intensely alive, held hers. As she poured from the magnificent silver service, Diana was struck how Lynn's hands were as lovely as ever and her face was still translucent in the filtered sunlight.

Visibly in pain, Alfred grabbed his abdomen and winced.

"Alfred dear," Lynn urged, "you must go back in the house at once and lay down."

"Dreadfully sorry, Diana." Alfred took her hand and studied the scar left by her stepfather. He kissed it tenderly. "You and Lynnie enjoy your tea. Then come up to the library and we'll have a nice talk."

She watched him sadly as he walked slowly back into the house.

"My darling Alfred has been in pain most of his life." Lynn sipped her tea. "Did you know when he was a lad of twelve he suffered from acute peritonitis and scarlet fever?"

"I was told only bits and pieces," Diana confided.

"Poor thing was sent home from the hospital to die. At wit's end, his mother summoned the doctor and demanded his life be saved. Shocking as it may sound, the doctor literally removed Alfred's appendix and a kidney," Lynn glanced up at the cottage some distance away, "right there on Hattie's kitchen table."

Lynn took another long sip of tea. "*My* first love was Teddy Byrne. He was tall and slim — a handsome apprentice lawyer," she reminisced. "I remember him waiting for me, standing on the Battersea Bridge with a raincoat draped over his shoulders. Oh, he was a sight to behold! He stole my heart away." She paused and smiled. "He grew up in Walthamstow, my neighborhood, you know. We were to be married." She drifted back. "But he joined the Royal Navy and was killed in action. I thought I would die!" She added, "We think we'll never love again, dear, but we do."

Jules brought a tray of Lynn's English trifle — made especially for Diana's homecoming.

Serving her a small portion of the dessert, Lynn sighed. "I could never have reached the heights of an actress and, more importantly, a human being had I never loved so deeply and known great loss and grief as a young woman." Lynn patted her hand affectionately. "You will find this to be true in your life as well."

All was quiet in the house as she mounted the stairs and gently rapped on the library door.

"Is that you, Diana?" From behind the door, Alfred's voice was stronger now. "Come in, dear."

Holding a magnifying glass over some papers, he was seated at his desk when she entered.

"Are you feeling better, Mr. Lunt?" She started to sit on the couch.

"No. No. No. Please, pull up a chair next to me." Alfred lit a cigarette, settled back, striking a Prufrockian pose. "Some years ago my English Rose and I reached deep into our souls and realized to have a child would be an impossibility. By all accounts we have lived a staged existence. As a result the theater became our family. Excuse me..." Alfred politely turned his head and coughed repeatedly into a handkerchief. "The only remote balance of normalcy in our lives occurred when Miss Fontanne and I were here at Ten Chimneys."

Uneasy, Diana reached inside her purse for a cigarette. "May I join you?"

"My God! Not you, too, Diana! It's a damned dirty habit!" He lit her cigarette for her. "You must quit. Promise me you'll give it a go." Alfred coughed again, a deep glottis rattle. "It's too late for me."

He patted his mouth and forehead with his hanky. "It has been bothering me senseless and took a long time for me to see the light." He struggled, trying to place his hanky in his breast pocket. "Truth is, I was threatened by a little girl. But most of all, jealous of her simple love for life. My agonizing quest for perfection has robbed Miss Fontanne and I of that luxury. I'm grateful to have learned that truth from you."

His left eye drifted, giving him a strange, vulnerable appearance. "This tired old hack will always love you for that."

"When I was young," she quickly exhaled, "I just thought you didn't like me for some reason."

His body wracked with another coughing spell. Diana jumped up to get him some water but Alfred gently forced her back into her chair.

"Years ago," he fixed his good eye on her, "I promised Lynnie I would atone for behaving badly toward you. From my heart, Diana, can you forgive this silly old boy?"

Overwhelmed, Diana embraced the theater legend.

Together they descended the spiral stairs. "I'm damned pleased. I feel a hell-of-a-lot better now. Let's walk up to the gardens, shall we? I must show off my zucchinis and squash. We'll bring some back for Jules to prepare for dinner tonight."

Once outside, Mr. Lunt's voice grew strong and empathetic as they walked arm-in-arm up the grassy knoll, holding baskets. "I only met your Dallas once. Enough time to know he was an exceptionally fine young man full of hope and promise — and he was mad for you. We can only pray one day the pain is replaced by a beautiful memory. It's easy for me to say but, truth is, I don't know what I'd do if I lost my Lynnie... ."

Almost a half-century later in Diana's jewelry box lay a bracelet of many charms and a piece of hay — Dallas had become a beautiful memory.

Chapter 61

"Will you marry me, Mina?" Humbly, Jules spoke into the Ten Chimneys' kitchen telephone. "I know this isn't a good time, darling. It never seems to be a good time."

For several minutes he listened. In a hushed, persistent tone he uttered, "Yes, of course you're right. Call me later this evening when you have more time."

Crestfallen, he hung up the phone. For a moment he stood at the sink collecting himself, then struggled to swing open the kitchen's double windows, a joyous task that was becoming increasingly difficult.

Over the years Alfred's gentleman's farm had downsized to a lovable menagerie. In the 1940s Ten Chimneys had maintained two horses, four cows, homing pigeons, chickens and pigs. Their stables were now empty and Alfred had closed the creamery the year before. Their three Jerseys were not replaced. Ben continued to maintain the chickens in their coop. Weather permitting, Lynn still fed her squirrels. Walter the Toulouse goose, to Alfred's disgust, lived to a ripe old age until a large raccoon did him in.

Alfred remained constantly busy that spring, but Lynn, no longer interested in dressmaking, became idle and bored. She felt deprived of the stage and complained to Jules, "Alfred would rather be weeding than acting."

'The Finns' were now deceased, but Alfred excitedly re-fashioned

Hattie's cottage for his brother-in-law George Bugbee, now a recent widower nearing retirement.

Lynn entered the kitchen with a small ball of black fur bounding at her knee. Her many dachshunds were now replaced only by one standard poodle. The puppy, affectionately named Winnie, was devoted to the couple, and slept at the foot of their bed.

"It's time for Alfred's medicine, Jules." In spite of Lynn's slowed movements and frail, diminutive stature, her voice was still resonant and she kept impeccably groomed, carrying herself with grace and poise. "He must have a bite to eat with his prescriptions before Ben drives us to Carroll College. Will you bring them with our lunch tray, please?"

"Medicine is already on his tray, Miss Fontanne." Jules was competent as ever. "I pressed his tux and it's hanging in the dressing room for his speaking engagement. And the Mercedes is parked in the courtyard, when you're ready."

Ben, now gray at the temples, entered in his chauffeur's livery. "You know, Miss Fontanne, I've been thinking about our discussion the other day. My nephew Richard could spare a few hours a week to assist Jules. And my eyes aren't as good as they used to be. He could also help me with chauffeuring."

"What a fine idea!" She smiled, reminiscing. "Perhaps I could instruct Richard how to properly announce dinner from the top of the drawing room stairs — like Alfred used to do."

After she left the kitchen, Jules took off his glasses and rubbed his eyes, relieved dinner wasn't required that evening. He lifted a gardenia from its vase on the window sill, smelled its sweet fragrance, then placed it on Alfred's serving tray.

Later, seated at the table on the back terrace near her lilac bush, Lynn in a large sun hat, was reading from a magnificently bound Dickens volume.

Her deep, throaty voice floated into the spring afternoon as she read Pip's final narrative. *"I took her hand in mine and we went out of the ruined place..."* With a gnarled hand from advanced arthritis, she turned the page.

No longer able to read with cataracts covering his right eye and an eye patch over his errant left, Alfred listened intently with a wistful smile on his lips as she continued, *"...and, as the morning mists had risen long ago when I first left the forge, so, the evening mists were rising now, and in all the broad expanse of tranquil light they showed to me, I saw no shadow of another parting from her."*

In the wooded silence, Alfred's mind wandered. He chuckled to himself. A quickly-penned letter from Noël that Lynn had read to him that morning had reminded him expeditiously, "...when you serve white fish don't serve it on a white platter!" His dear friend could always amuse.

Jules was aging rapidly, too. Painfully he straightened himself while carrying the luncheon tray of poached eggs on toast onto the terrace.

"That bald sexton Time!" Alfred sighed. "Oh, Jules, what I would give for a glass of aquavit and pickled herring!"

Before he could reply, Jules slumped forward and the tray's contents shifted. The delicate dishes, food and gardenia he so lovingly prepared only moments before, clattered to the ground, broken and shattered.

"My God, Jules!" Alfred strained to see. "Are you all right?"

Ten Chimneys' major domo stumbled again, dropped the now-empty tray and fell to the ground in an unconscious diabetic coma.

Alfred pleaded helplessly, "Lynn, what happened?"

CHAPTER 62

The advent of the 1960s ushered in many new social dynamics. Amidst the drug-induced culture of a generation, America lost her innocence, her President was assassinated and her young men went to war.

Adding to the nation's unrest, Los Angeles erupted in hopelessness. Known as The Watts Riots, amongst the city's black poor and unemployed, thirty-four people died in the streets, over one thousand were injured, four thousand were arrested, six hundred buildings destroyed and property damages were tallied at thirty-five million dollars.

During that decade, the Lunts received a Presidential Medal of Freedom from Lyndon Johnson, along with Walt Disney, Helen Keller, John Steinbeck, T.S. Eliot, Carl Sandburg and twenty-eight other luminaries. In The White House East Room noonday ceremony, Alfred and Lynn remained in the background until President Johnson called all the recipients forward to thank them for "making man's life safer, leisure more delightful, standard of living higher and dignity more important. They are the creators, we are the beneficiaries."

After the ceremony, Lynn and Helen Keller began an acquaintance which, through regular correspondence, bloomed into a friendship that lasted until Keller's death.

In California, Diana accepted a promotion and remained at Hughes Aircraft, now a burgeoning military contractor.

One afternoon, having been asked to be a bridesmaid at a friend and co-worker's summer wedding, she found herself paired with a shy groomsman, a Cal State University student. She watched as David plucked green olives from a heaping platter of appetizers, placing them on his bread plate.

"Aren't you going to eat those?" she asked.

"Never touch them, help yourself."

After a couple glasses of wine he overcame his shyness and refused to allow their evening to end before she accepted a date.

A few weeks later, David apprehensively opened the front door of his family's home. With baited breath, Diana waited as he called into the house, "We're here!"

Behind chairs, under tables and around corners, within the immaculate and orderly home, little heads popped up everywhere. A petite, well-groomed woman in an apron entered the living room from the kitchen. "Come along now, children." David's mother Roberta May 'Chic' spoke in a purposeful low voice. "Let's meet your brother's new friend."

Immediately, they all assembled, lining up from shortest to tallest, like stair steps.

"You're out of place — move over two spots!" Damian pushed his younger brother Dan.

Doting oldest sister Diane, tried in vain to gather a brother's long hair into a rubber band, "Duane," she warned, "if you don't get your hair cut by next week when you turn eighteen, Dad will kick you out!"

"Consider yourself warned!" Damian mocked their father, 'The Commander'.

Diana was soon to learn David's family was an endearing mix of eleven siblings controlled by a strict, retired Naval Commander of Irish Catholic descent.

"This is Dennis, Diane, Don, Debbie, Douglas — Yes, Diana, they all start with a D!" David smiled. "Just like yours."

"I'll never remember all their names," she whispered into his ear.

"The Commander and Mom didn't practice birth control," he whispered back with a teasing grin.

In stark contrast to The Commander, it soon became obvious Chic was the soul of the family. This soft-spoken mother efficiently ran her household and guided her eleven children with quiet wisdom. Her selflessness evoked not only an uncommon devotion from her children, but from all who knew her, especially Diana.

As the Vietnam War escalated, so did the draft. Young men in college, married, or with children, were no longer deferred. Everyone of age was being called into service. Many young women quickly married before their men were shipped overseas. After David was drafted out of college, Diana accepted his proposal of marriage. Her husband-to-be was a good man and she loved his solid, moral upbringing. With little assistance, she saved and planned for a tasteful wedding.

Years later on The Commander's living room wall, eleven portraits of each child's First Holy Communion hung in succession. On the opposite wall, were only nine 8x10 senior pictures. A major rift had developed when two of the brothers refused to cut their hair after their eighteenth birthday.

Wanting complete acceptance from her in-laws, Diana, after many months of study converted to Catholicism. A beloved priest Father George from David's alma mater Servite High School, tutored her privately after work for three nights a week. It wasn't much of a stretch from her Wisconsin-Lutheran upbringing, she reasoned.

During David's seven-day leave between Basic Training and Advanced Infantry Training, they were married. Diana's wedding party included, among others, a best man, maid of honor, two groomsmen, a flower girl and two altar boys — all her new brothers and sisters. At Virgel's insistence, Diana reluctantly asked Bob to give her away.

Eileen's initial reaction was not to "set foot in a Catholic Church." However, she did reconsider and attended her daughter's wedding. But her disdain for Jack's mother church would always torment her.

After a quick four-day honeymoon along the California coast —

with barely enough time to unpack and open gifts — Diana drove her new husband to the bus depot and, alone, returned to their apartment.

She wasn't alone, though. This was a common sight all over the United States. Diana immediately immersed herself in business as usual at Hughes, which was fast expanding its defense contracts.

Within the month she received a note from Mary Hammond:

> *Kirk and I want to congratulate your young man. We know you will be a fine wife.*
> *Love, Mary*

Three months later without any warning, her young soldier reappeared at her front door. She was told they had four days to drive coast-to-coast and find a small one-bedroom, unfurnished apartment near the Officers' Candidate School at Ft. Belvoir, Virginia. Fatefully, again, she was asked to relinquish her responsibilities at Hughes without notice.

With only seventy-five dollars between them, the newlyweds drove straight through to Washington, D.C. Her mother-in-law had packed a generous bag of sandwiches, fruit and cookies. Without funds to rest in the evenings in a motel, they took eight-hour shifts driving. While one drove, the other slept in the back seat.

Daily, for six months with military precision at six p.m., along with the other candidates' wives, Diana greeted her husband in a communal, chaperoned reception room at the OCS. After, she walked across the darkened parking lot to her car and drove home to an empty apartment. On Sundays, couples were encouraged to worship together at the Army base chapel, followed by a social afterwards.

The Herrolds, now transferred to Pet Milk Company in Portsmouth, often drove up to join them for Sunday services. Louise always brought a large cooked meal, with plenty of leftovers intended for Diana to eat during the rest of the week.

To supplement David's small allotment, the new bride soon found a job at Woodward and Northrup Department Store in downtown

D.C. Now working while David was in OCS, her only extravagance was to fly home once to Ten Chimneys.

Alfred thought it was very gallant and admirable Diana had become the wife of a soon-to-be officer. Before she knew it, she was pinning gold bars on David's uniform while Louise, Virgel and David's eldest sister, Diane from California, gazed on proudly.

Soon after her husband's commission, Jules received a letter from Diana and exuberantly announced to the Lunts the couple had arrived safely in Germany. They settled in Nelligan, a small village near the Bavarian Alps. To her joy, Diana was to learn she was living near the birthplace of her Opa Zabel. Their landlord, Frau Blessing, immediately offered her upstairs apartment to the young couple. Herr Blessing, however, was distant at first, recalling decades before when American planes bombed his countryside and held him prisoner. When he learned of David's passion for woodworking, he generously shared his time and workshop, but he refused to learn English. Frau Blessing, a sweet mother of four young girls, taught Diana her love for homemaking. For almost three years the newlyweds' rented a two-bedroom apartment without the luxuries of telephone or television, but their front entrance faced a lovely cobblestone village and their backyard, the bountiful green of German farmland.

'Back in the World' — as U.S. servicemen said — a temporarily successful surgery allowed Alfred to be rid of his eye patch during a tribute dinner for he and Lynn at the Beverly Hilton in Los Angeles.

Waiting for a play, the Lunts were free to travel and visit with old friends: Joan Crawford in Naples, Florida; Noël and the Chaplins at Montreux on Lake Geneva, Switzerland; Alec Guinness in their Manhattan brownstone. At Helen Hayes' suggestion, they decided to sail on the Kungsholm on a world cruise to Africa, the Far East and Hawaii.

"Where are our new generation of geniuses? Our young scribes of Broadway?" Alfred confided to Jules. "I truly have no desire to return to theater!"

Lynn was to film 'Anastasia' for NBC-TV that year, but she, too, was never again to act on stage.

During those years many letters and small gifts were exchanged between Ten Chimneys and Germany. Lynn cheered with happiness when she read Diana was to have a baby that fall. Jules humbly accepted the honor of being the newborn's godfather by proxy.

Not wanting to worry Diana, Jules and the Lunts withheld news of her godfather's declining health.

Chapter 63

In sharp contrast to the rest of the nation, within the tranquility of Ten Chimney's kettle moraine, there were few changes. The Lunts no longer had to work to maintain the lifestyle they loved. They owed not a penny on their Ten Chimneys and the New York Eastside brownstone and Lynn had a fortune in expensive furs and jewelry.

Alfred always remained frugal. A lifetime of financially supporting Hattie and three half-siblings had conditioned him.

Late one afternoon, a Sears van pulled into the Lunt's courtyard delivering a new RCA television set.

To which Alfred bellowed, "I'll not have it in the drawing room. Perhaps discreetly in a corner somewhere...? In the *library*!"

From Ten Chimneys the Lunts watched the Emmy ceremony during which they both received a coveted statuette for Hallmark Hall of Fame's 'The Magnificent Yankee'.

"It was too long. It's way past our bedtime," Alfred remarked when a Milwaukee Sentinel reporter called afterwards. "But we are awfully damned pleased."

Jules brought in a bucket of champagne for a congratulatory toast to which Lynn humbly uttered, "Why all the fuss over me — I'm just a little actress!" To Lynn greatness was being championed by her Queen, the Kennedys, Helen Keller and moon-walking astronauts.

"But for tonight, my darling, you and I are the best actor and actress on television!" Alfred rubbed his hands gleefully. "I wish mother was alive to see this!"

"Oh, Alfred, I'm sure our Hattie didn't miss a thing," Lynn replied ruefully. Although she was aware Alfred was happiest off-stage, she missed it desperately.

Hattie Sederholm would have been immensely proud. Fourteen million television sets had watched their winning performance of 'Yankee' and at least another seven million watched the re-run a year later.

On the way upstairs to their bedroom that night Alfred spouted. "Perhaps I should reconsider the value of television after all!"

"But Alfred, I hate the way I look on that small screen," Lynn fretted.

In spite of maddening critical accolades of his plays, during those war-ravaged years Noël Coward's wit enjoyed a newfound television celebrity and, in addition to his Caribbean estate, he purchased a home in Les Avant, Switzerland.

One of Miss Fontanne's lifelong goals was realized that year at Coward's Firefly Hill estate in Jamaica when she finally met her Queen Mum Elizabeth for tea.

Alfred insisted Noël come to Ten Chimneys to recuperate from a gall bladder surgery the following year. During his stay, the Lunts and Jules plied him with delicious food, tender care and outrageous humor.

"To cheer you!" One morning Lynn, wearing only a frilly apron, brought a breakfast tray into his guest room. She placed it on his lap and kissed him on the forehead. As she walked out of the room, he erupted in painful laughter at the sight of her exposed bare bottom!

The Lunts became entertained daily with episodic TV: "'Upstairs, Downstairs" literati, "Police Woman" intrigue, and indulgently amusing "Hollywood Squares". Alfred and Lynn enjoyed listening for Paul Lynde's caustic one-liners which could stop the whole game show with laughter.

Paul Lynde was actually a fine stage and film actor, however he was best known for his appearances on the immensely popular prime-time television show.

One season the celebrity was doing live theater in Chicago when the Lunts decided to invite him to dinner at Ten Chimneys.

"Do you mind if I bring along a couple cast members?" Lynde had asked Mr. Lunt.

A few nights later music blared over loud laughter as Paul Lynde's stretch limousine, arriving an hour and a half late, turned slowly into Ten Chimneys' winding courtyard.

Disgruntled, having just checked on their ruined dinner, Alfred and Jules peered out from their open kitchen window at the reveling partiers. It was easily apparent they had all been drinking when the dozen or more bit players piled out of the limo. Lynde was the last passenger to disembark, dressed in a full-length caftan, with gold necklaces, medallions and hurrachi sandals.

"They look like they just rolled in from Zimbabwe!" Alfred crowed.

"Disgraceful!" Jules was stunned. "All he needs is a bone in his nose..." He sniffed the air, "What on earth is that pungent smell?"

"I think they call it pot, Jules, and I'm told it requires a lot of food." Alfred tossed his hardened brioche into the trash. "The chateaubriand is past well-done and the sauce béarnaise has dwindled to half-cup!"

"Can you imagine! Mr. Lynde coming to dinner in a nightgown!" Jules asked incredulous, "Can't he afford a proper suit?"

"Absolutely, he's been smart-assing his way to millions for years!" Alfred responded. "There are too many people, Jules. This is going to be a long night. Please, go at once and pull something — anything — from the freezer!"

Alfred quickly exited the house to the courtyard where Paul and his theater company were milling about.

Desmond, a well-groomed black man also in a caftan, obviously continuing a conversation that had been taking place in the limo, asked in a strong Afrikaan accent. "Mr. Lynde, true or false: Research indicates that Columbus liked to wear bloomers and long stockings."

"It's not easy to sign a crew up for six months, Desmond!" Paul

Lynde detonated his crocodile grin and sassy wriggle as the cast members exploded in laughter.

Alfred pulled Paul aside into the Ten Chimneys' foyer. "Mr. Lynde, when we spoke on the telephone," he whispered, exasperated, "I understood a couple cast members to mean only one or two more guests!"

"I'm truly sorry, Mr. Lunt." Paul was sincerely apologetic. "Perhaps we should all get back in the limo and return to Chicago. I know I'm outrageous and should probably have analysis. I don't know who Paul Lynde is or why he's even funny. I prefer it to be a mystery to me." Now utterly ashamed, Lynde admitted, "There are some things about myself I'm better off not knowing."

"I'll hear no more of that nonsense!" Miss Fontanne's voice resonated into the foyer as she descended the staircase. "Alfred *dah-hling*, I'll take care of this." The grand dame of stage had made her first entrance. Silent, Paul Lynde watched her respectfully, wondering how the drama would play out.

She marched outside into the courtyard and approached the limousine. Bending her head through the driver's window, Lynn stated, "And you, deah sir. You will not go unfed this evening. I insist you join us for dinner."

Then, she escorted the unruly entourage and their limo driver around the house to the back garden terrace. "We shall have a marvelous evening! Jules, please serve our delicious hors d'oeuvres..."

"...And you!" Alfred grabbed Paul's arm. "You're coming with me!" The two men walked inside the house and up the spiral stairs to the kitchen. "I understand you're an excellent chef, so let's get you to work."

When they reached the kitchen, Alfred mumbled to himself, handing him a chef's apron. "We don't want to stain your — whatever do you call this."

"Oh, why not!" Paul exploded, flashing his toothy oversized grin. He gazed drolly at the apron. " I'm already deemed the gay icon who made the world a safer place for sissies!" He threw his arms up in the air as Alfred wrapped the apron strings around him.

Together, the two peeled potatoes over the sink.

"Alfred, may I call you Alfred? According to the renowned French chef, Julia Child, how much is a pinch?" When Alfred raised his eyebrows, Paul burst out, "Just enough to turn her on!"

Ten Chimneys' host was laughing so hard he had to sit down. Recovered, he began to peel another potato at the sink. "How's the theater production? Will it be a long run?"

To which Paul quipped, "Oh, I can't even get three weeks off to have cosmetic surgery!"

A short time later, thinly slicing the last of the potatoes, Paul exclaimed. "I have waited thirty years to dine with the great Lunts at Ten Chimneys." He poured scalded milk over the potatoes. "And it's come to this!"

"Can you keep a secret? For more years than I care to remember, I refused to bring a television into this house," Alfred confided. "But of late, Lynnie and I find ourselves dining in the library on TV trays just to watch you on Hollywood Squares."

"Olivier's divine celestials watch my squirrely half-hour game show?" Lynde was genuinely impressed. "On TV trays? Wow! Hard to imagine!"

"I only speak right on!" Alfred exclaimed.

"That's bitchen, Mr. Lunt!" Paul slapped Alfred on the back.

"No," Alfred quipped, "that's Shakespeare, Mr. Lynde." Alfred slapped him on the back, harder. "And our secret!"

During dinner that evening at Ten Chimneys, Paul with his straight man Desmond, was at the top of his game.

"When Queen Elizabeth swings her umbrella behind her back, immediately something happens," Desmond posed the question. "What?"

"Lord Snowden doubles up in pain!" Paul wisecracked, to which Lynn dissolved in laughter.

Jules brought in fresh garden salads with hot rolls meant for the next day's breakfast that were wolfed down in minutes.

"Diamonds should not be kept with your family jewels." Desmond quizzed in between bites. "Why?"

"They're so cold!" Paul shivered as he delivered his licentious zinger.

To a very appreciative assemblage, Jules served a delicious sole a'ma tanta Marie with mushroom puree and scalloped potatoes. Seconds were immediately requested.

"Onasis gave Jackie five million in jewelry in their first year of marriage alone." Desmond inquired. "True or false?"

"And it didn't cure her headache?" Paul giggled.

After Jules fed Winnie in the kitchen, she pranced into the dining room to sit at Lynn's feet, panting and begging for food.

Alarmed, Lynn bent down and gave her pet a small bite. "Why are you panting, my dear?"

Lynde, still on a roll, replied, "Because she can't talk dirty!"

Amidst howling laughter, Jules served crème broule. Already anticipating their requests, he had an additional tray at the ready in the kitchen.

"Will a goose help warn you if there's an intruder on your property?" Desmond remarked.

Lynnie knew the answer. "There's no better way!"

"In 'Alice In Wonderland' who kept crying 'I'm late, I'm late!'" Paul Lynde pointed to Alfred.

Alfred jumped up and gleefully rubbed his hands together. "Alice! And her mother's sick about it!"

Although the lateness of the hour had exceeded the Lunt's normal bedtime, exhuberant laughter rang out until midnight. Jules was to admit later this dinner party was one of their most memorable at Ten Chimneys.

When it was time to go, exhausted, Desmond hoarsely asked as they climbed into the waiting limousine, "Paul, can you get an elephant drunk?"

Paul fell into the backseat, stretched himself and yawned. "Yes, Desmond, but he still won't go up to your apartment!"

Unlike their arrival, the acting troupe, sated and quiet, returned to Chicago in the black limousine as it sped down Depot Road through Genesee's sleeping village.

A year after his last appearance on Hollywood Squares, for which he won two Emmys at age fifty-five, Paul Lynde died of a heart attack in Beverly Hills. It was rumored during a homosexual encounter, the 'poppers' he had taken caused a seizure.

Paul Lynde is still best remembered as the ultimate, keen, bitchy performer on Hollywood Squares. Among his most ardent fans were President Truman, Lucille Ball, Sammy Davis Jr., Greta Garbo and, of course, Alfred Lunt and Lynn Fontanne.

CHAPTER 64

Seated at her solitaire table awaiting lunch, Lynn glanced across the drawing room at her husband. She folded her playing cards. With the years her fragile stature, still stunning and meticulous, had begun to shrink and bow with age.

Alfred had a melancholy, far-away look in his eye as he stood at the window, staring into the kettle moraine.

Grasping her cane, she rose and walked across the room, gently taking his hand in hers. "Alfred, come with me. Let's see where..."

"...At least you can see," Alfred interrupted.

They settled on a couch nearby. She picked up a large volume on the side table. The book parted, revealing an engraved sterling silver bookmark.

She began to read her favorite poem, "'The White Cliffs", written by her feminist friend, Alice Miller. Although her body was small and frail, her voice was still a commanding contralto. With vowels pure and perfect diction, she would often drop pitch dramatically at the end of lines.

"At last - at last - like the dawn of a calm, fair day
After a night of terror and storm, they came —
My young light-hearted countrymen, tall and gay,
Looking the world over in search of fun and fame,
Marching through London..."

"It's time for Mr. Lunt's medicine," a matronly woman standing in the doorway, interrupted her. Their temporary maid held a glass of grapefruit juice and two pills in her hand, not at all like the appetizing trays Jules used to present.

"Couldn't you wait another fifteen minutes?" Alfred was extremely agitated. "Can't you see I have the greatest actress in the world reading to me!" He downed the sour juice and pills with an awful expression, grabbing his throat. "What is this?" he gasped, commencing into a fit of coughing.

"Grapefruit juice, sir," the maid answered.

"He prefers to swallow his medication with plain water," Lynn coolly advised the woman.

When the maid left the room, Alfred mussed to Lynn, "If she doesn't bring water next time, there'll be hell to pay."

"Whether or nor Jules' stay in the hospital is long or short," Lynn implored, "Alfred, you must settle down!"

"Please, my English Rose, begin again," he sat up ramrod straight, eyed her sheepishly and cleared his throat.

"If you are now calm, may I continue?" His faithful wife resumed her reading,

"Marching through London to the beat of a boastful air
Seeing for the first time Piccadilly..."

Once again they were interrupted. This time by a strange noise coming from the driveway. It was unmistakably a car's motor and a sparkplug misfire.

"What-the-devil's going on down there?" Alfred carped. "My God, it sounds like a sewing machine."

He stood up slowly and, with Lynn holding his arm, groped his way to the Flirtation Room's French doors and parted the lace curtains. He could see only the movement of blurred colored shapes below.

A dark blue Volkswagen sputtered and stopped in Ten Chimneys' courtyard. Overburdened with suitcases, a collapsed baby tram and a set of golf clubs, the tiny auto was barely visible under a tarpaulin secured by ropes.

Standing together at the parted lace, Lynn exclaimed, "I believe it's Diana, Alfred. She's a few days early. Look at her handsome military officer and — Oh Alfred! — her adorable fair-haired lad. In liederhosen!" Lynn clapped her hands joyously. "She's returned with her family."

Down below a little flaxen-haired toddler scampered up a footpath. His father chased after him and they both disappeared behind a knoll.

"Just like his mum used to do." Lynn cooed. "Completely at home — heading for the pool."

Below in the courtyard, Diana looked up at Jules' apartment and kitchen windows, surprised they were closed on such a beautiful day.

At the laundry room door, she saw only a woman's silhouette through the screen. "Is that you, Lola?" Diana opened the door and hugged her. "Where's Jules?" Disappointed he was nowhere in sight, "Is he back in the garden?"

"Oh, Diana, look how you've grown all up!" Lola stepped back and admired her for a moment. "Your Jules is at Passavant Hospital."

"The hospital!" She was alarmed. "I just got a letter from him. He didn't say anything about being ill!"

"He's not expected to live through the winter..." Lola was saddened to tell her.

Diana started to panic. "Where's Mr. Lunt and Miss Fontanne?"

"We're upstairs, dear!" Lynn's throaty tenor floated down into the entry hall.

With the help of her walking cane, Miss Fontanne advanced unhurriedly down the spiral staircase. "That will be all, Lola!" In a stern voice, she dismissed the laundress abruptly, irritated at Lola's indiscretion.

She put her hand through Diana's arm. "My dear, don't pay any attention to Lola," her eyes were bright and piercing. "Alfred and I have the finest doctors caring for Jules. We have been assured by Dr. Bigg that with his new pacemaker he will fully recover." Lynn patted her hand and together they slowly proceeded up the spiral stairs.

At the landing, even with his eye patch, Alfred was strikingly handsome with a full head of white hair and perfect posture.

"Welcome home, Diana!" His voice was fluid and clear, and he smiled broadly.

"Look at you, my dear! You're an elegant lady now!" Lynn gushed, "Alfred, look at her! *Dah-h-ling*, we must get you in the theatre!"

The ladies finally approached the top of the stairs.

"In the theater, you know, stairs are the best to make love and to die on! In fact..." Alfred glanced at Lynn, knowingly, "...if I suddenly start choking, kindly direct me to those very steps!" Mildly amused, his devoted wife helped ease her husband into the love seat and sat beside him. "That's how I met my darling Lynnie, you know! I literally fell for her — all the way down the stairs! Well, they weren't a flight of stairs, only a few steps, actually!"

Alfred had told the story many times, but Diana always enjoyed the retelling. She noticed these past four years had aged her cherished friends considerably.

"Mr. Lunt, you look wonderful!" Diana gave him a hug, and sat down. "The finest-looking man I know!"

"Oh no, dear! Not at all! I can't read, garden or cook anymore. My Lynnie does everything for me. She pretends not to, but I know better." Alfred lamented, "I'm afraid I've become a dreadful old bore!"

The maid brought in a tray of coffee and store-bought cookies from Russell's and quickly left the room.

As Alfred sipped his coffee, he contorted his face in agony. "Gawd-awful! Coffee you could walk on!" Mr. Lunt had not lost his flair for the theatrical. "We miss Jules so much. Nothing has been the same. Utterly irreplaceable ..."

"How serious..." Diana's voice broke.

"...He refuses to even discuss retirement." Lynn finished. "Ten Chimneys has been home to our Jules his entire adult life. Just like Alfred and I, he wants to die here. We have a predicament."

Alfred spoke in his shrill nasal, "Truth is, Diana, he won't survive another freezing winter in Wisconsin. Doctor Bigg says it will kill him! He can hardly go up and down the stairs." He placed his large hand at the side of his face and shook his head. "Absolutely cannot imagine Ten Chimneys without our Jules. All our loved ones are dropping like flies." With tears in his eyes, he turned to his wife, "Whatever will we do, Lynnie?"

"You must calm down at once, Alfred dear. Jules is going to be just fine." Lynn reassured him. Then to Diana, "Alfred always goes on like this."

"But where will Jules live?" Alfred agonized.

"Are you aware he has a sister in Los Angeles?" Lynn looked at Diana.

"Los Angeles! What about Wilhelmina Cooper in New York," Diana stated. "He and Mina have loved each other their whole lives!"

"Who's Wilhelmina!" Lynn was shocked. "Alfred, have you ever heard Jules speak of her?"

Remorsefully, Alfred said nothing, recalling Jules' telephoned apologies to 'his Mina' in Ten Chimneys' kitchen at Christmas long ago. It was the night of the fire when Carol Channing was visiting. There were of course other times, but that particular moment kept pricking his conscience.

"Mommy? Where Mommy?" Diana's toddler whimpered as he climbed the spiral stairs and fell forward onto his face at her feet. Her husband, David, followed behind and picked up the tired child.

"And what may I ask is your name my fine lad?" Miss Fontanne looked into the cherubic face.

The child stopped crying and replied triumphantly. "Bube!"

"I beg your pardon?" Lynn was surprised.

"It means little boy in German." David beamed proudly. "From the day he was born, everyone where we lived in Germany called him Bube!"

"I'm so sorry," Diana placed her coffee cup on the table. "My mind's on Jules right now. I would love to stay all afternoon, but we have to go to the hospital."

Miss Fontanne patted Diana's hand lovingly, "We understand, dear."

Holding the toddler while assisting Mr. Lunt to stand, David walked with him, as they proceeded down the spiral stairs behind the ladies.

Lynn whispered in Diana's ear, "For just a moment, your young man reminded me of my Teddy in uniform."

"I have missed you all so much." Diana held Lynn's hand tightly. "It's wonderful to be home at Ten Chimneys again."

At the bottom of the stairs Alfred in vain tried to reach for her. With tears in her eyes Diana touched his arm and, immediately, he awkwardly grasped her hand and kissed it.

Chapter 65

"…But we've come all the way from Germany!" Diana pleaded to Milwaukee's Passavant Hospital's Supervisor of Nursing.

"Children are not permitted in Intensive Care," the head nurse repeated the hospital's rules.

"Call Security if you wish," Diana demanded in hushed tones. "Jules may die and before that happens, he is going to meet his god son!" With the child in her arms, she resolutely walked past the nurse and down the hall.

The nurse shook her head and brusquely marched back to her station.

Diana peeked around the open door into Jules' room. The sun, shining through the window, cast an ethereal light around him. He had grown a gray beard and was sitting up on the raised bed reading his daily devotional. Close by, a rosary lay on a side table.

"Am I dreaming?" he spoke sweetly, adjusting his glasses upright on his nose, "Di, is it really you?"

She placed her son in David's capable hands, side-stepped the hospital monitors and tubes, and gently hugged her godfather, whispering, "This is my husband, David."

"So good to finally meet you!" Jules beamed weakly. "How proud I am for what you've done for our country."

"You served, too, I am told." David shook his hand in greeting.

Jules saddened immediately, "Di — Everyone is saying I have to leave Ten Chimneys and go back to Los Angeles." Quickly, his words tumbled out, "It's my home, my life. Mr. Lunt is so very ill right now. I'm the only one who should take care of him. My church is there, my window..." he broke with emotion, "...my Wilhelmina... everything I love... so far away... ."

The head nurse popped her head through the doorway. "Fifteen minutes, please."

"We love you, Jules." Diana held his hand tightly. "You always have a home with us." Then, she lightened the moment. "Did you get my latest letter? While waiting for our car to arrive from Germany, we spent a wonderful week in Virginia visiting my grandparents." Diana noticed severe intravenous bruising on Jules' arm. "They send all their love to you," fighting back tears she continued, "and now we're on our way to California. I'll have you know, we drove four states out of our way to see you!"

Charily, David sat the toddler on Jules' hospital bed.

"Jules," Diana beamed, "this is your godson, Bube!"

Grabbing his chest, Jules tried not to laugh, "Bube? Oh, Di!"

"It means 'little boy' in German," David again explained.

With small chubby hands, the child took a picture of himself from his pocket and placed it in his godfather's hand.

"Why, thank you!" As tears jumped into his eyes, Jules brightened. He took a deep breath and declared with new resolve, "The Good Lord is not going to take me now."

Chapter 66

It is said a good servant anticipates everything and a perfect one has no life of his own. For thirty-five years Jules Johnson was the perfect servant. His life's calling was to serve and care for the Lunts and their guests around the world and at Ten Chimneys.

The prevailing ill mood of the Los Angeles neighborhood following the Watts Riots was a strange, unwelcoming world to Jules. Forced to retire, he did not want to be a bother to his sister Mabel or her family, but he was always on edge. During the day he was disquieted by loud boom-boxes on corners and a daily police presence. At night, he was awakened by probing spotlights of helicopters and ambulance sirens.

Wilhelmina called often, her love and concern were genuine. But because she was younger, it was important for her to continue working. After a quick stop at Ten Chimneys, he visited New York that year to plan their future. They decided to begin their life together when she could draw social security along with his pension.

Late one night in nearby Orange County, Diana was giving Bube some cold medicine in his bedroom when the doorbell rang. In robe and slippers, she squinted through the door's peep-hole but couldn't recognize the man standing outside on her front porch.

"Diana, it's your dad!" Bob bellowed through the night's stillness. His hair was grey and thinning with a dominant bald spot. All he carried was a suitcase and his ever-constant cane.

Over fresh-brewed coffee in the kitchen, her father loudly complained, reeking of liquor. "I'm a little down on my luck and need a place to stay for a couple weeks." Ignoring Diana's request to speak quieter, he continued, "Janet and I are calling it quits."

Diana was not surprised. Although she barely knew her, it was obvious his fourth wife was far too reserved to tolerate Bob's unconventional lifestyle.

"All I can offer is the living room couch." Diana was still saddened by the collapse of his marriage to Leona. The best memories she had with her dad revolved around the three year union he had with Leona, with whom she had developed a close friendship.

Reluctantly, she agreed to what she thought was a passing inconvenience which ultimately stretched out to six months. His incessant smoking, drinking and watching TV at all hours of the night took its toll on Diana's family and home. Eventually, David's frustration with Bob's lack of interest to look for employment or offer any financial contribution to the household, resulted in his insisting he leave. It would be years before Diana heard from her father again.

Each Friday afternoon Diana, now working, picked Jules up from Mabel's house for weekend visits. One particular Friday, as she drove back to Anaheim, the two chatted happily, looking forward to that evening. Helen Hayes was to guest on the Tonight Show.

They watched Johnny introduce Miss Hayes as the 'First Lady of Theater' for which Helen quickly corrected him, "No, Mr. Carson, Lynn Fontanne is the First Lady of Theater!"

"Miss Hayes is one of the most generous women I've met," Jules acknowledged, rinsing dessert dishes in the kitchen sink afterwards. "Mr. Lunt will be pleased."

The next morning, they drove back into Los Angeles for a full day of sightseeing. Their plans included lunch at the Brown Derby and a matinee of 'Lady Sings The Blues' at the Grauman's Chinese Theater.

While they lunched at the popular restaurant, Diana gazed at its many handsigned 8x10 celebrity portraits decorating its walls. Jules, however, stared out of the window at a hippie strolling across Hollywood Boulevard.

"Di, see that young lady? She's called a flower child, isn't she? Such a far away look, completely harmless." He added, "So different from Mabel's neighborhood where everyone's angry all the time."

"She's stoned, Jules."

"Whatever do you mean?"

"Remember your Paul Lynde incident?" She changed the subject. "Hmmm. Would you prefer a cobb salad? Did you know, Jules, the Derby's most famous recipe was named after the owner, Bob Cobb?"

He couldn't look away from the stranger outside on the street. "Such a fresh young girl — where are her parents?"

"Many of them leave home, you know." She sipped her iced tea. "They think they're changing the world, but actually they're running away from it."

Later when the movie ended and they exited Grauman's, Diana attempted to find Chaplin's hand prints in the courtyard. After talking with the theater manager, she and Jules were devastated to learn that during the McCarthy hearings, the cement block with his imprints, and those of his signature bowler hat and cane had "mysteriously disappeared"!

Diana decided to visit Charlie's studio on Sunset where he made his early films before he bought United Artists. As they strolled through the English village designed by Chaplin, a utopian semblance of the 'E Street' of his childhood with its clapboard cottages and brick chimneys, Jules was unresponsive.

"Please tell me what's bothering you, Jules." She tried to break his silence. "Was the movie too heartbreaking for you?"

"No, Di, it's not Lady Day. Although I pray God bless her dear soul," he anguished. "Ben wrote me and said Mr. Lunt's health is failing." He removed his glasses and dabbed his teary eyes with his ever-present hanky. "I know his every need before he does. I can still feel his pain even though he's two thousand miles away."

He eased himself into her small Opal GT. She helped him settle into the low seat, belting him securely.

"I wish you didn't have to fuss so much over me." He dabbed at his moist forehead. "How can you remain so calm driving in all this traffic?"

She didn't answer him as she drove south on the Santa Ana Freeway, but instead asked, "I'm worried about you, Jules. Do you sleep well at night?"

"Oh, Di, it's terrible growing old! I'm tired all the time. I miss my own bed and apartment at Ten Chimneys. You know right now I'm sharing a bedroom in Mabel's small house with her teenagers." He sighed, "That loud noise they call music, arguing all the time, friends and girlfriends, in and out at all hours..."

Diana was alarmed. It was unusual for her godfather to complain about anything. But she realized even one as private and longsuffering as he, had limits.

Within the month she helped him move with his few possessions into a modest rental in Compton, arranged by Mabel.

The following Friday when Diana arrived at his apartment, the parking lot and adjoining streets were filled with cars. She was forced to park several blocks away.

When she approached Jules apartment, a belligerent group of young blacks stood in front of her like a wall, forcing her to walk around them.

"Who the hell is that?" one shouted. "She got some nerve, comin' roun' here!"

At Jules' apartment building, a black woman blocked her passage up the front steps. Thinking perhaps she was a neighbor, Diana started to speak.

The young woman exploded with pent-up angst. "Get the fuck outta my face!"

As Diana continued to climb the steep steps, the girl spat at her, "What you want, white bitch?"

"Jules? Are you there?" She called from his open doorway. Had he left it ajar in anticipation of her arrival, she thought, or had he just been robbed.

Groans could be heard from the living room. Horrified, she ran in to find him barely conscious lying on the hot grate of a floor heater.

"Oh, dear God!" Diana prayed as she lifted him, sickened by the smell of burnt flesh. The imprint of the heater's grate was seared on his back and shoulders.

"Di, don't be frightened," he aroused momentarily. "Just get me some orange juice."

She realized he had not been assaulted and immediately helped him drink a glass of juice. While holding him, she dialed the '0' operator.

"I felt it coming on." Now conscious, he admitted to the paramedics who arrived in minutes, "but I didn't get to the kitchen in time."

The severity of his burns, however, placed him in intensive care for two weeks. Diana and Mabel both agreed he could no longer live by himself.

"I think it's my turn to take care of you now," Diana declared. "I would love nothing more than to have my own child influenced, as I was, by your goodness and wisdom."

"Perhaps I can feel useful again," he smiled at her, weakly.

Shortly after David's discharge from the Army, thanks to the G.I. Bill, Diana and her young family had moved into a new four-bedroom home in Anaheim. David graduated from CSUF and began attending law school. When he wasn't studying, he spent most of his time woodworking in the garage to supplement their income.

Family dinners became a savory happening as she began to prepare meals under Jules' apt tutelage. Even her picky eater Bube now looked forward to finishing the food on his plate. During the next few months, her godfather's recipe for contentment returned as he worked his culinary magic in Diana's kitchen.

As Jules mended, he began taking walks again and, like he had done at Ten Chimneys with the Herrolds, he became friends with his new California neighbors. Warm and loving to all who knew him, he was also embraced by Diana's in-laws and friends. When in good health, Jules was to have many fun, memorable times while he lived with his goddaughter in Southern California.

Ferdinand Johnson was a rare jewel who brought out the best in people and lives were enriched beyond words in his presence. No one knew this more than Alfred Lunt. After a lifetime of love and devotion, his world in Wisconsin would never again be the same without his trusted friend, Jules.

Chapter 67

One Saturday morning while Jules and Diana were making waffles in her kitchen, the phone rang.

Helen Hayes' voice chirped over the wires from her suite at the Universal Sheraton in Los Angeles. "I was just thinking, Diana dear." She was in the midst of filming an ongoing series 'The Snoop Sisters' for NBC. "Would you and Jules enjoy visiting my set to watch Mildred and I film?"

"Good morning!" The security at the Universal Studios entrance gate welcomed them a few days later.

"Miss Hayes is expecting us," Diana gushed.

"Her chauffeur is waiting to drive you to her sound stage." The guard smiled and tipped his hat as a black limousine quietly pulled up to curbside.

By ten a.m. Diana and Jules were seated behind a cameraman and, with fascination, watched Helen and her co-star Mildred Natwick during taping.

When the crew broke for lunch, Miss Hayes, Jules and Diana were driven to the studio's commissary.

As the three entered, exchanging pleasantries, suddenly Walter Matthau, leaping three steps at a time on stilt-like legs, sprinted up the commissary stairs to open the door for Helen. Stooped and bent over at the waist, he towered over Helen's diminutive frame during her introductions. Shaking Diana's and Jules' hands warmly, his elastic face broke into a crooked, silly grin. He departed just as quickly as he had arrived.

Once seated inside, Helen immediately picked up where the three had left off at Ten Chimneys. "I just spoke with Lynn and, as usual, she's keeping Alfred's spirits up."

Diana was trying very hard not to stare at Michael Landon, who was only a foot away at the next table.

Amused, Helen whispered, "You're not alone, Di."

"I didn't realize..." Embarrassed, Diana said no more.

"Michael is considered royalty around here." Helen confessed. "Everyone wants to be near him."

As the three studied their menus, Jules asked, "Miss Hayes, your birthday's coming up soon. Have you made any plans?"

"Well, let's see. James is in Hawaii filming his own series," Helen replied. James MacArthur, Helen and Charles' adopted son, was starring in Hawaii Five-O. "I usually don't make a fuss on my birthday. Perhaps Mildred and I will have a quiet little dinner."

When the waiter arrived, Helen ordered lunch. "I'll have corned beef hash with two poached eggs on the top, please." She patted Jules' hand lightly. "Of course it's no comparison to yours!"

"The same, please!" Jules and Diana piped up together.

When lunch was finished Helen instructed her driver to give her grateful friends a private tour of Universal Studios while she completed filming for the day. "I've planned some stops for you to meet more of my friends," throwing kisses, "Good bye my loves!" she disappeared in her trailer.

As a personal favor to Helen Hayes, they were welcomed by a bevy of stars on their sound stages: Loren Green, George Peppard, Telly Savalas and Raymond Burr.

A few days later on October 10th, Jules and Diana surprised Helen with a day at Disneyland to celebrate her birthday.

"I have wonderful news!" Diana beamed while they lunched at the Blue Bayou in Disney's French Quarter. "I'm pregnant!"

Seven months later after a difficult pregnancy and thirty hours of hard labor, Diana proudly held a ten-pound, round-faced, strawberry-blonde baby girl in her arms. "Welcome to the world, my Heather Lynn."

"Oh, Di, Miss Fontanne will be so pleased." In the hospital room, Jules gazed lovingly at mother and daughter.

"I now understand Mr. Coward's phrase, 'the peace of the changing sea'."

That year Jules suffered a massive heart attack.

In April, a few months later as he continued to recover, he and Diana were excitedly stuffing mushrooms and artichoke hearts in her kitchen while champagne chilled in an ice bucket. Both of her children were sleeping blissfully in their rooms as the two sat down to watch the televised Oscar ceremony. The Hollywood tradition was a five-hour marathon from red carpet arrival to Best Picture presentation.

They were thrilled, their dear friend Helen Hayes was to co-host the event.

Returning to America only once at Oona's insistence, Charlie Chaplin was to receive his Lifetime Achievement Oscar that evening of April 10, 1972.

"May our Mr. Chaplin never have a limp green bean!" Diana laughed as she and Jules clicked flutes and toasted to their Ten Chimneys' friend.

Charlie thought America had forgotten him. For twenty years, he had refused to allow any of his eighty-one films to circulate. But when Jack Lemmon handed the living legend his signature bowler hat and cane, Sir Charles Chaplin was greeted with the longest and most enthusiastic standing ovation in its history. It was the single, most emotionally-charged moment in the history of Oscar — and it shook the Dorothy Chandler Pavilion to its rafters.

"Who is that, mommy?" Little David stumbled into the living room, rubbing his eyes. He climbed into his mother's lap.

"A dear friend, Bube." She reached for a tissue. "Shall we call the Lunts?" Remembering the time difference, she added, "Perhaps in the morning."

Jules removed his glasses and, with his ever-present white handkerchief, wiped the tears from his eyes. "I'm sure they're as overwhelmed as we are."

While Charlie Chaplin wept, Diana and Jules wept with him — and so did the world.

Chapter 68

Alfred Lunt stared into the Flirtation Room's gilded mirror, scowling morosely. A photographer snapped the reflection. It was to be a haunting image.

Guests and elegant dinner parties were becoming more and more infrequent at Ten Chimneys. New staff came and went those years and, although Lynn's dementia continued to progress and Alfred was diagnosed with cancer, the Lunt's never lost their wit or charm.

Helen Hayes received a call one afternoon from Alfred. "I have to tell you, Helen. That I've been laughing for a good hour about you and me. I've been recalling some of our times in "Clarence". And laughing so hard that I have to call and tell you. You know I can't see anymore. I can't read or play cards or watch television. I'm tired of the radio programs and I can't stand rock music," he carped. "My cooking has gone to pot because I can't see the ingredients. But I've found out what I like to do — I just sit and remember."

Shortly after he talked with Helen, he placed another call. "Is that you, Sonny Boy? Brilliant! Just called to wish you a happy 70th, old man! May you have many more — but of course you will — stodgy old s.o.b.'s like us live forever — Me? — Oh, hell yes. We're expecting your visit in a few weeks. I'm already preparing menus. No excuses, Rabbit's Bottom!" But Alfred and Lynn knew they might never again see their dying friend. "So long for now! Oh, yes, Lynnie wants to know how an old bugger like you got the Queen Mum to accept your invitation to tea!"

"At least she answered my invitation, you old sot!" Noël thundered across the wires. "You and Lynn just showed up!"

Alfred responded tenderly, "Well, Noëllie, we've had a magnificent long run, haven't we, old friend?"

With tears in his voice, Noël signed off, "Goodnight, my darlings. I'll see you tomorrow."

Dispirited, Alfred hung up the phone and looked at Lynn solemnly. "I want to die here at Ten Chimneys. Promise me, Lynnie."

The irreverent Noël Coward was finally recognized as a national treasure, receiving British knighthood, an honorary doctorate, a Tony, and an Oscar, all within three years of his death. His friends called it 'Dad's Renaissance' — he called it 'Holy Week'.

In early spring Sir Noël Coward died of a stroke, ending a fifty-two-year friendship with the Lunts. Noël was buried overlooking Blue Harbor at his Firefly Hill in Jamaica, 'A Talent to Amuse' etched on his tombstone. He was also memorialized in Westminster Abbey's hallowed Poets' Corner.

That year Diana passed through Genesee Depot on her way to Virginia to care for her ailing grandfather. With her two small children in tow, she spent a brief but heartfelt afternoon with the Lunts.

At her departure, Lynn kissed her on the cheek. "Remember us to your grandparents with all our love."

"Damned unfortunate you must say goodbye so soon." Alfred reached for her hand. "Lynnie was just reading to me the other day. Do you know 'Goodbye' began as an Old English phrase 'God be with you'? Repeated over the years, it simply became 'goodbye'. Goodbye, my Diana."

Weeping, they hugged tightly. Brokenhearted, she realized she might never again see that dear craggy, wonderful face, nor those deep, expressive eyes — mirrors to the most tender heart she'd ever known.

Upon arriving in Virginia, she was to face another heartbreak. Louise was in complete denial of Virgel's impending death of leukemia, refusing to see him in the Portsmouth Naval Hospital.

"I'm worried for Nana." Diana confessed to Virgel in his hospital room. "Shall I call my father?"

"Oh, God, no!" He answered forcefully. "Toots doesn't need that aggravation right now!" Then quietly he stated, "Remember, Di, you don't owe your father anything. I don't want to stay here. Please — bring me home."

"The marrow is gone and the bone so brittle," the doctor warned, "even if he turns the wrong way, his bones will break."

As he wished, she cleared Virgel's release through a reluctant doctor and took her grandfather home.

That night Louise called for a prayer vigil in the Herrold living room.

"Brother Virgel," the pastor began to shake and shout, "I rebuke that spirit of infirmity!"

While Virgel lay prone in his recliner, Louise drew her red living room drapes as the pastor and church elders encircled him to pray for a miracle. Surely, Diana thought, God would intervene for her saintly grandfather without such display if it were in His Plan.

Sometime later over coffee and cake in the kitchen, the pastor suggested, "Sister Louise, your granddaughter looks like she could use some prayer."

Surprised, but saying nothing, Diana was led to the Herrold's back porch where, fervently, the pastor and his elders spoke in tongues, placing their hands on her head and Bibles on her shoulders.

"Make, Lord Jesus, Your Perfect Will manifest in her life and give her peace." Their voices mounted with each new prayer as they pounded on her shoulders — until she fell to her knees.

Diana began to pray for God's quick intervention — to no avail.

After wishing the pastor and elders a goodnight, she gazed lovingly at her grandmother, now fast asleep on the couch while the light from the television continued to flicker across the room.

She tucked her fragile grandfather in his bed and, exhausted, fell asleep on a nearby rollaway. She awoke to a thump — and found Virgel lying on the floor. Not wanting to disturb her, he had tried to walk to the bathroom by himself and fallen.

"Don't wake your Nana, Di," he rasped in the darkness.

Just before sunrise an ambulance departed from the Herrold's driveway. Virgel had broken his back and was taken to the hospital. He died there two days later at midnight with his granddaughter and wife at his side.

In those early morning moments after Virgel's death in the hospital room's silence, brokenhearted, Diana realized her real father had died. Her grandfather's words would always remain with her. He was right, she didn't owe her birth father anything.

Diana studied her grandmother, her normal vitreous nature now peaceful, and marveled that God's perfect will was accomplished.

CHAPTER 69

"Of course they all know me at this hospital. I left my liver on the second floor, my aorta on the fourth floor, my kidneys on the fifth floor." Admitted to Northwestern Memorial Hospital in Chicago with advanced prostate cancer, Alfred placed a call to Carol Channing from his hospital bed. "I feel right at home," he proclaimed grandly. "After all, most of me is here!"

A day later, however, he secretly complained to Lynn after another excruciatingly painful episode with an X-ray machine. "Dreadful, slippery, cold... and they twist you into the most terrible, painful positions — over and over again. If they had photographed me, I bet I spelled J-E-S-U-S."

"I refuse the indignity of a third surgery in one week!" she whispered vehemently to Dr. Bigg.

That afternoon, quietly, Alfred slipped into a coma. For hours his wife of fifty-five years held her unconscious husband's hand.

Lynn left only at the doctor's insistence, determined to return early the next day.

In the wee hours of the next morning — at 4:05 a.m. on August 3rd, 1977, Alfred Lunt died — not at his beloved Ten Chimneys — but alone in a hospital room.

As the sun's rays greeted Genesee Depot over the kettle moraine that morning, the post office raised its flag at half-mast.

In California, unaware, Diana and Jules were humming along to the Carpenter's 'Top of the World' tune on her kitchen radio. While she attempted to duplicate the master chef's famous Ten Chimneys' cream puffs, Jules watched intently. She whipped the thin batter, poured it into the oiled cast-iron molds and placed it into the hot oven.

While she held her breath and watched her batter rise through the oven window, the familiar clatter of mail dropped into the front porch box, distracting her.

"I'll get it!" Jules left the kitchen, padded through the living room and opened the front screen door.

The mailman was startled for only a moment, "Oh it's you, Jules. The misses and I really enjoyed your muffins."

"How's your sciatica today, Harry?" Jules was concerned. "Have you tried witchhazel?"

Back in the kitchen the radio's music was interrupted by a news flash. "Theater giant Alfred Lunt dead at age eighty-two. Details at eleven."

Shaken — her mind reeling — Diana collapsed in a chair.

"It smells like it's time to take your cream puffs out of the oven, Di." Jules returned with the mail, excitedly holding up Ten Chimneys' familiar stationery. Setting the mail down, he put on a mitt, opened the oven and eyed what were supposed to be his signature seven-inch airy-light cream puffs.

"Don't worry, Di," he laughed, studying the flattened pastry as he lifted the heavy cast-iron out of the oven. "Alfred could never do it quite the same either." He finally looked at Diana. "What's wrong... ?"

"Jules, please sit down," Diana whispered, broken. "Mr. Lunt died this morning."

Ashen-faced, Jules stared at the envelope, addressed in Miss Fontanne's pen and sat down. Slowly he opened the letter. His retirement check, ignored, floated onto the kitchen floor. Every first of the month without fail Jules received a check from the Lunts. Without comment, Diana picked it up and placed it on the table.

Unfolding the letter, he began to read silently. His eyes slowly drank in the print, "Oh, my God, this letter is from Mr. Lunt, Di."

Through tears, he cleared his throat, then read aloud. "Dear Jules, Miss Fontanne and I wanted to express to you our sincere gratitude for your devotion all those years. I'm sorry I didn't tell you often enough, Jules. I never closed an eye all last night thinking about it..."

Jules wept. "...I am aware of your personal sacrifice. I was conscious of that, especially on holidays. Your private life was put aside for Ten Chimneys and it did not go unnoticed."

He couldn't continue, handing the letter to Diana.

Quietly, she struggled to find her voice, "Lynnie's writing this, as I will probably have to resort to signing an 'X' to its conclusion. I am as ever idling around while Lynn is whoopsing around the house in preparation for her dinner parties. What I wouldn't give to get outside at daybreak to pull weeds and hoe my gardens, prune my fruit trees or just to cook with you again, Jules. We had an awfully grand time, didn't we? My only real pleasure now, and I can almost die of pride, is that my Lynnie still takes a fancy to me. Enclosed is a note to Di." She barely whispered, "A million kisses to all, Alfred."

That Friday August 5, 1977, all Broadway theaters dimmed their lights at 7:59 p.m. At precisely the same time for one full minute, the Lunt-Fontanne marquee lit up the night sky. It was to be the world's salutation to a theater god.

On Saturday morning as was his custom, Jules was already up making breakfast. Diana in her bathrobe hurried into the kitchen, steadying her toddler on her hip. Forced to raise her voice above a grinding noise coming from the garage, she spoke, "I have Miss Fontanne on the phone in my bedroom." Wiping tears from her eyes, she placed the child in her youth chair and handed her a small glass of juice. "It's going to be impossible for us to fly back, Jules. O'Hare and Milwaukee airports are closed due to storms. Miss Fontanne would like to speak with you. Are you up to it?"

Weak from a sleepless night, he shuffled down the hallway to the bedroom telephone where Miss Fontanne was waiting on the line.

He could hear Winnie barking in the background when he picked up the phone.

"...can't console Winnie," Lynn grieved. "She trots, night and day, in and out of all the rooms, looking for our poor Alfred..."

A few moments later, Jules returned to the kitchen. "Could we please go to St. Mary's?"

Diana opened the back door and called into the noisy garage. "David, could you take a break?" Her husband turned off the lathe where he was turning a piece of orangewood into a candlestick and took off his goggles. "Could you watch the kids for a while? Jules and I have something very important to do."

Kneeling in front of the flickering candles at St. Mary's side altar, oblivious to confessions and a florist decorating for a wedding, Diana and Jules both lit prayer candles.

"Goodbye, my dear friend," she choked back her grief and repeated Alfred's last words to her, "God be with you."

"I should have been there..." Jules' voice broke in sadness. "He died alone, Di."

Alfred Lunt was buried at Forest Home in Milwaukee, a huge cemetery covering many blocks in the middle of the city. The torrential weather was as dramatic as Alfred. The ferocious winds, accompanied by lightning and thunder, poured rain so heavy his eighty-nine-year-old wife attended the chapel service, but was persuaded not to accompany the casket to the muddy burial site.

At Ten Chimneys a few hours later, a small group of friends gathered.

Fighting the inclement weather, Laurence Olivier finished an out-of-state matinee and rushed to Ten Chimneys, where, for two hours he comforted Lynn before returning to his eight o'clock evening performance.

Wearing her black mantilla, her shoulders stooped in age, Lynn Fontanne raised her glass. "To Alfred." She was very calm. "I will soon join him."

CHAPTER 70

After Alfred Lunt's death, Jules' health deteriorated rapidly. Diana noticed his light afternoon naps stretching into several hours and his appetite diminishing.

At one point when he was bedridden with a serious flu, he closed his eyes, "Miss Fontanne's friend Helen Keller once said 'anything done in the name of beauty is never lost.' I don't know how, but Ten Chimneys needs to be opened — to the public — somehow —"

He squeezed her hand tightly. "Di, remember when you were a child how I used to remind you to close the gates at Ten Chimneys? When Miss Fontanne dies, I can't bear the thought of the gates being closed forever. Mr. Bugbee can't possibly keep it up and this reality has been weighing heavy on my poor old worn-out heart."

His face was pallid with emotion. "I know this is asking a lot, but could you see to it my casket passes down Ten Chimneys' driveway, around the courtyard and into St. Paul's? Something simple in Genesee, Di," he smiled wistfully. "And Mina will take care of me in New York."

A few months later, while Jules and Diana walked through Eisenhower Park on a warm California day, they stopped and fed the ducks remnants from their picnic lunch. Feeling much better, he declared to his goddaughter, "I have a strongest desire to visit my Mina."

"Oh, Jules. Can't you wait a little longer? You're still unsteady and weak." She tried to talk him out of it — to no avail.

Apprehensively, she drove him to Los Angeles International Airport the next day.

"Call me when you get settled." She kissed him goodbye. From the terminal window she watched while he boarded the plane. He looked so fragile, she thought, but he turned around and smiled broadly at her with a sparkle in his eye.

A few days' later, Louise was softly weeping when she called. "Do you know that Jules died?"

"What?" Diana was stunned. "That can't be true! He's visiting with Wilhelmina in New York!"

"Ben couldn't find your phone number, so he called me. He must have called the Waukesha Sentinel with the news."

Louise read her dear friend's obituary,

"Ferdinand 'Jules' Johnson a beloved friend of many in The Depot during the thirty-five years he worked for the Lunts, passed away May 19, 1978, in New York at age sixty-nine."

Perhaps, Diana hoped, the last vestige of Jules was buried in a plot he and Wilhelmina had purchased years before together. She realized that, after a lifetime of sharing Jules, Wilhelmina finally had him to herself. And to end his life with his beloved Mina was exactly what Jules wanted. It was for him, a final blessing.

But for Diana, too many questions were to remain unanswered. Yes, she thought, Ferdinand 'Jules' Johnson was a most private man. But why so secretive about his lifelong relationship with Wilhelmina? Even to those closest to him, little was known of his ancestry or birth, and he had died with few possessions.

Throughout his life at Ten Chimneys he had shown tolerance to those who were at times haughty and impatient, but she knew his restraint never implied he was devoid of substance or intellect.

Like the Lunts, Diana acknowledged Jules had no peers. He had lived his life as a gentleman with honor, discretion and refinement.

Chapter 71

On a large corner table that Virgel had built, Louise set three 8x10 framed pictures: one of Diana and her children; one of her young Virgel with his wavy black hair; and one forty-year-old black and white portrait of the Lunts that read, "To our good neighbor Mrs. Herrold, Lynn Fontanne and Alfred Lunt."

In her California two-bedroom apartment the furniture and knickknacks from the time she and Virgel were first married were lovingly unpacked and placed exactly as they were in her Genesee Depot home. She now slept in Diana's canopy bed. Even Virgel's tools had not been left behind.

"Hello? Can you unlock the screen door, Nana?" Returning with more shelving paper and two KFC dinners, Diana peeked over a large grocery bag as her grandmother opened the door. After opening several cupboards she found two plates.

As the two women devoured their chicken, Louise joked. "The best part of moving to California, besides being near you, is how fresh and organized the kitchen becomes. And the worst thing about moving, especially so far away, is no one will come to my funeral!"

"What about me and Rhea? Are we no one?" Diana opened a moving box labeled 'BEDROOM'. "Nana, why did you bring Virgel's underwear!"

"There's still a lot of good wear in 'em." Louise possessively grabbed them and walked into the bedroom. She carefully folded her husband's white briefs and placed them in a chest.

"Besides they're the most comfortable I've ever worn! You should try one, Di," Lu giggled. "I'm wearing his socks with my tennies, too. They're old and soft — just the way I like 'em. Wanna see?" Louise kicked up her leg to make her point.

"How will you explain this to the ladies," Diana teased, "in the restroom over at the Senior Center?"

"Don't you dare ever bring me back to that place again!" Louise fumed. "There's nothing but a bunch of boring old people there!"

"Attendance at your funeral," Diana grinned as she poured Kool-Aid from an iced pitcher, "probably wouldn't be a problem if you go back there."

"Hell, all I'd be doing is going to funerals! But I plan on being around a long time. The smoke stack may be white but there's still fire in the furnace," Louise chided. "I want to do things I've never done before!"

On her prized stereo hi-fi the BeeGee's "More Than A Woman" was playing. She turned up the volume, "Do you know how to disco, Di?"

"Of course I do!" Diana was pleased that after Virgel's death, a little joy was returning to her grandmother's life.

Louise struck a John Travolta pose and, overwhelmed with laughter, Diana fell back on the sofa.

Her grandmother never returned to the Senior Center. Instead, she quickly met many young people within her apartment complex and at church who loved having her join them on their clubbing nights.

After church one Sunday Rhea Lemon, who was also now a recent widow, came to visit. "Lu, you're all dressed and beautiful. I was afraid you'd be too tired to go to lunch after your big night out with your energetic young friends."

"Energetic friends, my ass! They haven't even got out of bed yet upstairs." Louise had something else on her mind. "Rhea, I need you to go shopping with me today."

While her friend patiently waited in the alley, Louise carefully backed the old oversized 1965 Oldsmobile out of the tiny apartment garage. As she adjusted both side and rearview mirrors, straining to make sure she got not a scratch on her Virgel's pride and joy, an old foe returned. "U-u-u-mph!"

Two blocks from her apartment, they pulled into a gas station.

"We've got plenty of gas, Lu," Rhea complained, looking at the gauge.

"No," Louise retorted. "Virgel said don't ever let it get below half-tank."

The service station proprietor, a friendly middle-aged man, approached their car. "Mrs. Herrold, how are you on this beautiful day?" He smiled and winked at her. "Shall I check your water and oil while I'm at it?"

"Oh, that would be nice," Louise flushed and handed him her gas card. When he left, she whispered to her old friend, "You know, he's been trying to get me to go out on a date for weeks now! I'm worried he's going to find out I live so close and start bothering me. Sh-sh-sh! Here he comes."

"Louise, this is a fine old car," he smiled broadly as he returned her card. "You know, it's probably time for a tune-up."

"No, sir! My Virgel worked on it everyday, God rest his soul. He said it wouldn't need any more work for at least ten years, as little as I drive."

Louise pulled the car into the light flow of traffic on Tustin Avenue. "What a dumb cluck! Now he knows I'm a widow."

Ignoring an impatient driver honking behind them, she remained in the far left lane for a few more miles.

"I'm going to buy a white mink and a one-carat diamond today!"

"Are you crazy, Lu? That's a sight — a mink and diamond — to go with Virg's underwear! What are you gonna do with those things at our age?" Rhea teased, "Do you have a new boyfriend?"

"Of course not!" she spouted quickly. "But I swear on my mother's grave, that man at the gas station wants to have sex with me!"

"Why, he's half your age," Rhea hooted. "For cripe's sake, Lu, he doesn't want your body. He wants your car for repair bills!"

After a few minutes of silence, Louise admitted, "There'll never be another Virgel." Then, deep in thought, "Some days are good and some are just terrible, Rhea. I try not to burden Diana. Lord knows, she has enough to worry about." After a few minutes of quiet reflection Louise continued, "You know, I don't have anything nice to leave her when I'm gone. Something I can be proud to have her remember me by."

"Why, Lu, Diana would be the first to say she doesn't need that from you. I know she'd rather you spend the money on yourself — maybe a cruise?"

Louise steered the mammoth Oldsmobile into the Orange Mall parking area. "If Hank hadn't been so stingy, I wouldn't have to buy one to pass on to Di."

A group of teenagers were gathered nearby. One smart-alec with long muttonchops shouted, "Hey lady, you need a zip code for that white elephant?"

Face flushed with fury, Louise got out of the car. When she stomped toward them, they ran in all directions!

"I showed those little shits who's boss, didn't I," she proclaimed as they walked into the mall.

Finishing their lunch of hamburgers and french fries, she was still troubled. "Rhea, why do you and other people like you — without asking — get to see your husbands after they've passed on..."

Uncomfortable, Rhea didn't answer her friend as the ladies left the restaurant and strolled through the mall.

Louise continued, "And me — I've prayed for years — for Pa too — and nothing ever happens."

"Lu, are you sure you want to do this?" Rhea cautioned.

As the two elderly women entered the wholesale jewelry mart, Louise was still lost in her own thoughts.

"When I go, that's the first thing I'm going to ask the good Lord, I'll tell ya."

Chapter 72

"Is Bob here yet?" Louise, drowsy from pre-op sedation, asked from her hospital bed. After having complained to Dr. McCoy of a lingering pain in her abdomen for months, she was to have exploratory surgery.

"No, Nana, I'm sure he's tied up in morning traffic." Diana reassured her as she kissed her forehead. "He'll be here when you wake up and so will I."

Louise had prayed and was at peace as the hospital staff wheeled her down the hall. "Okay, dear."

Hours later a nurse led Bob into the hospital room where Diana had been waiting all morning. "Mr. Herold, your mother is in recovery now."

Without Virgel's blessing, he now called himself Bob Herold, spelled with one 'r'. Diana winced at the reality. His birth name had become too cumbersome due to past indiscretions and the relentless pursuit of creditors.

"Thank you," he reeked of liquor, "did you remember to pick up my laundry this morning?"

Unamused, the nurse looked at Diana. "Shall I bring in some strong coffee?"

For a year-and-a-half Bob had boasted how he was on the wagon and had been religiously attending AA meetings. Louise was proud of his rehabilitation, but now Diana realized nothing had changed — he had been lying all along.

When the nurse left the room, Diana spoke in firm, hushed tones. "I will not allow Nana to see you like this right out of surgery! You're not going to break her heart, again."

After a long icy stare, he left the hospital and, while she watched from a third-story window, crossed a busy street and walked into a bar.

Moments later Dr. McCoy entered, "I thought I'd find you here, Diana." He placed his hand on her shoulder and spoke compassionately, "Your grandmother has advanced colon cancer. I removed most of the diseased intestine which will give her about six more months..."

Unable to hear more, her mind went numb. Without realizing how she did it, she drove home.

For two weeks Louise convalesced in Diana's home. On the third week, Diana, stricken with the flu without anyone else to call, reluctantly phoned Bob's fifth and last wife. "Nana has everything she needs in her apartment. But someone has to help her with her meals and medications — just for a few days — until I'm better. Do you mind, Pat? If she catches this flu, it could kill her."

Early morning a few days later, Diana's bedside phone rang. "They want to go through my papers, Di!" Louise was angry.

"Who?" she asked. "Dad and Pat?"

"They keep asking me where the will is!" Louise moaned. "I keep telling them Diana knows what to do. Virgel made the arrangements years ago."

Late that night, her grandmother called again. "Honey, I'm sorry to call so late. But I can't get to my medicine."

"Where's Pat?" Diana was stunned, knowing with a catheter her grandmother couldn't move from her bed. "Have you eaten at all today?"

"I kept telling them, 'Diana knows what to do!' Finally he screamed at me, 'Well, if Diana knows everything, then Diana can take care of you!'" Louise's voice was fading. "They stormed out the door this morning, Di."

Chastising herself for even calling Pat in the first place, she made some inquiries from the phone book and was relieved to find a caregiver for a few more days.

Day and night for the next seven months, Diana was able to care for her grandmother in her own home with assistance from a visiting nurse and, eventually, hospice.

"My visitor came again last night in all white," Louise confided. "I can never make out a face."

"Nana," Diana sighed, "her name is Sarah and she's your visiting nurse."

"No, this one is luminous — in a floor-length hooded cape."

"Oh Nana, do you think it's your mother again?"

"No."

"Is it Jesus?"

"No."

"Could it be Virgel?"

"No. I wish it were."

"I think we should call Pastor Joe," Diana urged.

A few weeks later, during Pastor Joe's normal visit, Louise confided to him about the spirit. He asked her if it frightened her.

"Not at all, I hardly pay any attention to it anymore." She was actually comforted, "I think it's my angel waiting to take me home."

"If your grandmother was scared," Pastor Joe reassured Diana, "then we would have prayed about it." The gentle presence was to stay with her until she died.

When Pastor Joe left, Diana brought two mugs of coffee into the bedroom and sat down in Opa's old rocker Louise had newly-upholstered in red.

"Nana, there's something important we need to talk about."

Her grandmother sipped the hot brew.

"Promise me — please — if you want your great-grandchildren to grow up with a mother — no visits when you're gone." There, she'd said it. "If you want to spook someone, spook my dad!"

They both laughed until they cried.

"Only if you promise me two things." Her grandmother urged.

"That you will stop smoking immediately. And before the undertaker takes me away, call my nurse." She grasped Diana's hand tightly. "Have her make sure." Louise's biggest fear was being embalmed while in a deep coma. "And one more thing, Di. I want to look real classy. Like a Duchess."

"You will," Diana kissed her tenderly on the forehead.

Louise dropped off to sleep for about a half hour and awoke with an urgent thought.

"For twenty-five years me and Virgel and the Hammonds have kept a secret, Di." Louise took a deep breath. "While you were in the hospital, Eileen snuck into your purse and found a condom..."

"What was in my purse?" Diana was shocked.

"...because you were underage, she called the Hammonds ranting and raving you were raped by Dallas." Louise continued, "The only reason Virgel allowed you to go back to California was because your mother called and threatened to disown you."

"Oh my God, what did the Hammonds say? Nana, I don't know how it got in there! When Dallas came out of the gas station restroom..." she was trying to remember.

"I know the whole story — we all know the truth. Did you know he took your pillow off your bed and held it while we visited — made me promise not to wash it — he was comforted by your scent." Louise began to tear. "He loved you so much, Di. Our Dallas was always a gentleman."

"One of my biggest regrets in life is that we didn't make love," Diana confided. "We thought we had a lifetime together." She paused and took her grandmother's hand. "Another regret. I should have insisted Virgel give me away at my wedding. He deserved it. I'll never forgive myself for that."

Louise slipped into a deep sleep and suddenly awoke again, frightened. "He's going to try to turn you against me, Diana —" she fretted, "him and his demon drink."

"That will never happen," Diana hugged her. "My dad could never turn me against you."

As the cancer advanced, the familiar canopy was replaced by a hospital bed. When her grandmother's veins could no longer tolerate the intravenous pain medication, Diana administered morphine suppositories.

One Friday morning Dr. McCoy made a brief house call while Rhea was visiting. Louise's blue eyes were now a hazy gray, fixated and dilated, and the doctor felt she would only last a few more hours.

"Where's my Bobby... Where's my boy... ?" She was aroused momentarily from her coma as Diana turned her onto her side to insert the morphine.

"What do you think, Rhea? Should I call my father?"

"I don't think so, Di, she doesn't know what she's saying."

Two days later at exactly twelve noon on Sunday while nearby church bells tolled and a gentle summer rain began, Louise Herrold chose to leave when her granddaughter stepped out of her room for only a moment. Rhea held her lifelong friend's hand as Louise took her last breath.

Keeping her promise, Diana summoned the nurse who arrived minutes later.

Rhea lead Diana reluctantly into the kitchen as the morticians claimed Nana's body, placing it into a bag. "Oh, look outside, Di. The angels are crying happy tears."

But Diana could only hear the muffled, flat sound of rain on heavy plastic as the body bag was carried outside into the unassuming van.

Late afternoon at Fairhaven Mortuary, after a casket was chosen, the director suggested to Diana, "Tomorrow afternoon, you may bring Mrs. Herrold's clothing. Preferrably, high neck and long sleeves. We have a hair stylist, make up artist. Should you want a manicure..."

" ...I'll do it all," she interrupted him.

At dusk she went back into the apartment. In the darkening bedroom the impression of her grandmother's head lay on the pillow and the catheter still dangled at bedside. Strands of white hair in a brush lay on a nearby dresser. Holding her Nana's brush, she sat down on Opa's rocker and, in the darkness, finally released her tears.

Sometime later, she turned on the closet light. Louise's new three-quarter length white mink hung in a place of honor at the front of the closet. But when Diana tried to select a dress for her grandmother, she grew deeply ashamed, realizing Nana had not bought herself a new dress in many years.

With new resolve, she collected a triple strand of faux pearls from Louise's jewelry box. Nesting in a pair of Virgel's old white socks in her grandmother's lingerie drawer, she recovered the small velvet case where the one-carat diamond ring was hidden.

Immediately she drove to Louise's favorite shopping mall and before entering The Broadway, keeping her promise to her grandmother, Diana extinguished her last cigarette. On the second floor of the department store, a perfect dress was waiting. It was pink with soft ruffles at the neck and sleeve.

The next morning, Louise's body was already in the embalming room when she returned to the funeral home. Near her grandmother were two little girls laying on stainless steel tables. She was to learn the one-year-old had died of crib death and the three-year-old of leukemia.

"I can't tell the back from the front on this dress." The male embalmer complained, assuming she was an assistant. "I need your help over here for a minute."

"Oh God, no! I can't possibly... !"

As he held the baby, Diana took a deep breath and, shoring up her courage, placed the shear organza dress with bodice smocking over the little head of soft brown curls, put two small arms through capped sleeves and fastened a row of tiny buttons.

She looked next at her grandmother's lifeless face. Louise's body had been bathed and was covered in a white sheet. Her hair was freshly shampooed and set in rollers and her head was cradled on a wooden block.

"Nana, we can do this." Diana began by slipping the rollers out and tenderly combing her hair.

Before the funeral Louise's dignified body laid in repose for three days. Diana rarely left her side.

The day of the funeral her husband whispered. "Your father's here — in the back. What would you like me to do?"

"Tell him," she whispered back, "he's welcome to join the family in the front row."

Each guest filed past the casket while the organist played 'The Old Rugged Cross.'

At the end of the service Rhea hugged Diana. "Lu looks so beautiful. I'm told you did everything."

"Even down to Virgel's underwear!" Diana whispered.

They both smiled at each other, fighting laughter through tears.

As all the visitors slowly emptied the lovely weathered-gray brick church, only the immediate family remained. Bob and Pat had chosen to stand in the back during the service. With no show of emotion, Bob stepped forward, stood over his mother's body, looked down briefly, then walked past his daughter. No words of comfort were exchanged, only an overwhelming smell of alcohol. Her guilt about not calling Bob to her grandmother's bedside quickly evaporated.

Heather tucked a sealed note in her great-grandmother's casket and began to cry.

"Maybe you should take the children out to the limo." Diana kissed her husband. "I'll just be a moment."

She watched the last few cars leave the parking lot, then returned to the sanctuary alone.

The pale late afternoon sun was shining through stained glass windows as she placed a nosegay of flowers in her grandmother's hands.

"Standing room only, Nana." Diana gently touched her hair. "And you were afraid when you moved no one would be at your funeral."

Louise was glowing, dressed in her pale pink dinner dress and her strands of pearls. Diana slipped the one-carat diamond off her grandmother's finger. "Thank you, Nana." She bent down and kissed her one last time, "You are a Duchess, Louise Herrold."

CHAPTER 73

Miss Fontanne was to live six more years without her beloved Alfred. She quickly settled into a routine after her husband's death with the only remaining 'Finn' relative, Alfred's brother-in-law, George Bugbee, residing in Hattie's cottage.

The kettle moraine that October was ablaze with yellows, oranges and reds and the Ten Chimneys' courtyard was completely covered in a blanket of leaves.

To the annoying swells of a soap opera's organ, with Winnie at her heels, Lynn entered the library still in a dressing gown. Immediately, she turned off the television. George got up and poked at the dying embers in the fireplace. "The day would be a hell-of-a-lot more interesting if we watched 'Days of our Lives'," he grumbled to himself, "than Sugar-and-Spite every morning!"

"Others can't hear you when you mumble, George — Speak up!" When her breakfast tray arrived, she opened her newest Cartland romance novel and poured her tea. "Mrs. Miller, you may remove the poached egg, but leave the toast."

Satisfied to have put 'the bug' in his place, she bit into her butter-soaked toast. "I feel like double solitaire after lunch for a wager today. Although I tire of taking your money, George, when I win the wager, the library will be silenced from 'Days' for a full bloody week."

"The woodpile's low and Ben hasn't split logs in a while." George jabbed the paltry flames, accusingly. His unsuccessful bids to discredit Ben were obviously fueled by an intense ambition to take charge of Ten Chimneys.

"Just pick up the telley, George. And alert Mr. Bartel. Within an hour, he will deliver and the shed once more will be filled. There you are!" Irritated, she closed the book and left the library to dress for the day. As the sound of her footsteps faded up the stairs, waves of organ music once again filled the room.

Sometime later in the mudroom off the garage, Lynn lifted Winnie's leash from a hook and shouted up the stairs toward the kitchen. "Mrs. Miller, my barn coat is missing!"

Winnie, knowing it was time for her walk, whimpered excitedly and pawed at the back door.

From outside, opening the door, George countered. "Right where it always is, next to Alfred's! Ben didn't sweep the courtyard again this morning. It's slippery under the leaves. I'll clear a..."

"...Don't bother!" she intervened, brushing past him, annoyed that he was constantly underfoot.

"Winnie and I will manage very well indeed, thank you." She and her dog strolled instead behind the house along a narrow path to the main driveway and briskly walked to the wooden gate and back.

That afternoon while Lynn and George were playing double solitaire in the drawing room, Mrs. Miller interrupted. "Excuse me, Miss Fontanne. You have a long distance call from California. It's Miss Hayes."

Barely hiding his delusion that Helen had designs on him, Bugbee's eyes widened and followed Lynn as she left the room.

"We're wrapping up 'Sisters' and I terribly miss the seasons. Lynn, wouldn't it be divine to meet at The Plaza?" Helen chirred. The two old friends quickly made their plans, then hung up.

Lynn returned to the card game and sat down without a word. The two played in silence for several minutes.

Unable to contain his irritation, Bugbee blurted. "Did my Irish Charmer have any mention of me? You know, she flirts with me outrageously."

"Good Lord, George, she isn't anymore interested in you than she was in my Alfred! That was all rumors." Lynn sipped her glass of sherry. "Why, she uses you for sheer amusement, deah brother-in-law."

Not long after, she met with Helen Hayes and a group of ladies for tea and took in a performance of old friend Carol Channing's 'Hello Dolly' in New York City.

While at tea Anita Loos was horrified. "Charlie's body was exhumed!" she hissed. "And dumped at Oona's front door! They say, because he was a Jewish Communist!"

The ladies at table grew strangely quiet all realizing they were widows and vulnerable, just like Oona.

Lynn broke the silence, "And how *is* deah Charlie?"

As the widows squealed and tittered in laughter, only Helen mutely understood the reality of Lynn's progressing dementia and what was to become of her dear friend.

"Nothing's the same without Alfred," Helen stated. "How on earth are you managing, my dear?"

"I think it's time we all stopped crying." Lynn answered.

That same year Lynn traveled to London and threw a sumptuous dinner at the Dorchester for her Brit friends including John Gielgud. Showing her age, preferring not to dye her hair black, she still dressed with impeccable style for the occasion.

In 1980 Lynn Fontanne received Kennedy Center Honors with Leonard Bernstein, Agnes DeMille, James Cagney and Jason Robards. Beverly Sills lead two thousand people in singing "Happy Birthday" to her while she sat next to former President Jimmy Carter.

During their lifetime Alfred Lunt and Lynn Fontanne were awarded honorary degrees from New York University, Dartmouth, Russell Sage College, Emerson College, Yale, Temple, Brandeis, the Art Institute of Chicago, Smith and UCLA.

At Ten Chimneys, in addition to her new cook, Mrs. Miller, Ben's nephew Richard was now Lynn's chauffeur and butler, and Harriet Owens, her secretary.

Eventually, paranoia began to torment her. Because she was afraid to be alone, Brent Fintel a Genesee local, was moved into

Jules' apartment at her insistence. Brent was often engaged in looking under beds and into closets before she would settle down for the evening. Sometimes, at Miss Fontanne's request, he slept across the hallway in the Hayes' bedroom to guard her slumber.

As her dementia progressed, there were wretched times of confusion. One evening Lynn stepped out of her closet, nude, sporting an old hat. Seated in front of the vanity mirror, she called to the Ten Chimneys' maid.

When the maid entered the room, Lynn asked coquettishly, "What do you think of this hat?"

A lifelong friend, Chuck Bowden, Tennessee Williams' producer, came often to visit her during those years.

"There are three people outside staring at me!" Lynn said to him over dinner one evening in Ten Chimneys' second story dining room.

"Only three, Lynnie?" Chuck consoled her. "There must be thousands outside adoring you!"

Chapter 74

In the early spring morning, with dew still covering grass and leaves, Katherine Hepburn, fresh from her Oscar win for "On Golden Pond", strode down Ten Chimneys' back road toward the main house.

Still possessing a spirited tomboyish beauty in signature chignon, hiking boots and britches, Miss Hepburn was fit and lean for her seventy-five years. Having instructed her chauffeur to drop her at the Perkins' drive in The Depot, she preferred instead to walk through the kettle moraine.

Martha Roland, Lynn's new nurse, had been anticipating Miss Hepburn's arrival via the main drive for more than an hour and was surprised to see her approach the house from a convergent direction. For days, beyond Bugbee's watchful eye, Lynn had been secretly preparing for this moment. Quickly, Martha alerted Miss Fontanne in the library.

"We must expect the unexpected from Kate," Lynn scratched Winnie's ears affectionately while her devoted pet whimpered for attention at her feet.

Having sent 'the bug' to Waukesha at day break on an all-day errand, Lynn was confident nothing was to ruin the epicurean meals she'd planned in Ten Chimneys' garden room.

Martha escorted their admittedly odd but illustrious visitor up the spiral stairs and into the library.

"I waaked pahst the gahden expecting to see Lynn cutting flowahs on this beautiful day." Miss Hepburn commented in her familiar Connecticut twang.

"I'm sorry," Martha replied, "Miss Fontanne hasn't ventured out of the house much these past few months."

"Good gawlly!" Kate's aversion to idleness and her Yankee eccentricity was stirred. "Well, that's about to end!"

Upon entering the library, she was struck by how diminished Miss Fontanne appeared in her fireside chair. Lynn had taken particular care in dressing that morning, resplendent, in a white silk suit with her now gray chignon, elegant make-up and graceful eyelashes.

The two legends settled down for breakfast in Ten Chimneys' garden room with its corner fireplace and bright florals on walls and curtains.

"Whaat a real thrill to see you in this beautiful house. Very unusual." Kate looked around her, impressed. "It's indeed lovely. And so aah you. Unique creetcha. Lovely to look at. Such a wonderful atmospheah you create around you."

"Do you take sugar, dah-h-ling?" Lynn's hand trembled as she tried to pour from the heavy Olivier tea service.

"No sugah, thank you. Allow me." Kate took the burdensome pot, attempting to pour, but it began to shake even more. "Oh, hell..."

For a moment, Martha entered the room to check on Miss Fontanne.

"Oh, therah you aah!" Kate beckoned to her. "Please take all this away and pourah aah tea in the biggest coffee mugs you can find."

Within minutes Lynn was awkwardly sipping from an oversized breakfast mug Alfred had used only for their hungry field hands. "Do you take sugar, dah-h-ling?"

"No sugah, Lynn, thank you," Hepburn repeated adamantly, her head wobbling on its axis. "I have Paahkinsons, you knowah. I think people aah beginning to think I'm not going to be around much longah."

"How is your Spencer?" Lynn smiled sweetly, her dementia returning.

"My dea-ah! Spencah pahssed ah long time ago." It was rumored Lynn suffered from Alzheimer's disease, but Kate was nonetheless alarmed. "We aah what is known as gradually disintegrating, aahn't we?"

Hepburn's self-possessed talkative nature was enlivening as she sipped more tea from her giant cup. "'Buck up, Kate,' Spence would say. 'Know your lines and don't bump into the furnitcha.' So tell me, Lynn, how have you dealt with the grief aftah Alfred's pahssing?"

"As I deal with everything," Lynn admitted. "I go into my garden, pick flowers and create marvelous bouquets to place throughout our Ten Chimneys. I could never continue on without the hope of reuniting with Alfred."

"Well, fowah me, death when it comes, is final." Katharine rose, and abruptly zipped up her jacket. "I never could figure out religion. I mean, I can't see Him so I wonder. I think somebody did something or maybe something happened. But it doesn't interest me much, things that aah unfigurable. I don't really... I think if you die, you die. Personally, my therapy has always been writing in my journal. Enough of this nonsense, let's get you out of those clothes and into something sensible fowah your gahden."

While the women strolled up the knoll and beyond The Studio with Winnie at their heels, Lynn, breathing in a fragrant nosegay of lilies of the valley, was still mildly protesting. "Dr. Bigg has ordered me not to wander about. He says my bones are brit..."

"Brit — shit!" Kate interrupted, leading her old friend by the arm. "Lynn, if you obey awll the rules, you'll miss awll the fun. You don't have to ride your bicycle, owah be silly like me and swim in the freezing ocean evrah day. But you must make yourself walk. Isn't that right, Winnie?"

The old dog barked and trotted happily behind them in the sun-dappled morning.

With the noon sun at its arc, the women continued to busy themselves in the back orchard, Lynn positioned as sentry and Kate marching up and down a ladder picking fruit.

"After all this fuss," Kate had worked up a sweat, "I expect a lemon meringue pie for dessert tomorrow night."

As Lynn added another lemon to her already filled bushel basket, she apologized. "I must warn you, Ten Chimneys hasn't produced a decent lemon pie since our poor Jules left." There was an intense spark in her eyes. "We were married fifty-five years, you know."

"I don't believe in marriage. It's bloody impractical to love, honor and obey!" Kate straightened her shoulders. "Well, I've just done what I damned well wanted to and I made enough money to support myself. I was just out for me. And I got me, you knowah. Then I met Spencah, at a time when I was in a position to be adorable to someone else."

"I believe you must live with someone many years before you truly fall in love..." Lynn couldn't finish, her eyes had dimmed.

"Rubbish!" Kate hooted. "The ideal institution would be to live next doah to one anothah and just visit now and then." She grabbed one last lemon.

After a picnic lunch delivered by Martha, Lynn, now in a coat, preferred to sit demurely on a blanket nearby, while Kate moved the ladder to a peach tree and again vigorously mounted its steps. "Spence was a complex and difficult man. Even I who knew him best was never able to fathom the demons that seemed to drive him. I was with Spence for neahly three decades." She swayed back and forth precariously on the ladder for a moment, but quickly caught her balance.

At times Lynn's mind could vividly recall a memory of long ago. "But, dah-h-ling, what about your love for Mr. Hughes?"

"Oh my God, poor Hah-wah-d! The only person I've evah known that matched my own independence. We werah very much in love. But in retrospect, we werah in love with the idea of each othah. He was glamorous and, at that time, I loved glamour." She stretched on tip-toe to pick a particularly appetizing fruit. "I've always had a kind of missionary streak but I nevah thought that I could cure him. I'll let you be the judge to that. When I broke our engagement, his condition wasn't so exaggahrated as it became later on. He hadn't gone to the land of coo-coo yet."

Kate descended the ladder, produced from her pocket an old

Swiss-Army knife, unfolded the blade and cut a juicy morsel for both of them.

"Of awll my life's relationships," there was a glint in Kate's eye as she took another bite, "Hah-wah-d was assuredly the most adventurous and lustiest. He was up for anything. But that was in my thirties. When I was as ripe as this peach!"

Delighted, they both bit into the fruit and laughed uproariously.

With the sun touching tree tops, the women walked past The Studio on their way to afternoon tea. Lynn, stilled in her tracks, gazed at the sign 'Lynn and Alfred live here'.

"This door hasn't been opened in ages. Let's send up for tea here." Invigorated, Lynn proclaimed, "And two brandy old fashions before dinner!"

Once inside, Kate inquired. "What waas Alfred thinking? So many fireplaces in corners without mantles."

Lynn didn't answer. In the center of the darkening room, she was lost in thought, staring longingly up at the loft.

Sipping a brandy, Kate sighed. "Hah-wah-d protected Spence and I for years, you knowah, by buying up all the rag photos. Spence didn't give a damn, but it saved my career. Cost him a fortune. I'll always love him for that." She raised her glass and, with one swig, finished her brandy. "Did you catch my intahview on television?"

Confused, Lynn lifted her glass, too.

Kate continued, "If you didn't — you didn't miss much."

"Miss what, deah?"

"My television intahview!" Kate glanced at her friend sympathetically. "When Bahbra Walters asked me if I will evah wear ah dress, I told her I will wear one to her funeral! And how possible is that?"

Hepburn eyed Lynn for a long moment. "They'll miss us, you knowah," she confided. "Like an old monument. Like the Flatiron Building. We were all four personalities. Show me an actor who isn't a personality, and I'll show you an actor who isn't a star."

"Stardom and film never entered our minds." Lynn's eyes brightened again for a moment, "We strove for perfection on stage and, for my poor Alfred, it came at a deah price."

As the two walked back to the main house for dinner, "I have many regrets and I'm sure ev-rah-one does. The stupid things you do you regret. If you have any sense. And if you don't regret them, maybe you aah stupid."

They walked past the rose garden and Kate once again opened her knife and cut a fragrant blossom. Smelling it she asked, "Is there anything you regret, Lynn?"

Lynn admitted sadly. "I would have cherished the title Dame. They thought I was American, but I was always British."

Too tired for the opulent dinner she had originally planned, Ten Chimneys' mistress was forced to retire early that evening.

In a small pool of light near curtains billowing in a soft cross-breeze, Kate seated herself at Noël's writing desk in his favorite bed-room.

She wrote one last entry in her journal to Spencer:

> *"Living wasn't easy for you, was it? What did you like to do? Sailing — especially in stormy weather. You loved polo, but tennis, golf, swimming — no, not really. Walking — no, that didn't suit you — that was one of those things where you could think at the same time. Of this, of that... of what, Spence, what was it? Was it some specific thing, like being a Catholic and you felt a bad Catholic? You concentrated on all the bad, none of the good which your religion offered. It must have been some-thing very fundamental, very ever-present. And the incredible fact that there you were, really the greatest movie actor — you could do it, and you could do it with that glorious simplicity, that directness. You couldn't enter your own life, but you could be someone else. You were the character in a moment, you hardly had to study — what a relief, you could be someone else for a while, you weren't you, you were safe. And then back to life's trials: 'Oh hell, take a drink. Yes. No. Maybe. And then stop taking those drinks — you were great at that, Spence, you could just stop. How I respected you for that — very unusual. But why the escape hatch? Why was it always open? To get away*

from the remarkable you. I always meant to ask you. Did you know what it was? Are you having a long rest after all your tossing and turning in life? Are you happy finally?"

During her lifetime Katharine was nominated for twelve Academy Awards. She won four, three after she was sixty years old. At the onset of the 21st century, no other actress had achieved Miss Hepburn's four Oscars. She starred with Spencer Tracy in nine films and won an Emmy playing opposite Laurence Olivier in 1975, again, after she was sixty.

The loves of their lives were both born in Milwaukee and Miss Fontanne and Miss Hepburn both died at age ninety-six. Whether ironic or providential — or perhaps a mixture of both?

"I'll let you be the judge to that," Kate would say.

CHAPTER 75

Lynne Fontanne raised her head from the pillow to cough. Her breathing was rattled and shallow.

It was an unusually cool July day in 1983, and she didn't think she was well enough to take tea in the library. On better days she read there, stopping to gaze at her favorite portrait of Alfred and reminisce.

When noon came, she was feeling stronger and decided to get up. With assistance, Lynn descended the stairs slowly and shuffled into the library.

"My *dah-h-ling* Larry phoned today?"

Frequently Mr. Olivier called, but not that day. Martha nodded her head. She turned on the television and stoked the fire, settling Lynn into her down-cushioned chair near the fire's warmth with a tray of soup and crackers set before her.

Facing Alfred's portrait with remarkable reserve and dignity in spite of her senility, Lynn spoke. "I miss his beautiful indulgences. I miss everything about him."

Her food untouched, she was lost in thought. "I would enjoy a nap now — bring Alfred's portrait into the bedroom with me today — and ask Jules to please bring two gardenias from the kitchen window sill. One for me and one for little Diana."

Martha pampered her without question, immediately bringing in only Alfred's portrait, realizing the flowers were from another time.

At four o'clock the nurse brought in her usual afternoon tea. As she plumped her pillows and set the tea tray in front of her on the bed, Miss Fontanne looked up and whispered. "Would you please put on Chopin?"

While Lynn slipped into a deep sleep, George Bugbee, was summoned to her room. She appeared to be failing fast, so he turned off the phonograph.

Lynn immediately opened her eyes. "Alfred, *dah-h-ling*! Don't stop the music!"

The soft strains of Chopin again filled the room.

In the early cool hours of morning, a soft fragrant breeze gently blew the lace curtains at the windows. A robin's faint song rang out in the distance as Lynn's hand dropped and hung limply off the bed.

Martha found her, eyes open, focused on Alfred's portrait. Her expression was calm, peaceful. Lynn and her Alfred, the consummate couple, were finally together again.

She was buried to her beloved Alfred's right and, of course, to his left was his adored mother Hattie.

Contrary to Alfred's tumultuous burial the decade before, Miss Fontanne's funeral was held on a bright summer day, fragrant with flowers. It was a beautiful English day, just like her.

For many years George Bugbee lived in Hattie's cottage, unable to maintain the large estate. After his death, a local sheriff glanced at the thistles now growing in Lynn's once perfectly groomed rose garden, then chain-locked the old wooden gate.

A great golden era had passed.

Chapter 76
- May 26, 2003 -

After a short drive from Milwaukee's General Mitchell Airport, Diana waited at the Genesee Depot tracks for a freight train to pass.

The conductor was no longer the old lovable gray-haired gentleman of 'The Goose' passenger train who threw candy to her as a child. Instead, he was now a young man who looked straight ahead down the track, not the least bit interested in The Depot.

When she shored up nerve to knock on the front door of her grandparent's old cottage, a woman answered.

"Excuse me, I used to live here years ago..." she began.

"Diana? Is that you!" Diane Sickle screamed. "My parents bought the house from the Herrolds," she explained, "and now I own it."

They walked through the enlarged living room and kitchen. Louise's glass shelves and mirrors were still there but the downstairs was no longer her grandmother's. Noticably absent was the charming, apple blossom wallpaper her Nana had loved. Her dad's mural over the bathtub had disappeared under layers of paint and the shower was now being used as it was intended.

Stroking the banister, admiring Virgel's loving woodwork, Diana followed her childhood friend as they ascended the stairs. Upstairs, the old attic bedroom was the only room in the house unchanged. She gazed at the glass-enclosed shelves, dormer windows and pink bathroom and was silent for a few moments, remembering.

"Oh!" She glanced at her watch. "I really must go! I have to meet the curator at Ten Chimneys." She hugged Diane and they promised to write.

In minutes she stood at the familiar wooden gate where Molly Hannah, the curator, met her for a private tour.

As they strolled down the drive, Diana was overwhelmed by the restored beauty of her beloved Ten Chimneys. "Jules worried that after Lynn's death the estate could eventually be destroyed. He wished to have it open somehow to the public. He must be very happy. It was his home, too, you know — for thirty-five years." Then, as they continued walking, "Joe Garton is seriously ill, isn't he?"

Sadly, Molly answered, "Yes — cancer, I'm afraid."

With tears in her eyes, Diana noted the bare veranda columns at the front of the main house. "This was always covered with morning glories and English ivy." She pointed upstairs, "And overflowing flower boxes were there. Joe understands Alfred's fondness for detail and I'm sure he wants to know. There's so much I have to tell him and so little time..."

The two women entered the house. In the kitchen, Lynn's hand-sewn red and white gingham curtains were present, but Diana saddened when she noticed the matching shelf edging was missing.

"Alfred would be devastated. This kitchen was his sanctuary, Molly. He told me Lynn's gingham made it the 'prettiest kitchen in the whole world!'"

They exited the house and continued walking up the stone stairs toward The Studio. "Someone moved the sign. It's in the wrong place." Perplexed, Diana noticed the plaque 'Lynn and Alfred live here' had been moved up to the second story of The Studio's rough exterior.

Molly jotted copious notes on a pad. "Do you have a picture of its original placement?"

"Yes. I'll send it." Diana remarked, "I was with Alfred when he agonized over it. He wanted it just to the right of the doorway, where he had seen so many in Europe."

"I must go now." Molly jotted one last note. "Here's my pencil and pad, Diana. Please note anything else you remember that needs to be addressed. I have tons to do before the celebration!" She said excitedly, "Joe is so looking forward to seeing you this evening!" She waved goodbye, shouting, "Can you believe it's actually happening tonight?"

In the stillness of the late afternoon — Alfred's gloaming hour — Diana sat down on the old wooden stairs at the back of the house.

Directly above Lynn's lilac bush, nesting on Jules' window sill, were two baby robins, staring down at her from their perch. Boldly, their mother, a magnificent bird with bright orange-red breast and long tail feathers, landed inches from her on the steps.

The stately, mystic creature burst into song, so poignant and shrill, it echoed through woods and beyond.

Once again, she thought, Ten Chimneys was a sanctuary. Like Jules, the confident bird guarded it and, like the Lunts, the brood nested above it all, watching.

CHAPTER 77

That evening the tiny hamlet of Genesee Depot was bumper-to-bumper with luxury cars and limos. Alone in her rental car, dressed in a full-length black dinner suit and Lynn's single pearl earrings, Diana sat in traffic, blinded by headlights. Reminiscent of a Broadway theater premiere, flood lights shone and criss-crossed into the starlit sky.

Wisconsin had been plagued with torrential rains and thunderstorms the entire month. Only yesterday, Molly had revealed, the skies had cleared to bless Ten Chimneys' grand opening.

Nestled in the woods, directly across the street from the Lunt estate, she pulled into the new, three-story Ten Chimneys' Cultural Center drive.

Moments later standing in the lobby, Diana found herself amidst a sea of strangers. There was glamour everywhere — strains of 'Stardust', flutes of champagne, trays of hor'dourves — all hosted in black tie. Waves of reporters jostled each other, attempting to interview and photograph the beautiful people in their sparkling jewelry, gowns and tuxedos.

Directly to the left of the reception area on the entry wall was a larger-than-life black and white image of the newly-wed Lunts, dressed casually, frolicking on the estate. To the right was another huge image of an older Alfred proudly removing his cardamon bread from the oven.

Diana smiled and sighed to herself. Alfred would be "damned pleased".

She noticed a young man with a camera slung around his neck and approached him with childish excitement. "Could you please take my picture next to the Lunts? Here's my..."

"...I'll get in trouble, lady," he interrupted curtly.

"...camera," she finished weakly.

Not listening, he stated, "I'm with the Milwaukee Sentinel."

"Oh, I'm very sorry. I had no idea you were from the newspaper. I thought you were..."

He interrupted her again. "Ask the boss over there," he pointed his thumb in the direction of a busy newspaper executive. "She's the only one who tells me what pictures to take. She has a list of the important people, somewhere."

Diana was so embarrassed, she seriously considered returning to the bed and breakfast. Maybe this wasn't meant to be afterall. She told herself perhaps she should leave and come back Monday morning for the ribbon cutting ceremony.

Remembering what Miss Fontanne had told her four decades before, she took a deep breath and repeated to herself, "I come in faith with hope high mounting," and quickly grabbed a glass of champagne from a passing tray.

Nearby, Dr. Joe Garton was being interviewed by the press. "I welcome you all here this evening on Alfred Lunt and Lynn Fontanne's 81st wedding anniversary. The restoration of this living monument was, for me, a leap of faith. This unique site and museum will resume its historic role for artistic creation, education and inspiration. Our Foundation will offer estate tours and exhibitions. The Ten Chimneys' renaissance is complete — my goal is accomplished."

He looked proudly at his docents who had gathered, "You, our docents, hold the key. Your oral history spoken to each visitor will perpetuate the legend of our beloved Lunts."

Martin Dable, now a Ten Chimneys' docent, and his wife, Shirley, were having cocktails with Molly Hannah.

"We're all so happy for Joe," Molly sipped her wine. "Such a grand turnout!"

"Where do you suppose all these gorgeous people came from, Molly?" Martin straightened the knot of his tie.

"All over, I presume," Molly answered. "I met with someone this afternoon, all the way from California. She used to live up the hill."

"There were only four houses up the hill. Could that possibly be my next door neighbor?"

"Her name is Diana," Molly affirmed.

Martin was overjoyed. "How will I ever find her in this crowd?"

In a narrow hallway, swept along by the spirit of the evening, Diana found herself in a long line awaiting a sumptuous display of crème vichyssoise, endive salad and rack of lamb — all Alfred's favorite delectables.

"I don't believe I've met you." A friendly, smartly-dressed, professional young woman and man were standing next to her. "My name is Karen Dummer and this is my fiancé, John. And you are?"

"I'm Diana," she tittered, "And I don't have a date."

The three smiled at each other.

"Well, my date John would love to dance with you," Karen offered.

From the hallway, they entered a grand ballroom decorated in the soft whites and greys of 1940s art deco. A Big Band in World War II military uniform was playing 'Moonlight Serenade'. Suspended from the ceiling, encircling the room, were enormous pictures of the Lunt's depicting their various stage portrayals throughout their lifelong theater career.

The three sat down at a white-linened table set for a formal dinner, overflowing with white tulips. At her placesetting Diana found a silk organza gift bag filled with mementos of the evening and a circa 1920s dance card.

"Allow me to be the first to sign your dance card," John graciously obliged.

Relieved, Diana took another sip of champagne. "It's so nice to find some friends tonight."

At dinner's end, a white wedding anniversary cake was presented, complete with engraved napkins. Dr. Garton gave a brief, eloquent toast, cut the cake, and quickly disappeared behind a crowd as everyone merged, seeking to talk with this man of the hour.

Intrigued by her many years with the Lunts, Karen revealed to Diana, "I'm on the Board of Trustees and must introduce you to Charles Bray, our Chairman. I know he would love to talk with you." As the evening progressed, Karen introduced her to Mr. Bray and many other fascinating people.

Upstairs in a replica of the Lunt-Fontanne Theater, Molly approached Martin, "Did you ever find Diana?"

"No." Tired, he loosened the knot of his tie. "Too big a crowd."

In an opposite wing on the same floor of the Cultural Center, Diana and Joe Garton sat on a 'pouf', a circular settee in the middle of an authentic recreation of the Lunt's dressing room. Now bald from chemotherapy, Dr. Garton was markedly thin and frail. Sipping sherry together, they both watched a montage of the Lunt's home movies playing on a television screen.

"Could that be you, Diana?" Joe asked.

In black and white, in front of them, a little blonde child danced gleefully in what appeared to be a dress made of newspaper.

"It looks like me," she stared, stood up and approached the television. "Miss Fontanne did make me a newspaper dress when I was a little girl."

Dr. Garton quickly summoned a woman who appeared with a 35mm camera.

As the Lunt home movies continued, Jules' image suddenly appeared, pulling bread out of the oven in the Ten Chimneys' kitchen.

"Oh Jules," Diana was overwhelmed. "I'm so glad I'm here to witness this wonderful celebration!"

"Every life needs a purpose - a dream," Joe uttered. "I have been allowed to live long enough to see my dream realized. Ten Chimneys has come alive. I want to thank you for traveling so far to join me, sharing your many years of memories with Jules and the Lunts." He smiled, wistfully, "Through our docents, Diana, your Jules will live on with Alfred and Lynn."

"There is no one else alive to do this," Diana hugged him. "In all humility, on Jules' and the Lunts' behalf, I thank you Joe. You have made this miracle possible."

"Not only me. There are hundreds of people here who have given generously of their money and time to create this evening." Joe took her arm. "Right here. Right now. I would give anything to be you tonight. I never met the Lunts. Only you understand what this means to them. You should write a book, Diana."

He lead her to another exhibit in the room. "I'd like to show you something." He read aloud, Noël Coward's poem, framed and placed on a wall near Alfred's dressing table.

"When I have fears, as Keats had fears,
Of the moment I'll cease to be
I console myself with vanished years
Remembered laughter, remembered tears,
And the peace of the changing sea.
When I feel sad, as Keats felt sad,
That my life is so nearly done
It gives me comfort to dwell upon
Remembered friends who are dead and gone
And the jokes we had and the fun.
How happy they are, I cannot know
But happy am I who loved them so."

Diana smiled through tears. "Tonight, this is your poem, Joe."

Dr. Joseph Garton was to die of cancer eight weeks later at age fifty-six.

He left a priceless living, breathing memorial to theater and the arts, effectively writing the book on how to gracefully accomplish what others deemed an impossible task.

CHAPTER 78

The following Monday, mid-morning, hundreds of volunteers, docents, and invited friends, including Diana, gathered at the Ten Chimneys' Cultural Center and together walked across Depot Road to the Lunt's estate.

Behind them, a commotion erupted. An uninvited couple had tried to join them, unnoticed.

As a male docent escorted the pair off of the property and an electronic gate closed in front of the two, the bearded overweight man shouted, "I've lived here for sixty years..."

"Shut up, Butch! Let me do the talking!" The woman next to him whacked him in the back of the head.

"Tours begin this week for the public," Molly assured them. "You may call the Cultural Center tomorrow for tour reservations."

Dr. Garton and his handpicked predecessor, Sean Malone, symbolically opened Alfred's scrolled iron courtyard gate.

Once inside, the invitees congregated around a vintage limousine where, in the back seat, Lynn's theater glasses had been placed atop long white gloves near Alfred's top hat. All the while, in front of Hattie's cottage on the hill, journalists and photographers gathered to document images of the apex of Dr. Garton's distinguished career.

After the ceremony as Diana milled through the crowd, she noticed a tall, reserved black man standing alone, gazing up at Jules' apartment. Intrigued, she attempted to approach him but, in the crush of celebration, he disappeared.

In the tree-filtered sunlight as the group returned to the Cultural Center for a champagne brunch to be served in the ballroom, Diana found herself strolling next to an elderly Genesee Depot volunteer.

"I must tell you, my dear, I had the privilege of polishing the beautiful silver tea set given to the Lunts by Laurence Olivier and Vivien Leigh. Why, it must be fifty years old, if it's a day!" She smiled kindly. "By the way, my name is Louise."

"It's probably more like sixty years, actually." Diana hugged her. "What a beautiful name — Louise."

After the buffet, a visibly weary but jubilant Joe Garton tapped his crystal flute with a silver knife and announced to everyone. "I insist you refill your champagne glass or coffee cup. We have a rare treat for your viewing pleasure." The lights in the large hall dimmed. "The Lunt's enchanting 1931 film 'The Guardsman' is about to begin!"

Diana watched her cherished Genesee neighbors by magic of lens and celluloid and wept. To see them again in splendid costumed finery, bantering and playing with each other, pierced her to the heart. Yet, how utterly incomplete was this hour of film. Anguished, she realized how little of the Lunt's large body of stage work or their full, eventful personal lives was immortalized on film.

Immediately when the lights were raised and the black and white images faded on screen, from across the room someone yelled, "Diana!"

Unabashedly, Martin ran to her and lifted her off the ground, twirling her around in a bear hug.

"Martin! Is that you?" She winced in pain, thinking her ribs might break. Instantly, they were childhood friends again as he dropped her unceremoniously.

To catch her breath she sat down on a lobby couch. "Tell me Martin, are you still afraid of the dark and ghosts?"

"We all had fears, didn't we Di?" he smiled sitting next to her. "But I faced mine head on."

"How's that?" she wondered.

"I'm a mortician!" He beamed at her. "My wife and I recently retired. We owned a funeral home for many years. How about you?"

Her face grew pale. "I'm afraid I'm a work in progress."

Still engrossed in conversation, they were surprised to hear the Ten Chimneys' grandfather clock chime in the lobby to summon Martin's scheduled docent tour.

"Oh, no, I have to go. My group is waiting," he announced sadly. "Let me see if I can..."

"Don't worry, Martin. Joe's already made touring arrangements for me."

They hugged each other. Like her promise to Diane Sickle, she and Martin agreed to keep in touch.

It was four o'clock — tea time — when Diana's tour, the last of the day, concluded and the docents and guests began to leave.

With Joe's kind permission, Diana walked the grounds alone, once more drinking in the renewed splendor of her childhood paradise. For some final moments, she leisurely wandered from orchard to courtyard during Alfred's gloaming hour. She picked a nosegay of lilies of the valley and walked up the shaded, winding drive to return to the Cultural Center. Hearing footsteps behind her, she was surprised to see a guest had remained behind.

With long, even strides, the same black man she had tried to approach earlier, quickly caught up to her.

"This must have been a wonderful day for you, Diana. My mother spoke highly of you, you know." He extended his hand in greeting. "I'm Dr. Cooper. I recognize you from a photo of my mother's."

"Cooper?" she gasped. "Wilhelmina Cooper?"

"Wilhelmina was my mother." A shadow of sadness crossed his face. "We had planned to visit Ten Chimneys together this weekend. She had promised to enlighten me. All I know of my family is oral history," he continued, "like so many black families of my generation, I'm afraid."

"Wilhelmina is no longer living?"

"She passed away last month — in April — Easter Sunday." The sadness crossed his face again and his eyes filled with tears.

"I'm truly sorry." Diana studied this man she had just met. His eyes were familiar deep brown pools of quiet wisdom.

They passed the old wooden gate, now guarded by the steel of modern electronics.

"We should close the gate, don't you think?" he asked.

"A wise man told me often to do that very thing," she replied. "It's almost suppertime. I've decided to walk to The Depot to an old hotel that's been turned into a lovely restaurant. Care to join me?"

"Is it far from here?" he inquired.

"Only three minutes on a red Schwinn bicycle..." she laughed.

The kettle moraine was silent, except for a robin's song echoing above the trees as they strolled down the hill.

"Genesee-quoi," she pronounced the word with a soft 'G' like Mr. Lunt had done so many years ago. Taking a deep breath, she closed her eyes. "This healing pastoral countryside — this magnificent kettle moraine — that's the miracle of Ten Chimneys."

All around her were the ephemeral greens of nature's leaves peaking their first fruits. Not yet their most beautiful, she pondered. Their latter fruits of reds and golds were yet to come. Much like a life richly lived.

"Genesee-quoi?" The unfamiliar word rolled off the young man's lips. "Could it work for me?"

The insulated wood and its comforting silence surrounded her once again. She opened her bright, clear eyes and smiled, "Oh my dear Dr. Cooper, you have no idea."

In Milwaukee, before her flight home to California, Diana stood alone in the Forest Home Cemetery. Surrounded by old turn-of-the-century trees, lie Wisconsin's military heros, powerful industrialists, politicians, pioneering women and the city's 19th century beer dynasties of Valentin Blatz, Frederick Pabst and Joseph Schlitz. She studied the huge granite monument simply entitled 'LUNT' with the engraving,

> *"Alfred Lunt and Lynn Fontanne were universally regarded as the greatest acting team in the history of the English speaking theater. They were married for fifty-five years and were inseparable both on and off the stage."*

In front of her was a row of five small, unassuming headstones.

"Thank you for loving a child," Diana whispered, placing a cluster of Lynn's lilies of the valley on her grave.

"From your orchard, Alfred." She set a twig of apple blossoms on his stone. "I hope you have finally found peace in a perfect place."

Across the heavens lightning struck, thunder cracked and Wisconsin's torrential storms resumed. With raindrops streaming down her face and cheeks, she looked up. She repositioned the hood of her overcoat and began to leave. Her high heel sank into the wet grass, forcing her to stop in front of Harriet Sederholm's headstone.

"Oh, how could I have forgotten you, Hattie?"

Dripping wet, she fished around in her purse, found a tube of lipstick and put it near Hattie's epitaph.

"It isn't your fire engine red to bon motts with Nana — but I hope it will do."

As Diana walked away she glanced back and whispered to all, "See you in a blink."

Our Sincere Thanks To

Ten Chimneys Foundation:
Dr. Joseph Garton
Deirdre Garton
Sean Malone
Erika Kent
Molly Hannah
Cait Dallas
Amanda Shilling
Richard Quick
Karen Dummer-Robison

And

The people of Genesee Depot:
Martin and Shirley Dable
Diane Sickle-Vick
Bill Pronold
Mary Jo Pronold-Hultman
Bill McKinsi
Larry Bartell

And

Louise who shined the silver

PICTURES

To our good neighbour Mrs Herrold
Lynn Fontanne
Alfred Lunt

Newlyweds, Virgel and Louise Herrold
Genesee Depot, Wi.

The Herrolds and Lemons: newlyweds, best friends and neighbors

Newlyweds, Hank and Beatrice Luckert with young Robert (Diana's father)

Jules Johnson and Louise
Genesee Depot, Wi.

Louise and Rhea Lemon at
the Herrold home

Diana, Maxine and
their mother Eileen
at the Herrold home

THE NINETEEN FIFTIES

Diana and her sister Maxine at the Herrold home

Virgel and Louise Herrold at home in Genesee Depot

Jules Johnson at the Herrold home

Great grandpa Herman 'Zabel' Luckert at the Herrold home

Pet Milk Company North Prairie, Wi.

Great grandpa 'Zabel' and Diana

Diana and Maxine with Virgel trying to plow his garden

Great grandpa 'Zabel' at the Luckert Minkery in Marinette, Wi.

Virgel with Diana before she delivered her first pie to Ten Chimneys

Hank and Beatrice Luckert
with new daughter, Lynn

Diana plays her accordion
at the Herrold home

Lynn Fontanne and Diana poolside at Ten Chimneys
(Taken from stilled frame of home movie camera)

THE NINETEEN SIXTIES AND SEVENTIES

Jules and Diana in the courtyard of Ten Chimneys

Jules on the grounds of Ten Chimneys

Jules with Diana's son David at
Sea World in San Diego, Ca.

Jules at home in Anaheim, Ca.

Last picture of Jules with Diana and her children,
David and Heather, at home in Anaheim, Ca.

Diana in Ten Chimney's Flirtation Room, 2003

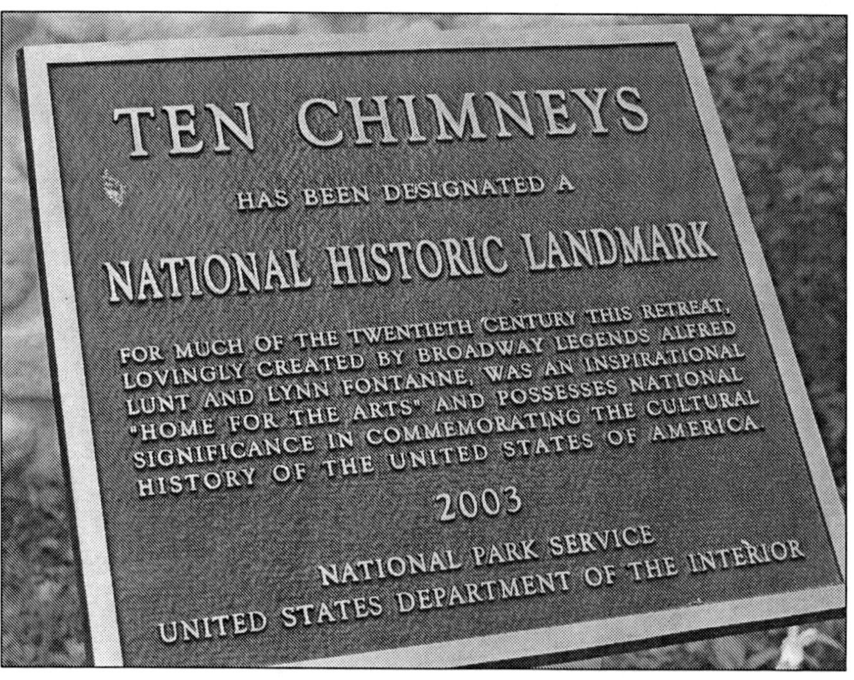

Ten Chimneys National Historic Landmark plaque

SELECTED NOTES

p.11 Sears and Roebuck (tm) catalog, Richard Sears and Alva C. Roebuck Co., founded 1893.

p.18 *"Well, my darlings..."*, Noël Coward quote, c.1943, from Christine Plichta, docent, Ten Chimneys Foundation.

p.18-19 *The White Cliffs of Dover*, Glen Miller (performed by)/ Walter Kent (music by)/Nat Burton (lyrics by), Music Publishers, NYC, 1941.

p.20 Eleanor Roosevelt, *My Day*, syndicated newspaper column, 1935-1962.

p.20 *"...too emotionally moved..."*, Charles Chaplin telegram, c.1940.

p.21 *"If Alfred starts talking..."*, Charles MacArthur quote: Margo Peters, *Design for Living*, Alfred A. Knopf, New York, 2003.

p.22 *Scotch is a curious spirit..."*, Eugene O'Neill toast from his play, *The Iceman Cometh*, Vintage, 1999.

p.23 Chateau d'Yquem, Jacques de Sauvage, established 1593, Bordeaux, France.

p.27 *"Mother, I had..."*, Alfred Lunt letter to Hattie Sederholm, Hotel St. Regis, NY, Sept. 8, 1943.

p.27 *"all arse..."*, Alfred Lunt letter to Sederholm, April 24, 1944.

p.27 *"We had a heavenly..."*, Alfred Lunt letter to Sederholm, The Savoy Hotel, London, c.1944.

p.27 *"...high old time..."*, Alfred Lunt letter to Hattie Sederholm, July 2, 1944.

p.28 *"Take it up!"*, Alfred Lunt quote: Clifton Daniel, *With the*

Lunts on the (Buzz-Bombed) Road, New York Times Magazine, Feb. 9, 1945.

p.33 *"...fear of separation...",* Alfred Lunt quote: Clifton Daniel, *With the Lunts on the (Buzz-Bombed) Road*, ibid.

p.37 *The Guiding Light*, ABC Television, Irna Phillips (creator), 1952.

p.38 *Stardust*, Hoagy Carmichael/Mitchell Parish, Columbia Music, 1931.

p.39 English Oval cigarettes, Phillip Morris, Inc. USA.

p.40 Le Cordon Blue cooking school, established 1896, Paris, France.

p.41 *Stars and Stripes Forever*, John Phillip Sousa (composer), Gershwin Publishing Corp., NY, NY, 1935.

p.42 Toni (tm) home permanent, The Toni Company, 1950.

p.43 *On Wisconsin* (state song in 1959), *W*illiam T. Purdy (music by)/J.S.Hubbard & Charles Rosa (lyrics by), 1913.

p.45 Popsicle (tm), Frank Epperson, 1924, rights sold to Joe Lowe Co., New York, NY.

p.46*You're A Grand Old Flag,* George M. Cohen (composer), Library of Congress, Music Division, Nov. 9, 2005.

p.46 *When The Saints Go Marching In*, Louis Armstrong (performed by), EPM USA, 1928.

p.48*"no story, no situations...",* Lynn Fontanne quote to Robert Sherwood, June, 1947.

p.53 Whitman's (tm) chocolates, Stephen F. Whitman, founder, 1842.

p.54 Sears and Roebuck, ibid.

p.56 *God Bless the Child*, composers Herzog-Holiday, arranger Sammy Nestico, MCA Music Publishing, 2005.

p.58 *Lily of the Valley*, traditional hymn, The Broadman Hymnal, Broadman Press, Nashville, TN, 1940.

p.65 Kodak Brownie (tm) movie camera, Kodak Co., 1951.

p.66 *Lorelei*, Heinrich Heine (written by), Friedrich Silcher (composer), 1827.

p.72 Philco (tm), ten inch black &white television set, model year 1949.

p.72 *The Hopalong Cassidy Show*, NBC Television, 1952.

p.72 *The Roy Rodgers Show*, CBS Television, 1952.

p.77 Lucky Strikes cigarettes, R.J.Reynolds, 1871.

p.79 *"chock full of fireplaces..."* Lynn Fontanne quote to Hugh Beaumont, Dec. 12, 1949.

p.81 Tootsie Roll (tm), Leo Hirshfield, Sweets Company of America, 1896.

p.81 Bit o' Honey (tm), Schutter-Johnson Co. of Chicago, 1924.

p.81 Bazooka (tm) bubble gum, Topps Chewing Gum, Brooklyn, NY, 1938.

p.85 Necco wafers (tm), New England Confectionary Co., early 1900s.

p.85 Smarties candy pills (tm), CeDeCandy, Inc., 1949.

p.85 Smith Brothers (tm) cherry cough drops, William Andrew Smith (founder), 1949.

p.90 Edna Ferber inscription emailed to Diana Enright by Ten Chimneys' curator, Cait Dallas, May, 2005.

p.94 *Confidential Magazine* (aka the scourge of Hollywood), Niche Media, 1950.

p.95 Kool-Aid (tm) cherry flavor, Edwin Perkins (founder), Perkins Products Co., 1927.

p.96 Sweet Acidophilus (patent), Purity, 1976.

p.96 Kool-Aid (tm) popsicle, ibid.

p.98 *Melody of Love*, orig. music by Hans Engleman/lyrics by Tom Glazer, 1903; Doubleday (Zephyr Books), 1988.

p.98 Sunbeam (tm) toaster, John K. Stewart/Thomas J. Clark (founders), Sunbeam Corporation, Chicago, 1946.

p.98 *My Man*, Channing Pollack (English lyrics), Maurice Yvain (music by), Billie Holiday (performed by) with Buster Harding's Orchestra, Decca, 1949.

p.98 Here's My Heart cologne, David McConnell (founder), Avon (tm) Cosmetics, New York, 1886.

p.99 Sarah Coventry (tm) jewelry sets, Charles H. Stewart (founder), Emmons Home Fashions, Chicago, 1949.

p.99 *The Hidden Staircase*, Nancy Drew mysteries, original text by Mildred A. Wirt, 1930.

p.99 Maybelline (tm) cake mascara, T.L. Williams (founder), The Maybelline Co., New York, 1917.

p.109 *Someday My Prince Will Come*, Frank Churchill and Leigh Harline (composers).

p.115 *"A bump..."*, William Shakespeare, *Romeo & Juliet*, Act I, Scene 3.

p.115 *Amphitron 38* playbill, Giraudoux's translation adapted by Sam Behrman, c.1936.

p.115 *"I look like I swallowed..."*, Alfred Lunt quote to Diana Enright, c.1950.

p.116 Alfred Lunt *Parsifal* (Greek opera) miniature stage set gifted to Museum of the City of New York, Dec. 1946.

p.116 *"I worked my God...head off..."*, Alfred Lunt quote to Robert Sherwood, Dec. 26, 1946.

p.117 *"Good morrow, brother Clarence..."*, William Shakespeare, *Henry V*, Act IV, Scene 1.

p.119 excerpts from *Hamlet,* Act III, William Shakespeare.

p.120 *Fire Over London*, A.E.W.Mason (novel); 1937 film: Clemence Dane (screenplay), William Howard (director).

p.120 *Gone with the Wind,* David Selznick film, MGM Studios, 1945.

p.121-122 excerpts from *Hamlet*, Act III, William Shakespeare.

p.123 *A Streetcar Named Desire,* Tennesee Williams stageplay, London Production, 1945.

p.123 *"Happiness to their sheets..."*, William Shakespeare, *Othello*, Act II, Scene 3.

p.123-125 excerpts from *Henry V*, Act V, William Shakespeare.

p.125*Caesar & Cleopatra* film, Gabriel Pascal (director)/ George Bernard Shaw (written by), postwar Britain, 1945.

p.125 *"He and she are so beautiful...again with them."* Noël Coward quote from Lynn Fontanne to Graham Robertson, Ten Chimneys, Aug. 2, 1947.

p.128 *'Melody of Love'*, ibid.

p.130 *The Guiding Light*, ibid.

p.134 *The Old Rugged Cross*, Reverend George Bennard (composer), traditional hymn, 1913.

p.137-141 excerpts from *Taming of the Shrew,* Act II, William Shakespeare.

p.141 *Life* Magazine, Time-Life Building, New York, NY, published since 1883.

p.143 Hamm's Beer (tm), Theo and Louise Hamm (founders), Hamm Brewing Co., St. Paul, MN.

p.150 Burberry (tm) cashmere scarf, Thomas Burberry, Bansingstoke, England, 1856.

p.155 *O Holy Night*, Adolphe Charles Adden (music by)/Placide Chappeau (lyrics by), traditional hymn, mid-1800s.

p.163 *The Bridge On The River Kwai*, Pierre Boulle (credited screenwriter)/ Carl Foreman and Michael Wilson (blacklisted writers), David Lean film version, 1957.

p.168 *When I Have Fears*, Noël Coward poem, Orion Publishing Group, 2000.

p.177 *Smile*, Charles Chaplin (music), Modern Times, 1936.

p.186 *"It was to be...",* Helen Hayes quote: *On Reflection* an autobiography with Sanford Dody, Lippincott, New York, 1968.

p.187 *"When I first met him..."* Helen Hayes quote, *On Reflection*, ibid.

p.189 *"Oh God, Oh God",* Alfred Lunt quote: Margo Peters, *Design for Living*, ibid.

p.192-193 *Lynn Fontanne notes* to Louise/Virgel Herrold, gifted by Diana Enright to the Ten Chimneys Foundation, 2003.

p.194 *"I usually come through...",* Lynn Fontanne quote to Noël Coward, May 19, 1949.

p.195 *"O Gertrude, Gertrude...",* William Shakespeare, *Hamlet*, Act IV, Scene 5.

p.196 *"Sweet Vivian...",* Laurence Olivier quote to Lynn Fontanne, Italy, 1953.

p.199 *"I'd rather have lived...",* Vivian Leigh quote to Radie Harris, 1967.

p.200 *"Our dear Viv's tragedy..."*, Lynn Fontanne quote: Margo Peters, *Design for Living*, ibid.

p.200 *"I pray for..."*, Olivier quote: *Love Lives - Laurence Olivier and Vivien Leigh*, article by Michael Sauter, 2006.

p.200 *"This, this..."*, Olivier quote: *Love Lives - Laurence Olivier and Vivien Leigh*, ibid.

p.207 *"To be hauled out..."*, Alfred Lunt quote: Margo Peters, *Design for Living*, ibid.

p.208 *"On The Street Where You Live"*, Don Freeman (artist), Helen Hayes gifted art to the Lunts, 1958.

p.208 *My Fair Lady*, Alan Jay Lerner (novel and lyrics)/ Frederick Loewe (music by), Broadway production, 1956.

p.210 *Ladies Home Journal*, O.Cyrus/H. Curtis (founders), Louisa Knapp (editor), Meredith Publishing, December, 1883.

p.211 *I Know My Love*, Stewart Chaney (set design)/Alfred Lunt (director), Broadway production, 1949.

p.233 Lanz (tm) flannel nightgown, Lanz of Salzburg, Albany, NY, 1922.

p.238 *Leaves of Gold* booklet, Clyde Francis Lytle, Leroy Brown Publisher.

p.241 Pendleton Woolen Mills, Pendleton Oregon, founded 1863 by Thomas Kay.

p.241 Bass Weejan (tm) penny loafers, George Henry Bass (founder), Bass Co., St. Louis, MO, 1876.

p.242 Weejan (tm) loafers, ibid.

p.243 *Sweetheart of Sigma Chi*, composers Stokrs, Byron, D.Vernor and F.Dudleigh.

p.243 *Red Red Robin*, Harry Woods (written by), 1926, Al Jolson (performed by), Bing Crosby (recorded by), 1962.

p.243 Marlboro (tm) cigarettes, Phillip Morris Co., introduced 1920.

p.243 *Red Red Robin*, ibid.

p.245 Candlelight Club, Roanoke, VA, burned down in 1970.

p.245 *Peppermint Twist*, Dee Glover (composer)/Joey Dee & The Starlighters (performed by), Roulette Label, 1961.

p.245 *When I Fall in Love,* The Lettermen (performed by), Topic/Lute Labels, 1962.

p.245 *I Can't Stop Loving You*, Ray Charles (performer)/Don Gibson (lyrics), 1962.

p.245 Johns Hopkins, private institution in Baltimore, MD, founded 1876.

p.247Christian Dior perfume, Christian Dior, Normandy, France, 1946.

p.249 Duke University, Durham, NC, founded 1838.

p.249 William and Mary College, Williamsburg, VA, founded 1693.

p.262 *The Lawrence Welk Show*, ABC Television, 1955.

p.264 *"Teddy Byrne...",* Lynn Fontanne quote: Margo Peters, *Design for Living,* Alfred A. Knopf, New York, 2003.

p.269 Dickens 'Pip' quote: *Great Expectations*, Avenel Books, New York, 1978.

p.269*"when you serve white fish..."*, Noël Coward letter to Alfred Lunt: Margo Peters, *Design for Living,* ibid.

p.269 Swedish aquavit beverage, founded by O.P.Anderson, 1891.

p.270 Presidential Medal of Freedom, Lyndon B. Johnson, Sept. 14, 1964.

p.276 *"too long...awfully damned pleased...",* Alfred Lunt quote to *Waukesha Sentinel*, Jan. 28, 1965.

p.277 *Upstairs Downstairs*, British serial drama, Sagitta Productions, PBS Television (American version), 1974-1977.

p.277 *Police Woman*, NBC Television, 1974-1978.

p.277 *Hollywood Squares*, NBC Television, 1966-1980.

p.279-281 Paul Lynde selected quotes to Peter Marshall on NBC *Hollywood Squares*, 1967-1975.

p.283-284 *The White Cliffs*, Alice Duer Miller poem, recited by Lynn Fontanne, Victor Records, NBC, 1941.

p.297 *The Snoop Sisters*, NBC Mystery Movie, 1971-1977.

p.301 *"I have to tell you...",* Alfred Lunt quote to Helen Hayes: Helen Hayes, *My Life in Three Acts*, Harcourt Brace Jovanovich, c1990.

p.302 *"Goodnight my darlings...",* Noël Coward quote d.1973, www.corsinet.com, 2005.

p.302 "Dad's Renaissance...Holy Week", Noël Coward quote, c.1973.

p.305 *"Of course they all know me...",* Alfred Lunt quote to Carol Channing: *The Fabulous Lunts*, Jared Brown, 1945.

p.305 *"J-E-S-U-S",* Alfred Lunt quote to Bob Browning, 1977.

p.305 *"I refuse the indignity...",* Lynn Fontanne quote: Margo Peters, *Design for Living*, ibid.

p.306 *On Top of the World,* The Carpenters (performed by)/Richard Carpenter (lyrics by), A &M Records, 1972.

p.308 *"I will soon join...",* Lynn Fontanne quote from Jim and Gloria Irwin to Thomas H. Garver, interview, c1977.

p.310 *"Ferdinand 'Jules' Johnson..."* obituary clipping of Diana Enright's from *Waukesha Sentinel*, May, 1978.

p.311 KFC, Kentucky Fried Chicken fast-food restaurants, established by Harlan Sanders 1930, division of Tricon Global Restaurants.

p.311 Inscription on Lunt 8x10 portrait gifted to Ten Chimneys Foundation by Diana Enright, 2003.

p.312 Kool-Aid (tm), ibid.

p.312 *More Than A Woman*, written and performed by BeeGees, Barry Gibb, Robin Gibb and Maurice Gibb, 1977.

p.320 Broadway Department Store, renamed Federated Dept. Stores Foundation, 1995.

p.322 *Days of our Lives,* Irna Phillips/Ted Corday (creators) NBC Television, 1965.

p.324 *"Charlie's body...",* Helen Hayes with Katherine Hatch, *My Life in Three Acts*, ibid.

p.324 *"and how is dear Charlie?",* Lynn Fontanne quote to Helen Hayes: *My Life in Three Acts*, ibid.

p.324 *"I think it's time...",* Lynn Fontanne quote to Alan Hewitt, Nov. 10, 1977.

p.324 *"paranoia began...",* paraphrased from Brent Fintel statement to Thomas H. Garver, July 7, 1998.

p.325 *"Only three Lynnie?"*, Charles Bowden quote: unpublished pages of his visit to Ten Chimneys, c.1983.

p.327 *"What a real thrill..."*, Katharine Hepburn to Lynn Fontanne May, 1982.

p.327-330 Katharine Hepburn selected quotes from Australian Radio National transcript, June, 2003 and from BBCi Films, 2005.

p.330 Swiss Army Knife (tm), Carl Elsener (inventor), Victorinox & Wenger Cos., 1891.

p.331 *"They thought I was American..."*, Lynn Fontanne quote to Bunny Raasch, Milwaukee Channel 12 (WISN), July 30, 1981.

p.331-332 *"Living wasn't easy for you..."*, 1986 documentary, Katharine Hepburn journal entry.

p.340 *Moonlight Serenade,* Glenn Miller (composed and performed by), 1935.

p.342 Noël Coward poem, *When I Have Fears*, ibid.

Printed in the United States
89830LV00003BC/2/A

9 781592 992836